AF660844

Fundamentals of Entrepreneurship

SANGRAM KESHARI MOHANTY
Faculty Member and Trainer-Motivator
Institute of Entrepreneurship Development
Bhubaneswar

PHI Learning Private Limited
Delhi-110092
2014

₹ 195.00

FUNDAMENTALS OF ENTREPRENEURSHIP
Sangram Keshari Mohanty

© 2005 by PHI Learning Private Limited, Delhi. All rights reserved. No part of this book may be reproduced in any form, by mimeograph or any other means, without permission in writing from the publisher.

ISBN-978-81-203-2867-9

The export rights of this book are vested solely with the publisher.

Tenth Printing ... ... **October, 2014**

Published by Asoke K. Ghosh, PHI Learning Private Limited, Rimjhim House, 111, Patparganj Industrial Estate, Delhi-110092 and Printed by Mudrak, 30-A, Patparganj, Delhi-110091.

To

My Parents

Contents

Foreword

When I grew up as a student, the only thing that I knew about entrepreneurs was that they are the folks who take risks and set up businesses. In general, Orissans appear to be less entrepreneurial, partly because they come from humble backgrounds, and in those days, they appeared more so. But the changing time has seen their emergence as people capable of not only taking risk but also competing and succeeding. An elegant example of this is the author of the book, *Fundamentals of Entrepreneurship*, himself. Mr. Sangram Keshari Mohanty has taken a big step by spending enormous time in compiling a lot of information on theory and practice of entrepreneurship, from Max Weber's perspective of the bygone era to SBI's 20th century Stree Shakti Package on women. An economist by training and a teacher of entrepreneurship by profession, he has just the ideal background to write such a book. Risk and return are the two sides of the entrepreneurship coin. Mr. Mohanty has already taken the risk. I feel that the information contained in the book would be well-received by the readers, including potential entrepreneurs, and the author would get the richly-deserved return on sweat equity. I wish the book all the success.

BANIKANTA MISHRA
Professor
Xavier Institute of Management
Bhubaneswar

Preface

Entrepreneurship acts as a critical factor for accelerating economic development of a country. In a developing country like ours, its role is more important than that in developed countries so far as the creation of self-employment opportunities and reduction of unemployment situations are concerned. With the objectives of creation of enterprise and generation of employment avenues for the millions, a number of entrepreneurial institutes like NIESBUD, EDI, NISIET, IEDs/CEDs have been set up through government and non-government initiatives to train the youths for taking up entrepreneurial activities as their career option. In course of time, a few universities and autonomous colleges have incorporated Entrepreneurship and Small Business Management into their course curriculum so as to provide necessary exposure to the students to the entrepreneurial and industrial climate of the country. Further, nowadays, entrepreneurial development training programmes for new entrepreneurs and entrepreneurial education for college students are gathering momentum. But the available books, training manuals and literature on entrepreneurship are limited. Therefore, the author, being an accredited trainer-motivator and expert in the field of entrepreneurship development and training, has identified this problem and made an humble attempt to write this book in the most comprehensive and analytical manner to suit to the needs of trainees, trainers and above all, the students pursuing their graduation in commerce and management.

This book, entitled *Fundamentals of Entrepreneurship*, has been written strictly according to the syllabus of Utkal, Berhampur, Sambalpur, Fakir Mohan and North Orissa Universities for B.Com. students. This book would also cater to the needs of B.Com., B.B.A., M.B.A. and B.E. students of different universities. This book would also be equally useful to the EDP trainers, entrepreneurs, economists, bankers and development professionals assured with the task of entrepreneurial and industrial development.

This book has been written in a short span of time. Though due care has been taken in writing the book, still lapses of commission and omission are likely to remain. The author will be extremely indebted if the teachers and trainers in the field of entrepreneurship development and above all, the students and other readers who would go through the book point out the deficiencies and send their valuable suggestions for further improvement.

SANGRAM KESHARI MOHANTY

Acknowledgements

At the outset, I express my deep sense of gratitude to my wife **'Dolly'** whose persistent inspiration and moral support helped me to make this endeavour a success. I am greatly indebted to my daughter **'Soumya'** and son **'Soumitra'** for their unstinted assistance, especially in the form of collection of reference materials from different journals, magazines and scriptures for incorporation in the book.

I extend my thanks to Mr. Sujit Acharya, Academic Consultant of DDCE, Utkal University, for his valuable suggestions and kind assistance during the course of writing the book. I also express my gratitude to Prof. Banikanta Mishra, Xavier's Institute of Management, Bhubaneswar, for his valuable suggestions and foreword. I also express my thanks to Mr. J.K. Mohanty, Director, Orissa Computer Centre, Bhubaneswar for having helped in making the DTP of entire text in a flawless manner.

I am thankful to Mr. Ashirbad Das, Mr. Dibylochan Swain and Ms. Tanisha Pattnaik, three students of B.J.B. (Autonomous) College, pursuing B.Com. studies, for their constant persuasion to write this book. I express my deep gratitude to the publisher, Prentice-Hall of India, who have taken ample care for bringing out the book in a short span of time.

SANGRAM KESHARI MOHANTY

"May everybody surmount difficulties; may everybody have goodluck. May everybody realize his ambitions; may everybody rejoice everywhere."

— Kalidasa
(Vikramorvashiyam)

CHAPTER 1

Entrepreneur and Entrepreneurship

CHAPTER CONTENTS

1.1 ENTREPRENEUR: DEFINITION AND CONCEPT

The word ***entrepreneur*** is derived from the French word, ***'Entreprendre'*** which means to 'undertake', i.e., the person who undertakes the risk of new enterprise. The word entrepreneur, therefore, first appeared in the French language in the beginning of the sixteenth century. The word was also applied to the leaders of military expedition. But it was **Richard Cantilon**, an Irishman, living in France who first used the term ***entrepreneur*** to refer to economic activities. According to Cantilon: "An entrepreneur is a person who buys factor services at certain prices with a view to selling its product at uncertain prices". Thus, to Cantilon, an entrepreneur is a bearer of risk which is non-insurable.

One of the most renowned French economists **Jean Baptiste Say** defined the term ***entrepreneur*** in a meaningful manner. According to J.B. Say: "An entrepreneur is the agent who unites all the factors of production and who finds in value of the products the re-establishment of the entire capital he employs, and the value of wages, the interest and the rent which he pays as well as the profits belonging to himself. He may or may not supply capital but he must have judgement, perseverance and the knowledge of the world of business. He must possess the art of superintendence and administration".

Adam Smith, the father of classical economics, did not use the term ***entrepreneur*** anywhere. Instead, he used the words like ***employer***, the ***merchant***, the ***undertaker*** and the ***master***.

Alfred Marshall wrote about the capitalists and management but he was silent about their difference. As such, the classical economists ignored the term ***entrepreneur*** entirely.

According to **A.P. Usher:** "Specialization or division of labour necessitates an entrepreneurial function the crux of which is to coordinate different economic activities, This view on entrepreneurship was very narrow and it reduced the entrepreneurship activities to no more than a managerial function".

F.H. Knight, in his article on *Risk, Uncertainty and Profit* propounded the maxim that "entrepreneurs are a specialized group of persons who bear risks and deal with uncertainty." He also identified social, psychological and economic factors which govern the supply of entrepreneurship.

According to **David Ricardo**, a contemporary of **J.B. Say**: "The foremost motive of a risk taker is to amass capital and capital accumulation is the sinequanon of economic development".

J.S. Mill viewed the word ***entrepreneur*** as organizer who was paid for his non-manual type of work. According to him: "Extra-ordinary skills acted as the bedrock in production process that ought to be possessed by the entrepreneur".

Leon Walrus, in his papers, *The Theory of Social Wealth* (Allen and Unwin, London, 1954) pointed out that entrepreneur is the coordinator of basic factors of production. He treated '***entrepreneur***' as the fourth factor of production who combines other factors such as land, labour and capital.

In 1882, **F.B. Hawley** contemplated ***risk taking*** as the prime characteristic feature of the entrepreneur which was comparable to the elementary agents of production like land, labour and capital. All classical and neoclassical economists believed in the significance of entrepreneurial action but did not incorporate the term 'entrepreneur' into their theories and thus entrepreneurship remained as a clandestine factor.

With **J.A. Schumpeter**, the term ***entrepreneur*** had received a wide acclaim. He defined the entrepreneur as an ***innovator*** who carries out new combinations to initiate the process of economic development through introduction of new products, new markets, conquests of new source of raw materials and establishment of a new organization of industry. He said, "The carrying out of a new combinations we call ***enterprise***, the individuals whose function is to carry them out we call ***entrepreneurs***". He has put emphasis on ***profit,*** which is the product of innovation and the prime mover of economic development. According to **Schumpeter**, "The process of development is a deliberate and continuous phenomenon which is actively promoted by the escort services of a change agent who provides economic leadership. This change agent is what is called ***entrepreneur***."

Cole described entrepreneur as an individual who undertakes 'to initiate, maintain or aggrandize a profit-oriented business unit for production or distribution of economic goods and services.'

Oxford English Dictionary defined entrepreneur as one who undertakes an enterprise. Especially a contractor-acting as an intermediary between labour and capital for production is an entrepreneur.

According to **McClelland:** "An entrepreneur is someone who exercises some control over the means of production and produces more than what he can consume in order to sell (or exchange) it for individual (or household) income."

An entrepreneur, as defined by **Robert E. Nelson**, is a person who is able to look at the environment, identify opportunities to improve the environment, marshall resources and implement action to maximize those opportunities.

In a nutshell, an entrepreneur, is described as a capitalist employer seeking profit; a risk taker, a monopolist, a coordinator an innovator and an organizer of means of production. A person of all these attributes in operation may be termed as entrepreneur. He is a person who organizes, operates and assumes the risk of a business venture.

The Entrepreneur: Some Important Definitions

---

1. According to **F.A. Walker:** "Entrepreneur is one who is endowed with more than average capacities in the task of organizing and coordinating the factors of production, i.e. land, labour capital and enterprise".
2. **Marx** regarded entrepreneur as social parasite.
3. According to **Galbraith:** "An entrepreneur must accept the challenge and should be willing hard to achieve something".
4. **Peter F. Drucker** defines an entrepreneur as one who always searches for change, responds to it and exploits it as an opportunity. Innovation is the basic tool of entrepreneurs, the means by which they exploit change as an opportunity for a different business or service.
5. According to **E.E. Hagen:** "An entrepreneur is an economic man who tries to maximize his profits by innovation, involve problem solving and gets satisfaction from using his capabilities on attacking problems".
6. According to **Mark Casson:** "An entrepreneur is a person who specializes in taking judgemental decision about the coordination of scarce resources".
7. **Frank Young** defined entrepreneur as a change agent.
8. According to **Max Weber:** "Entrepreneurs are a product of particular social condition in which they are brought up and it is the society which shapes individuals as entrepreneurs".
9. **International Labour Organization (ILO)** defines entrepreneurs as those people who have the ability to see and evaluate business opportunities, together with the necessary resources to take advantage of them and to initiate appropriate action to ensure success.
10. **Akhouri** describes entrepreneur as a character who combines innovativeness, readiness to take risk, sensing opportunities, identifying and mobilizing potential resources, concern for excellence, and who is persistent in achieving the goal.

1.2 CHARACTERISTICS OF ENTREPRENEUR

Entrepreneur is a key figure in economic progress. He is the person who introduces new things in the economy. He is considered as the business leader and not as simple owner of capital. He is a person with telescopic faculty, drive and talent who perceives business opportunities and promptly seizes them for exploitation. **M.M.P. Akhouri**, formerly Executive Director, National Institute for Entrepreneurship and Small Business Development (NIESBUD), New Delhi, describes entrepreneur "as a character who combines innovativeness, readiness to take risk, sensing opportunities, identifying and mobilizing potential resources, concerns for excellence and who is persistent in achieving the goal." The above definition of Akhouri provides distinguishing characteristic features of entrepreneur. However, to be successful, an entrepreneur should have the following characteristic features:

1. ***Need to achieve:*** Entrepreneurs have got strong desire to achieve higher goals. Their inner self motivates their behaviour towards high achievement; most of the people dream of success but do not take any action towards achieving these dreams. Entrepreneurs with high n-Ach factor act continuously to achieve the goal and make their dreams come true. For them, winning is achievement.
2. ***Independence:*** Most of the entrepreneurs start on their own because they dislike to work for others. They prefer to be their own boss and want to be responsible for their own decisions.
3. ***Risk-bearing:*** Entrepreneurs are the persons who take decisions under uncertainty and thus they are willing to take risk, but they never gamble with the results. They choose moderate risk rather than play wild gamble. They, therefore, undertake calculated risk which is high enough to be exciting, but with a fairly reasonable chance to win.
4. ***Locus of control:*** Closely consistent with McClelland's theory of need for achievement, is the belief in internal locus of control. According to Rotter's locus of control theory, an individual perceives the outcome of an event as being either within or beyond his personal control. Entrepreneurs believe in their own ability to control the consequences of their endeavour by influencing their socio-economic environment rather than leave everything to luck. They strongly believe that they can govern and shape their own destiny.
5. ***Perseverance:*** Entrepreneur has got the quality of sticking to job he decides to undertake. Once committed to a specific goal and course of action, entrepreneurs become absorbed to it. They personally solve the problems that come across their way while setting up the project. They also work sincerely until the whole project is successfully implemented.
6. ***Positive self-concept:*** Entrepreneurs are always positive in their action. Being an achiever, he directs his fantasies and dreams towards achievement of worthwhile goals and sets extraordinary standard of excellence in what he is doing. This is based upon his awareness of SWOT analysis, i.e. his strengths, weaknesses, opportunities and threats. He utilizes his positive knowledge to support his thinking. He never exhibits any negative attitude.

7. ***Ability to find and explore opportunities:*** Entrepreneurs are always alert to opportunities. They are very much quick to see and grab opportunities. They exhibit an innovative turn of mind and convert the problems into viable opportunities. They plan intellectually and anticipate carefully how to achieve their goals in realizing an opportunity.
8. ***Hope of success:*** Hope of success is a significant quality of entrepreneurial personality. Entrepreneurs set their goals with a hope of success rather than fear of failure. This is because they set their goals on the basis of facts and their ability to manoeuvre them to their advantage.
9. ***Flexibility:*** Most of the successful entrepreneurs measure the pros and cons of a decision and tend to change if the situation demands. They never feel reluctant to revise their decisions. They are the persons with open mind without rigidity.
10. ***Analytical ability of mind:*** Entrepreneurs are unaffected by personal likes and dislikes. They stand beyond these types of prejudices as they are realistic in their approach. At the time of their need they select experts rather than friends and relatives to assist them. They usually avoid emotional and sensitive attitude towards their business or problem.
11. ***Sense of efficacy:*** Entrepreneurs are always oriented towards action for accomplishment of their goals. Being confident of their abilities, they find themselves as problem solvers rather than problem avoiders. They chalk out their goals for future and make planning to achieve them.
12. ***Openness to feedback and learning from experience:*** Successful entrepreneurs like to have immediate feedback of their performance. They modify their plans on the basis of the feedback they receive from the environment around them. They learn from their experience and never get discouraged having received unfavourable information. On the contrary, they are stimulated by unfavourable information to involve themselves sincerely in their own tasks to reach their desired goals.
13. ***Confronting uncertainty:*** Successful entrepreneurs are always optimistic and take every odd as the opportunity. They manoeuvre their environment in such a way that the works get accomplished rationally. Thus, they win by the application of their extraordinary insight and skill.
14. ***Interpersonal skills:*** Entrepreneurs are always comfortable while dealing with people at all levels. During the course of their action, they come across a cross section of individuals with whom they have to deal. They interact with raw material suppliers, customers, bankers, etc. for different activities. As successful entrepreneurs, they should be persons who like working with others possessing the much needed quality of interpersonal skill to deal with people.
15. ***Need to influence others:*** Once the entrepreneurs set their goals, they have to play the roles of manager too. For influencing others (n Power), a low need to establish emotional relationship (low n Affiliation), and a high need to discipline one's own self (to inhibit overexpression of their personality) are essential.
16. ***Stress takers:*** Entrepreneurs are capable of working for long hours and solving different complexities at the same time. As the captain of an industry or an enterprise, an entrepreneur faces a number of problems and in right moment he takes right

decisions which may involve physical as well as mental stress. He can face these challenges if he has the capability to work for long hours and keep himself cool under monotony.

17. ***Time orientation:*** Entrepreneurs anticipate future trends basing upon their past experience and exposure. They stick to the time pragmatically while doing their jobs.
18. ***Innovators:*** Successful entrepreneurs are innovators. They constantly put their efforts in introducing new products, new method of production, opening new markets and reorganizing the enterprise.
19. ***Business communication skill:*** In order to motivate others in the business, entrepreneurs must possess good communication skill. Both written and oral communication skills are necessary for the entrepreneurs for running enterprise efficiently.
20. ***Telescopic faculty:*** Successful entrepreneurs always tend to think ahead. They have got telescopic faculties which make them think for the future. Future orientation make them quite alert to the changing conditions of the time and they tend to produce goods and commodities as per the changing demands.
21. ***Leadership:*** Entrepreneurs should possess the quality of leadership. Leadership is the ability to exert interpersonal influence by means of communication towards the achievement of goals. Entrepreneurs as the leaders should provide the necessary spark to motivation by guiding, inspiring, assisting and directing the members of the group for achievement of unity of action, efforts and purpose. According to George R.Terry: "Leadership is the activity of influencing people of strive willingly for group objectives". Thus, entrepreneur, as the leader of the group, can ensure high performance by creating a well-to-do environment among others. They must have the capability to arrive at prompt and correct direction and win the confidence of their subordinates. Being the leader of the organization, they should possess the following characteristics:

    (a) Existence of followers
    (b) Assumption of responsibility
    (c) Empathy towards followers
    (d) Exemplary conduct
    (e) Developing teamwork
    (f) Common objectivity
    (g) Facilitating change
    (h) Building morale
    (i) Maintenance of discipline
    (j) Active participation

    Hence, entrepreneurs by their own leadership styles and behaviour reduce the problems with careful listening and proper handling of situations. Good administrative work depends upon effective leadership of the entrepreneur.
22. ***Business planning:*** Planning implies deciding in advance what, when and how to do a thing. Entrepreneurs should be adept in planning their business and planning

is an intellectual approach to solution of the various problems. Therefore, entrepreneurs should be equipped with skill and knowledge to prepare their business plan. A successful entrepreneur always follows the principles of management while planning for his business. This is because the success of a small enterprise depends upon one's doing the right thing at the right time. As such, through the instrument of planning, the entrepreneurs determine the following things:

(i) Objectives
(ii) Policies and procedures
(iii) Budget
(iv) Strategies
(v) Rules
(vi) Programmes

Apart from these, while planning for setting up a small enterprise, entrepreneurs have to follow the procedures and regulations such as:

(a) Product identification and project selection
(b) Preparation of techno-economic feasibility report
(c) Accommodation and other infrastructural facilities
(d) Power/water connection
(e) Procurement of machineries and raw materials
(f) Financial support
(g) Marketing of the products or services
(h) Availing incentives and subsidies declared by the Government for development of SSI sector
(i) Procurement of pollution control certificates, etc.

Thus, the planning can act as a bridge between the present position and expected future shape of an enterprise. It provides a sense of vision to the entrepreneurs to cope with risky and uncertain situation.

23. ***Decision making:*** Decision-making skill is a fundamental characteristic of an entrepreneur. This implies the function of choosing a particular course of action out of several alternative courses for the purpose of achieving specified goals. It reflects the quality and competence of the entrepreneur and is very much necessary at every stage of creation of an enterprise. The stages are as given below:

(i) Setting of goals
(ii) Formulation of policies
(iii) Designing organizational structure
(iv) Motivation
(v) Communication
(vi) Control, etc.

Hence, decision making is necessary at all times and mostly at conditions of uncertainty and risk. As the entrepreneurial decision-making process modally involves two aspects such as nature of the problem situation and qualities of the decision maker, successful entrepreneur should possess the following traits to become a good decision maker:

(a) He should be systematic and logical.
(b) He must have a spirit of enquiry.
(c) He should be analytical in his approach while thinking.
(d) He should control his emotion and be objective.
(e) He must be well conversant with the subject matter.
(f) He must not be reluctant to gather knowledge from others if the subject matter is outside his comprehension.
(g) He must conceive the desired end results clearly.
(h) He must concentrate on optimization of output whether qualitative or quantitative.
(i) He should also concentrate on how best his decisions can be implemented.
(j) He should choose appropriate means to achieve his goals.

24. ***Ability to mobilize resources:*** Entrepreneurs must have the ability to marshall all the inputs to obtain the end product. They have to mobilize 6Ms, i.e. Man, Money, Material, Machinery, Market and Method effectively to realize the final product as entrepreneurship is a function of gap filling and input completing.
25. ***Self-confidence:*** Entrepreneurs must have self-confidence to accomplish the task effectively and efficiently. They must take decisions on their own in uncertain and risky situation and should stick to it confidently even if there occurs initial setbacks.

Table 1.1 depicts the characteristic and traits giving the working profile of entrepreneurs prepared at a workshop on entrepreneurship conducted at the East-West centre, Honolulu in 1977.

Table 1.1 Characteristics and Traits of Entrepreneurs

Characteristics	*Traits*
Self-confidence	Confidence, independence, individuality, optimism
Task-oriented	Need for achievement, profit-oriented persistence, perseverance, determination, hard work, drive energy, initiative
Risk bearer	Risk-taking ability, likes, challenges
Leadership	Leadership behaviour, gets along well with others, responsive to suggestions and criticisms
Originality	Innovative, creative, flexible (openness of mind), resourceful, versatile, knowledgeable
Future-oriented	Foresight perceptive

Table 1.2 illustrates McBer's 21 entrepreneurial core competencies and associated personal entrepreneurial characteristics.

Table 1.2 Personal Entrepreneurial Characteristics

	Core competencies	*Entrepreneurial activities*
1.	Initiative	Does things before asked for or forced to by events and acts to extend the business to new areas, products or services
2.	Perceiving opportunities	Identifies business opportunities and mobilizes necessary resources to make good an opportunity
3.	Persistence	Takes repeated or different actions to overcome obstacles
4.	Information gathering	Consults experts for business and technical advice. Seeks information on client's or supplier's needs. Personally undertakes market research and make use of personal contacts or information networks to obtain useful information
5.	Concern for quality work	States desire to produce or sell a better quality product or service. Compares his performance favourably with that of others
6.	Commitment to contractual obligations	Makes a personal sacrifice or expands extraordinary effort to complete a job, accepts full responsibility in completing a job contract on schedule, pitches in with workers or work in their place to get the job done and shows utmost concern to satisfy the customer
7.	Efficiency orientation	Finds ways and means to do things faster, better and economically
8.	Planning	Various inter-related jobs are synchronized according to plan
9.	Problem solving	Conceives new ideas and finds innovative solutions
10.	Self-confidence	Makes decisions on his own and sticks to it inspite of initial setbacks
11.	Expertise	Possesses technical expertise in areas of business, finance, marketing, etc.
12.	Self-critical	Aware of personal limitations but tries to improve upon by learning from his past mistakes or experiences of others and is never complacent with success
13.	Persuasion	Persuades customers and financiers to patronize his business
14.	Use of influence strategies	Develops business contacts, retains influential people as agents and restricts dissemination of information in his possession
15.	Assertiveness	Instructs, reprimands or disciplines for failing to perform
16.	Monitoring	Develops a reporting system to ensure that work is completed and quality norms
17.	Credibility	Demonstrates honesty in dealing with employees, suppliers and customers even if it means a loss of business

(Contd.)

Table 1.2 Contd.

	Core competencies	*Entrepreneurial activities*
18.	Concern for employee welfare	Expresses concern for employees by responding promptly to their grievances
19.	Impersonal relationship	Places long-term goodwill over short-term gain in a business relationship
20.	Expansion of capital base	Reinvests a greater portion of profits to expand capital base of the firm
21.	Building product image	Concerned about the image of his products among consumers and does everything possible to establish a niche for his products in the market

1.3 ENTREPRENEURSHIP: DEFINITION AND CHARACTERISTICS

Development of the economy in any form is the result of human activity. This activity in man envisages three important roles:

(i) organizer
(ii) worker
(iii) user of goods produced

Of these roles, the role of man in coordinating and organizing the means of production is considerably significant. Unless the skill and resources provided by the nature are fully harnessed and transformed into viable production units, man's labour will remain largely unproductive and keeps his level of consumption low. These considerations focus on the importance of entrepreneurship in the development of any nation. Thus, entrepreneurship plays a critical role in the growth path of a country.

According to **J.A. Timmons:** "Entrepreneurship is the ability to create and build something from practically nothing. Fundamentally, a human creative activity, it is finding personal energy by initiating, building and achieving an enterprise or organization rather than by just watching, analysing or describing one. It requires the ability to take calculated risk and reduce the chance of failure. It is the ability to build a founding team to complement the entrepreneurial skill and talents"

1.3.1 Definitions

Various authors have given various definitions on entrepreneur and entrepreneurship. It is the knack for sensing an opportunity where others see chaos, contradiction and confusion. It is the know-how to find marshall and control resources and to make sure the venture does not run out of money when it is needed the most.

A.H. Cole has defined entrepreneurship as "the purposeful activity of an individual or group of associated individuals, undertaken to initiate, maintain, or earn profit by production and distribution of economic goods and services."

According to **Heggins** "Entrepreneurship is meant the function of seeking investment and production opportunity, organizing an enterprise to undertake a new production process, raising capital, hiring labour, arranging the supply of raw materials and selecting top managers of day-to-day operations".

Joseph A. Schumpeter has given an important definition on entrepreneurship. According to him, entrepreneurship is essentially a creative activity. It consists of doing such things as are generally not done in ordinary course of business. An entrepreneur is one who innovates, i.e. carries out new combination or enterprise. **McClelland,** like other specialists, identified two characteristics of entrepreneurship, i.e. first, doing thing in a new and better way, secondly, decision making under uncertainty. **McClelland** more explicitly emphasized achievement motivation as the most critical factor for the growth of entrepreneurship.

Peter Drucker has given a very comprehensive definition of entrepreneurship. According to him: "Entrepreneurship is neither a science nor an art. It is a practice. It has a knowledge base. Knowledge in entrepreneurship is a means to an end. Indeed, what constitutes knowledge in practice is largely defined by the ends, that is by the practice. Entrepreneurship is not just about making money. It is about imagination, flexibility, creativity, willingness to think conceptually, readiness to take risks, ability to mobilize agents of production and the capacity to see change as an opportunity. It is also about marrying passion and process with a good dose of perseverance".

In our country entrepreneurship movement is gathering momentum now-a-days and a plethora of support agencies are coming forward to drive the movement a long way for success. A high sense of responsibility is an essential ingredient for development of entrepreneurship in India. As such:

Entrepreneurship	=	Entrepreneur	+	Enterprise
↓		↓		↓
(Process)		(Person)		(Object)

1.3.2 Characteristics of Entrepreneurship

Entrepreneurship as an economic activity emerges and functions in socio-economic and cultural settings. It is a complex and multifaceted subject. The following are the important characteristics of entrepreneurship.

1. ***Decision making:*** Decision-making activity is one of the fundamental characteristic features of entrepreneurship. A decision is a course of action which is consciously chosen from among a multiple of alternatives to achieve the desired result. As entrepreneurship involves both risk and uncertainty, decision making is crucial on the part of the entrepreneurs to establish and run the enterprise successfully.

2. ***Accepting challenges:*** Entrepreneurship means accepting challenges amidst risk and uncertainty. While accepting entrepreneurship as a career, the entrepreneur accepts the challenges of all odds and puts his efforts to convert the odds into viable business opportunities by pooling together the resources for building and running the enterprise.
3. ***Risk taking:*** One of the important characteristics of entrepreneurship is risk taking or risk bearing. This characteristic feature implies assuming the responsibility for loss that may occur due to unforeseen contingencies of the future. Entrepreneur, by his deep insight and scientific approach, analyses the situation objectively and reduces the risk considerably on one hand and enhances the profit factor on the other.
4. ***Building organization:*** Entrepreneurship presupposes the initiative and skill on building organization. It is by delegation of authorities and proper leadership that organization can be built up. As per the views of Harbison, organization building is the most critical skill needed for entrepreneurship as it facilitates the economic use of other innovations.
5. ***Skillful management:*** Entrepreneurship involves skillful management. The basic managerial skill is the most important characteristic feature of entrepreneurship. For effective management of an enterprise, the role of an entrepreneur to initiate and supervise design of organization-improvement projects in relation to upcoming opportunities is very much important.
6. ***Innovation:*** **David McClelland** identified two important characteristics of entrepreneurship—first doing things in a new and better way, which is synonymous to ***innovation*** given by **J.A. Schumpeter**, and second, decision making under uncertainty. So ***innovation*** is one of the most important characteristics of entrepreneurship.
7. ***Mobilization of resources:*** Resource mobilization is also a fundamental characteristic feature of entrepreneurship. Resources are the help needed to carry out activities resulting in accomplishment of goal. They are found in scattered manner in the environment and required to be perceived, identified and mobilized by entrepreneurs to attain business goal. Thus, entrepreneurs make themselves distinct from the rest of population because of their innate capability to mobilize resources. This is because resources are needed to ensure success which has the highest priority in the minds of entrepreneurs.

1.4 EMERGENCE OF ENTREPRENEURIAL CLASS

Emergence of entrepreneurial class is as old as our ancient history itself. It dates back to the pre-Vedic period when Harappan culture flourished in India. However, history of entrepreneurship and emergence of entrepreneurial class in India may be viewed under the following periods.

- Period I: Entrepreneurship in Ancient period

- Period II: Entrepreneurship in pre-Independence era, i.e. before 1850
- Period III: Entrepreneurship between 1850–1947
- Period IV: Entrepreneurship in 1947 and onwards—post-Independence period

1.4.1 Period I: Entrepreneurship in Ancient Period

The review of ancient literature proved that ancient Indians took up a variety of commercial vocations akin to present-day entrepreneurial activities. The first phase of entrepreneurship emerged when the Aryan conquerors settled down in this country by suppressing the non-Aryans. They appropriated the products of village communities to themselves leaving a little for the villagers or natives. Thus, the main conflict of ancient Indian society began. The Aryans were faced with the problem of innovating new crafts and occupations and also evolved some kind of division of labour for the new handicrafts, breeding of cattle and cultivating land. All these occupations did not exist at the time of conquest by Aryans. They were the products of entrepreneurial actions. Commenting on the earlier phase of entrepreneurial evolution **Walter Ruben** observes:

"The problem was to evolve some kind of law and order to regulate this division of products. The question was: Who had to till the field, breed the cattle and to work in handicrafts and what part of the product would be given to the various social classes? Immediately after the conquest, the settlement of the Aryans began and together with it the formation of states and the establishment of laws. The need of *Dharma* was expressed in the oldest upanishads and the oldest *Dharma sutras* followed. They avoided the speaking of class struggle as mentioned above, but used the terminology of the four ranks (*Varnadharma*), which is quite characteristic of despotism. In the same period, science began in India especially medicine and astronomy. Astronomy was connected with religion and magic, but medicine stood in some kind of conflict with it. The *Asvins* were regarded by the Brahmanas as somewhat 'impure' and there was some competition between magician and the physician both claiming to the proper healer of the diseased. But in this long run, Brahmanas succeeded in uniting most of the branches of science and religion".

Ancient literature like *Manusmriti* has provided a clear idea about entrepreneurial class of people during ancient period (pre-Vedic). According to Manusmriti, "people belonging to *Vaisya* caste were regarded as entrepreneurs who are specialized to maintain livestock, to give charity, perform sacrifices, study scriptures, undertake business and banking." Hence, *Vaisyas* are the specialized class of people carrying entrepreneurial activities in these days. They carried on trade in agriculture, industry and banking sectors. Agriculture, crafts and handicrafts were the basic sources of the occupation for the people in Gupta and post-Gupta period. The occupational development during this period comprised ownership of land pasture grounds, trees, forests, water reservoirs, mines, etc. There is clear evidence about the use of technical knowledge in water use namely, Persian water (Arahatta) in Northern India during the early medieval period. With introduction of entrepreneurship, the towns and cities developed.

***Vaisyas as Entrepreneurs**

A *Vaisya* should always be in the corals, iron and iron-made things, clothes (cotton, silken or woolen), perfumery and salt (329). He must have first-hand knowledge about sowing seeds, the merits and demerits of the soil (in a particular area) measurement and weight and how to handle them (330). He must be well acquainted with the merits and demerits of Mercantile commodities, knowledge of different countries (what things should be bought and sold profitably, in which country the commodities which can potentially yield some profit or incur loss, the ways and means of multiplying the cattle, how to employ servants and fix and pay their salaries, knowledge of different languages of different places, knowledge of suitable places to store the commodities safely and thorough knowledge of purchase and sale (331–332). A *Vaisya* should always make efforts to multiply his wealth through righteous means."

**Manusmriti,* Charter I, 328, 329, 330, 331–332.

1.4.2 Period II: Entrepreneurship in Pre-Independence Era before 1850 A.D.

During pre-Independence era, agriculture was the main-stay of the people of India. It is said that besides agriculture, a class of businessmen specialized in manufacturing of handicrafts, metalworks, stonecarving and jewellery designing, etc. had dominated the industrial entrepreneurship sector in rural areas. Those communities were known as *Banias* (Hindu and Jain), Parsis, Chheriars and Gujaratis, etc. These communities actually laid the foundation of entrepreneurship by carrying on trade and commerce at initial stage and later they started establishing manufacturing centres. These centres were located either near river banks or near ports for ease of transportation. The following types of industries were found in those period.

(i) *Cottage industries* manufacturing woodcraft items, jewellery designing, stonecarvings, ironworks, hornworks, etc.
(ii) *Village industries* comprising handloom and textile production, brass and bell metalworks developed in clusters

Indian handicrafts, which were once considered the best in the world, had received a severe blow due to the British colonialism. Industrial revolution in Great Britain had reduced in India to the status of materials supplier and a consumer market for the finished products manufactured in Britain.

Manufacturing entrepreneurship in India did not develop till 1840. The introduction of railways in 1840 led to the beginning of industrial entrepreneurship through factory system. In India in 1854, the first and foremost textile mill was established. Before this, in 1847, R. Chotulal, a Nagar Brahmin envisaged to manufacture textile on the basis of modern factory system.

From the very beginning, the Britishers devised a discriminatory economic policy for the Indian entrepreneurs, as a consequence of which industrial entrepreneurship suffered a great deal. The following reasons are attributed to the slow growth of entrepreneurship in India during this period:

(i) The enterprises were not given proper protection by the British Government.
(ii) Only those industries in which the British Government put their own capital were given encouragement.
(iii) The railway freight charges were higher for locations not nearer to the ports. This proved that the transportation of goods manufactured for the Indian markets was more expensive than goods meant for export.
(iv) The British imposed exorbitant tariffs on India-made goods.
(v) Entrepreneurs were constantly harassed for getting licences and finance to establish and run industries.
(vi) There were almost no facilities for technical education which alone could strengthen Indian industrial entrepreneurship.
(vii) The Indian indigenous entrepreneurs faced fierce competition from machine-made goods exported to India.
(viii) Lack of transportation and communication facilities acted as the stumbling block in the way of industrial growth.
(ix) The British Government did not encourage the establishment of heavy industries like heavy machinery, iron and steel which are necessary for rapid industrialization.
(x) Political turmoil and abolition of princely courts discouraged the growth of entrepreneurship.
(xi) Prevalence of multi-currency system affected the business environment and blocked the growth of enterprise.

Inspite of the above problems, the export trade of textile in 17th century was on ascending trend. During this period, grouping of Indian merchants into joint-stock associations for the purpose of managing the supply of textiles to the European companies was very significant. This helped in exporting huge volume of textiles to the European markets leading to favourable terms of trade. But in subsequent years, the demand for Indian textiles decreased due to discriminatory custom policies adopted by the British Government. Till 1850, growth of entrepreneurship means only growth of British private enterprises like plantation, coal mines, banking and insurance.

1.4.3 Period III: Entrepreneurship during 1850–1947

The mid-nineteenth century opened up the path for rapid industrialization. With the introduction of railways in 1853 in the country, the scope of industrial entrepreneurship had gone up. Britishers started harnessing the natural resources of India to their own advantage simultaneously developing the roads, railways ports and other infrastructural facilities. In course of time, Britishers along with mercantile class of India have built a conducive atmosphere for investment of trading as well as manufacturing activity.

However, during 1850–1947, entrepreneurship in India can be analysed in the following manners:

(i) Entrepreneurship in eastern part of the country
(ii) Entrepreneurship in western part of the country

In eastern part of India, the entrepreneurship was mainly European who engaged in export-oriented industries like jute, textiles, tea, coal, etc. But the entrepreneurship in western part of India was mostly among the Indians. It is, of course, due to its relatively longer political independence and the advantages availed by all the communities of western India. British exploitation was not directly imposed. When East India Company started its political and commercial activities, Indian merchants were not eliminated from the field of finance and trade.

Entrepreneurship was in abundance in Indian businessmen, but it could not offer sufficient scope for its exercise. However, Indian history indicates that Indian traders had trade relations with Greece, Yemen and other Arabian and African countries.

Emergence of Parsis as Entrepreneurs

In India, an emergence of manufacturing entrepreneurship is viewed by some social scientist as the consequence of arrival of East India Company followed by colonial British rule. It gave new stimulus to businessman by injecting various changes in economy and accelerating the export of raw materials and import of finished goods. However, the Parsis were greatly influenced by the East India Company.

During this period, Parsis established a good rapport with East India Company. They acted as brokers, suppliers of commodities and craftsmen in ship-building industry. Parsis built vessels for the company. In 1852, a Parsi foreman of a gun factory belonging to the company established a steel industry in Bombay. All the above examples prove that the starting point of manufacturing entrepreneurship laid with emerging entrepreneurial talents among the Parsis in the country. On the strength of the historical evidences produced by Brimmer, Lamb, Gadgil and Tripathy, the illustrious historians, it could be observed that Parsis, along with Marwaris and Gujaratis trading castes, took to entrepreneurial behaviour in the last decades of the 18th century in Calcutta, Bombay and Madras. Britishers and Parsis observed the impact of industrial revolution in Britain and thus they started exploiting Indian natural resources and promoted indigo plantation, leather manufacturing and steelmaking.

Swadeshi Movement and Birth of Indigenous Entrepreneurship

In 1905, Indian leaders adopted concept of ***Swadeshi and boycott*** to counteract the discriminatory policy of the British Government. The *swadeshi* method was based on *atmashakti* (the principle of self-reliance) which meant manufacturing and using indigenous goods by the Indians. The basic objectives of the ***Swadeshi Movement*** were the following:

(a) To promote indigenous industries by the Indian entrepreneurs
(b) To rejuvenate the cottage and handicraft sector
(c) To provide employment opportunities to the craftsmen of India
(d) To open up a vast captive market for sale of products manufactured indigenously through a network of *swadeshi* stores

The movement acted as an antidote to the British policy and encouraged the Indians to plunge into entrepreneurship. Jamshedji Tata established his first iron and steel industry with the help of '*Swadeshi contribution*'. P.C. Roy founded the Bengal Chemical Works. V.O. Chidambaram Pillai set up the indigenous Steam Navigation Company at Tuticorin, Tamil Nadu. Hence, due to this movement indigenous entrepreneurship developed in many types of activities such as textiles, soap, matches, oil, tanneries, potteries, etc. Even banks and insurance companies grew up through *swadeshi* endeavour. During this period, the Europeans took active efforts particularly in plantations and jute.

Indian entrepreneurs were given the opportunities to produce more during the First World War because of the following two reasons.

(i) Increase in demand for India-made goods
(ii) Reduction of import of goods from Britain

Managing Agency System

In the post-war period, the policy of protection by the Government provided stimulant to certain industrial activities. A remarkable feature of the post-war period was the introduction of *Managing Agency System*. This system was initiated by Sri Dwarakanath Tagore who glorified the formation of joint stock companies and emphasized that the management of enterprise must be retained in the hands of the ***firm*** rather than in the hands of any individual. According to Brimmer: "The persons of Indian business communities (Indian agency houses) were the real entrepreneurs. They introduced new methods of production, new sources of raw materials, new products and new markets".

During this period, though the Indian entrepreneurs grew in numbers and made great headway in cotton textiles and steels, they still faced a number of problems such as:

(a) Shortage of technical manpower due to lack of technical and vocational education
(b) Lack of managerial skills
(c) Lack of technical know-how
(d) Low level of confidence in accomplishing the jobs

In view of the above-mentioned problems, the Tatas were forced to employ foreign technicians and managers. However, industries such as cement, sugar, cotton textiles, paper, coal, iron and steel were developed after Second World War. As such, indigenous entrepreneurship grew at a rapid pace with the emergence of entrepreneur classes such as Parsis, Marwaris and Gujaratis in the country on the eve of Independence of India.

1.4.4 Period III: Entrepreneurship in 1947 and Onwards—Post-Independence Period

In the post-Independence period, the Government of India identified the need for rapid industrialization. According to V.R. Gaikward and R.N. Tripathi, socio-economic background of the persons played a decisive role in the process of entrepreneurship. Thomash Timberg has traced the growth of entrepreneurship in the context of leading business community of

Marwaris. During post-Independence period, Marwaris emerged as big investors and industrialists from the status of petty shopkeepers and moneylenders. India adopted the mixed economic system where both private and public sector enterprises play crucial role. In free India, the Government itself emerged as a strong force to take up entrepreneurial ventures by establishing new occupation and industries.

The first Industrial Policy Resolution (IPR) was announced in 1948 which provided clear-cut guidelines for industrial and entrepreneurial development.

Emergence of Marwaris as a Great Business Class

Marwaris had developed a lot in building new and small enterprises in the beginning of post-Independence era. It is believed that 60 per cent of the assets of the Indian industries was in the hands of the Marwaris. The Monopolies Inquiry Commission listed 147 large industries of ***Marwaris*** in almost all areas which proved their entrepreneurial talent. Thus, Marwaris made a successful bid to fill the vacuum left by the British in the business sector.

After Independence, the Birla group set up the rayon mill at Gwalior which had been the largest mill of its kind till 1964. In 1964, the Bajaj group laid the foundation of Hind Lamps and in 1949 Dalmia group established a cement factory in Orissa. Before Independence, the Marwaris controlled only 6 companies; but after Independence, they had 618 directorships which rose to one-fourth of the total in 1951. The report of the Monopolies Inquiry Commission, 1964 has mentioned 37 large industrial houses from which the traditional strength of different communities can be revealed (see Table 1.3).

Table 1.3 Community of Leading Industrialists

Community	*No. of firms*	*Assets in billions (Rs)*
Marwaris	10	7.5
Gujaratis (Hindu)	13	3.8
Bengalis	2	1.5
Parsis	2	4.7
Others	10	2.1
Total	37	19.6

Source: *Monopolies Inquiry Commission Report,* 1964, pp. 119–121.

Table 1.4 reveals the frequency distribution of industrial companies controlled and also the directorship held by communities from 1911–1951.

This Marwaris community emerged as a giant entrepreneurial class in the post-Independence period. The ***houses*** of Birla, Singhnia, Bajaj and others have created their image in the international market in the field of industrial development in India.

Table 1.4 Communities and the Companies.

Communities	*No. of companies controlled*			*No. of directorship held*		
	1911	1931	1951	1911	1931	1951
British	202	416	382	652	1335	865
Parsis	15	25	18	96	261	142
Gujaratis	3	11	17	71	166	232
Jews	5	9	4	17	13	–
Muslims	–	10	3	24	70	66
Bengalis	8	5	20	48	170	320
Marwaris	–	6	96	6	146	618
Mixed control	28	28	79	102	121	372
Total	261	510	619	1016	2282	2622

Source: Adopted from M.M. Mehta, *Structure of Indian Industries*, 2nd ed., p. 352, 1961.

The Industrial Policy Resolution of 1956 emphasized on the need for rapid industrialization through the establishment of heavy industries and expansion of public sector and co-operative enterprises. This had given rise to a complete metamorphosis of socio-economic and industrial environment in the country. Besides the mercantile class, several new communities slowly entered into the entrepreneurial activity and widened the entrepreneurial and industrial base of the country.

In post-Independence period, entrepreneurship has been dispersed both socially and geographically. This has been possible because of infrastructural development, foreign collaboration, technical know-how, expansion of vocational and technical education, export promotion, import substitution and above all, the favourable policy of the Government towards industrial development. The Government by providing incentives, subsidies and other inputs at concessional rates induced the entrepreneurs to set up small scale units. Hence, entrepreneurial growth under planned economic development of the country has reached a new height. With the induction of educated youths in industry, the composition of entrepreneurial class changed significantly.

Emergence of new entrepreneurial class and the growth of entrepreneurs can be attributed to the following aspects:

(a) Establishment of institutional support system such as promotional agencies and financial support agencies
(b) Panchayati Raj institutions for village development
(c) Nationalization of commercial banks in 1969 for the purpose of nation building
(d) Development of money market and capital market
(e) Formation of specialized institutions like NSIC, KVIB, KVIC, MSME, TCOs, SFCs, etc.
(f) Establishment of entrepreneurial development institutions at both national and state levels such as NIESBUD, NIMSME, EDII and IEDs and CEDs respectively.

Thus, a large number of people belonging to the middle or lower middle classes were encouraged to set up their own industrial ventures due to the above-mentioned measures adopted by the Government for promotion of enterprises. This has given a new dimension to entrepreneurial growth. The development schemes, adopted by the government, were aimed at the following objectives to promote new breed of entrepreneurs:

(i) To encourage a proper distribution of economic power between public and private sectors
(ii) To increase the tempo of industrialization by spreading entrepreneurship from the existing industrial centres to other cities, towns and villages
(iii) To spread entrepreneurship from a new dominant entrepreneurs to a large number of industrially potential people of varied social strata

As such, in post-Independence period, the base and magnitude of entrepreneurship in India developed manifold. Entrepreneurs recognized the business not only as a money-spinning activity but also a medium to acquire social status. The family entrepreneurship units such as Tatas, Birlas, Mafatlals, Dalmias, Kirloskars, Desais, Somanis, Ambanis, Kotharis established new frontiers and expanded the existing units.

1.5 COMPARISON OF ENTREPRENEUR WITH ENTREPRENEURSHIP, ENTERPRISE AND MANAGER

The term *entrepreneur* is used synonymously with the term *entrepreneurship*, but they are completely different in their meaning and connotation. Their differences are given in Table 1.5.

Table 1.5 Distinction between Entrepreneur and Entrepreneurship

Entrepreneur	*Entrepreneurship*
1. Entrepreneur is a person.	1. Entrepreneurship is a process.
2. Entrepreneur is an organizer.	2. Entrepreneurship is the organized form of initiative.
3. Entrepreneur is a risk-taker.	3. Entrepreneurship is risk-taking activity.
4. Entrepreneur is an innovator.	4. Entrepreneurship is the process of innovation
5. Entrepreneur is a good planner.	5. Entrepreneurship is the planning for successful performances.
6. Entrepreneur is a leader.	6. Entrepreneurship is the crux of leadership.
7. Entrepreneur is a decision-maker.	7. Entrepreneurship is nothing but a decision-making activity.
8. Entrepreneur is a visualizer.	8. Entrepreneurship is the vision.
9. Entrepreneur is an administrator.	9. Entrepreneurship is the administration.
10. Entrepreneur is an initiator.	10. Entrepreneurship is taking an initiative.

Tables 1.6 and 1.7 compare the entrepreneur with enterprise and manager, respectively.

Table 1.6 Distinction between Entrepreneur and Enterprise

Entrepreneur	*Enterprise*
1. Entrepreneur is person.	1. Enterprise is the business unit.
2. Entrepreneur is risk-taker.	2. Enterprise is the unit involving risk and uncertainty.
3. Entrepreneur is decision-maker.	3. Enterprise serves as the framework within which decision concerning what to produce, how much to produce, where to produce are taken by the entrepreneur.
4. Entrepreneur engages himself in producing and selling the product.	4. Enterprise implies the harmonious interrelation or service of functions and staff primarily for the purpose of making/selling product or service.
5. Entrepreneur procures raw materials and other inputs for production.	5. Enterprise utilises the raw materials and other inputs in the process of production.

Table 1.7 Distinction between Entrepreneur and Manager.

Entrepreneur	*Manager*
1. Entrepreneur is an innovator	1. Manager keeps in managing the business on established rules, polices and procedures.
2. Entrepreneur is a moderate risk-taker.	2. Manager does not undertake risk.
3. Entrepreneur is not guided by the motive of profit. He continuously puts his efforts for achieving the goal—reward of the entire process in connection.	3. Manager is interested in salary. His salary is fixed and certain.
4. Entrepreneur is self-employed and his own boss.	4. Manager is a salaried person and dependent upon his employer.

EXERCISES

A. Long answer type questions:

1. Who is an entrepreneur? What are the characteristics of a successful entrepreneur?

2. Distinguish between entrepreneur and manager.

3. Define entrepreneurship. What are the characteristic features of entrepreneurship?

4. Define entrepreneur. Explain briefly the characteristics and traits of an entrepreneur.
5. Define entrepreneurship. How is it different from the word entrepreneur ?
6. Explain briefly the emergence of entrepreneurial class in India.
7. Explain the growth of entrepreneurship in post-Independence period.
8. What are the barriers for non-development of entrepreneurship during pre-Independence era?

B. Short answer type questions:

1. Write short notes on the following:
   (a) Entrepreneurship and enterprise
   (b) Vaisyas as entrepreneurs
   (c) Decision making and business planning
   (d) Risk taking and leadership
2. Distinguish between:
   (a) Entrepreneur and professional manager
   (b) Entrepreneurship and enterprise
   (c) Entrepreneur and entrepreneurship
3. Define the following terms:
   (a) Innovation
   (b) Creativity
   (c) Locus of control
   (d) Decision making
   (e) Entrepreneur
   (f) Entrepreneurship

CHAPTER 2

Classification and Functions of Entrepreneur

CHAPTER CONTENTS

2.1 INTRODUCTION

In modern day world, various types of entrepreneurs are found engaged in various types of activities. They are not only found in industrial activities but also in agricultural and commercial activities. One can very well recognize the entrepreneurs working in industry, service and business sectors which are technically called as ***ISB*** sectors. However, Clarence Danhof, on the basis of his study of the American agriculture, classified entrepreneurs into the various categories, which are discussed in the next section.

2.2 DANHOF'S CLASSIFICATION

1. ***Innovating entrepreneurs:*** This category of entrepreneurs is characterized by the smell of innovativeness. These entrepreneurs sense the opportunities for introduction

of new ideas, new technology of production, opening of new markets and creating new organizations. Innovating entrepreneurs are very much helpful for their country because they bring about a transformation in lifestyle.

2. ***Adoptive or imitative entrepreneurs:*** These entrepreneurs imitate the existing entrepreneurs and set up their enterprise in the same manner. Instead of innovating, they just imitate the technology and methods innovated by others. These entrepreneurs are very much helping in less developed countries as they contribute significantly in the growth of enterprise and entrepreneurial culture in these countries. Further by adopting the technology, which is already tested, they generate ample employment avenues for countries and therefore they are treated as the agent of the economic development.
3. ***Fabian entrepreneurs:*** These entrepreneurs are very much sceptical in their approach in adopting or innovating new technology in their enterprise. They are not adaptable to the changing environment. They love to remain in the existing business with the age-old techniques of production. They only adopt the new technologies when they realize that failure to adopt will lead to loss or collapse of the enterprise.
4. ***Drone entrepreneurs:*** These entrepreneurs are conservative or orthodox in outlook. They never like to get rid of their traditional business and traditional machineries or systems of the business. They always feel comfortable with their old-fashioned technology of production even though the environment as well as the society have undergone considerable changes. Thus, drone entrepreneurs refuse to adopt the changes. They are laggards as they continue to operate in their traditional way and resist changes.

In recent years, some new classifications have been made regarding entrepreneurs, which are discussed further.

1. ***Solo operators:*** These entrepreneurs prefer to set up their business individually. They introduce their own capital, intellect and business acumen to run the enterprise successfully. They operate their business mainly in the form of proprietorship type of concern.
2. ***Active partners:*** Entrepreneurs of this type jointly put their efforts to build enterprise pooling together their own resources. They actively participate in managing the daily routine of the business concern. As such, the business houses or the firms which are managed by the active partners become more successful in their operation.
3. ***Inventors:*** These entrepreneurs primarily involve themselves in Research and Development (R and D) activities. They are creative in character and feel happy in inventing new products, technologies and methods of production.
4. ***Challengers:*** Entrepreneurs of this type take challenges to establish business venture as mark of achievement. They keep on improving their standard and face boldly the odds and adversities that come in their way. They use their business acumen and talent to convert the odds into opportunities thereby making profit. According to them, if there is no challenge in life, there is no charm in life. Challenges make them bold, and thus, they never hesitate to plunge themselves into uncertainties for earning profit.

5. ***Buyers (entrepreneurs):*** These entrepreneurs explore opportunities to purchase the existing units which may be seized or are in running condition. If the units they purchase are sick they turn them around using their experiences, expertise and business acumen. By purchasing these units they make themselves free from the hassles of building infrastructures and other facilities.
6. ***Life timers:*** These entrepreneurs believe that business is the part and parcel of their life. They take up the business to reunite successfully as a matter of ego satisfaction. They have a strong desire for taking personal responsibility. Family enterprises which thrive due to high personal skill are included under this category.

2.3 OTHER CLASSIFICATIONS

Apart from the categories discussed in the previous section, there are various types of entrepreneurs which are classified on the basis of age, sex, types of business, use of technology, etc. These categories are discussed further.

1. ***Industrial entrepreneurs:*** Industrial entrepreneurs include large scale, medium scale, small scale and tiny entrepreneurs who operate large, medium, small and tiny business. It also includes micro-entrepreneurs who manufacture and sell the products by establishing micro-enterprises. These entrepreneurs primarily take up manufacturing activities.
2. ***Service entrepreneurs:*** Entrepreneurs of this category involve in service sector activities like repair and maintenance, engineering workshop, beauty parlours, etc., where the entrepreneurs can provide services to the people. This type of enterprise needs skill and vocational training for its success.
3. ***Business entrepreneurs:*** In recent years, business entrepreneurs are treated as trading entrepreneurs. They are not concerned with manufacturing activity. They only undertake trading as their enterprise or business. They identify viable market opportunities and convert them into profitable business concerns to stimulate the demand for their product in the market. Enterprises like stationary store, medicine shop, cloth store etc. come under this category.
4. ***Agricultural entrepreneurs:*** These entrepreneurs engage themselves in agricultural activities like plantation crops, exotic flower production, cash crops, horticulture, floriculture, animal husbandry, dairy, poultry etc. These entrepreneurs come forward to use modern methods of production, modern irrigation facilities, pesticides, HYV seeds, etc. for more volume of production and more amount of profit than that in traditional agriculture.
5. ***Corporate entrepreneurs:*** Corporate entrepreneurs exhibit their skills and intelligence by promoting—corporation. A corporation for business organization is formed and registered under a statute, which gives it a separate legal entity. Corporate entrepreneurs, therefore, undertake their business activities under legally registered company or trust.

6. ***First generation entrepreneurs:*** These entrepreneurs do not possess any family business background beforehand. They start their enterprises on their own using their own skill, experience, expertise and exposure. They are, in fact, self-made entrepreneurs.
7. ***Classical entrepreneurs:*** These entrepreneurs are traditional and stereotype in their approach. They are motivated by their economic gain and persistently aim at optimizing profit.
8. ***Pure entrepreneurs:*** Pure entrepreneurs believe in their own performance while undertaking business activities. They strive to prove their excellence in ventures. They are guided by the motive of profit and apply their business skills to earn more and more profit.
9. ***Induced entrepreneurs:*** These entrepreneurs are induced by the promotional agencies to set up enterprise with the help of the government. From time to time, the government announces industrial policy in which subsidies and incentives in various forms are provided to the persons interested to start small-scale business ventures. By providing basket of facilities like financial assistance, land at cheap price, scarce raw materials, tax exemption, skill training, etc. these agencies usually provide inducement to the persons to become entrepreneur.
10. ***Spontaneous entrepreneurs:*** These entrepreneurs start their own enterprise spontaneously. They are self-confident and positive in their approach. Their inner urge and inborn talent drive them to establish their own venture.
11. ***Women entrepreneurs:*** Women entrepreneurs are defined as the women or the group of women who initiate, organize and operate a business enterprise. According to Government of India views, a woman entrepreneur is defined as an enterprise owned and controlled by a woman and having minimum financial interests of 51 per cent of the capital and giving at least 51 per cent of the employment generated in the enterprise to women.
12. ***Rural entrepreneurs:*** Entrepreneurs selecting rural-based industrial opportunity in either khadi or village industries sector or in farm entrepreneurships are regarded as rural entrepreneurs. According to Khadi and Village Industry Commission (KVIC), village industry or rural industry means any industry located in the rural area, population of which does not exceed 10,000 which produces any goods or renders any services with or without use of power and in which the fixed capital investment per head of an artisan or a worker does not exceed a thousand rupees. This definition has recently been modified by the government. Accordingly, any industry located as village industries in rural area, village or town with a population of 20,000 and below and an investment of Rs 3 crores in plant and machineries classified as village industries. Thus, rural entrepreneurs are given ample scope to establish village industry for bringing about regional balance.
13. ***Modern entrepreneurs:*** Modern entrepreneurs always produce goods and services in accordance with the changing needs of the time and adopt the changes very quickly. They undertake those economic activities or business, which suits to the current demand of the market.

14. ***Non-technical entrepreneurs:*** These entrepreneurs are more concerned with the non-technical aspects of the products, which they deal with. They persistently try to develop alternative marketing and distribution strategies to promote their business. They plan their strategy in such a way that the demand for their goods/services increases
15. ***Technical entrepreneurs:*** Entrepreneurs of these types are technically educated or experienced. They have got the quality of craftsmanship and they depend upon their skill in production techniques. These technically trained manpower are the greatest strength of the country so far as the entrepreneurial development is concerned.
16. ***Individual entrepreneurs:*** Individual entrepreneurs are usually found in small scale sectors. These entrepreneurs introduce their own fund, intelligence and skill to establish their small business units. Such entrepreneurs have the advantages of flexibility, quick decision and the favour from the government as well as the promotional agencies. Individual entrepreneurs bear the risk to earn profit.
17. ***Institutional entrepreneurs:*** In case of business enterprises which need some complex decisions due to the bigger size of the scale of operation, institutionalization of the entreprise is needed. Here, a group of entrepreneurs has to be developed to handle the complex process of decision making in the matters of finance, investment of capital and marketing of products.
18. ***Entrepreneurs by inheritance:*** The right of inheritance is the basic factor which makes a person inherit the business of the family through succession. In our country, the family-controlled business barons like Tatas, Birlas, Ambanis come under this category. In this case, firms are passed from one generation to another.
19. ***Forced entrepreneurs:*** Entrepreneurs of this category are forced by the environmental conditions to become entrepreneurs. Unemployed persons without a job or persons with comparatively low educational background enter into the field of entrepreneurship. Since in the former case, many people take to enterprise building either through government patronage by availing schematic finance through IRDP, SEEUY, PMRY, SGSY, etc. They are called forced entrepreneurs.
20. ***Professional entrepreneurs:*** These entrepreneurs take active interest in establishing new enterprises but never stay in that business for a long time. They sell out the existing business and start new ventures with the increased sales. Such entrepreneurs are dynamic and keep on identifying innovative ideas and convert them into commercially-viable projects.

2.4 INTRAPRENEURS

In recent years, an emerging group of persons left big corporations and started their own small business in America either because their ideas were not accepted by their top bosses or because the ideas were innovative enough to offer ample scope of making good profit. These persons were turned to entrepreneurs and achieved great success in their new ventures. These entrepreneurs came to be known as ***intrapreneurs***.

Gifford Pinchot III, an American management specialist, in his book *Intrapreneuring*, used the term *intrapreneurs* to depict the persons who resigned from their well-paid executive positions to launch their own ventures. Intrapreneurs are also innovators like entrepreneurs. They also introduce new products, ideas and services within the framework of a company to grow and succeed in a changing environment. Table 2.1 portrays the distinction between entrepreneur and intrapreneur.

Table 2.1 Distinction between Entrepreneur and Intrapreneur

Entrepreneur	*Intrapreneur*
1. Entrepreneur is independent.	1. Intrapreneur is semi-independent.
2. Entrepreneur raises their funds on his own initiative.	2. Intrapreneur depends upon the industry in which he works for getting the finance.
3. Entrepreneur takes the profit of the business.	3. Intrapreneur does not take profit out of innovations but he can be provided with a variety of perquisite for their innovation.
4. Entrepreneur bears the full risk of his business.	4. Intrapreneur bears the risk of the business which is a small part of the entire business.
5. Entrepreneur is the real owner of the business.	5. Intrapreneur is not the real owner of the business, rather he works for the business.
6. Entrepreneur operates from outside an organization.	6. Intrapreneur operates from within the organization.
7. Entrepreneur converts the ideas of intrapreneur into viable opportunities.	7. Intrapreneur takes the responsibility of creating innovation of any kind from within the organization.

2.5 ULTRAPRENEURS

The concept of entrepreneurship is an evolved thing. Even though it has been there for a long time, its performance and execution evolve with the prevalent economic condition of the day. The entrepreneurs of 90s are a different breed in relation to their immediate predecessors from the 80s. Thus, the path of successful entrepreneurship is ever changing as the art and science of entrepreneurship is taking a new colour. This new breed of entrepreneurs is challenging the old notion that entrepreneurs are born, not made. There are several reasons to this change. This may be due to global competitiveness, tight financing concept or for unforgiving business environment. Now-a-days, new products and services are conceived, created, tested, produced and marketed very quickly and with great speed. Therefore, today's entrepreneur needs to have a different mindset about establishing and operating a company. The mindset is what is called ***ultrapreneuring***.

According to **James B. Arkebauer**, the concept of ultrapreneuring is to identify a business opportunity, determine its viability and form a company. It requires assembling a supercompetent management team who then develop, produce and market the product or service. They then sell the majority interest in the company, all of this with maximum resource leverage of both talent and money in the shortest optimum time period.

Gone are the days of developing a company to die with and no more cradle to grave management thinking. Ultragrowth companies are not made to pass on to the next generation. Ultrapreneurs create them and then sell out, merge or combine. Their life-long challenge is to do it again and over again.

The following are some of the characteristics of an ultrapreneur.

(a) Achievement
(b) Action orientation
(c) Commitment
(d) Energy
(e) Goal setting
(f) Growth orientation
(g) Honesty
(h) Innovation
(i) Intelligence
(j) Leadership
(k) Risk tolerance
(l) Self-confidence

2.6 FUNCTIONS OF ENTREPRENEURS

Entrepreneurs is an opportunity seeker. He is also the organizer and coordinator of the agents of production. He has to execute many a good functions while establishing a small-scale enterprise. He not only perceives the business opportunities but also mobilizes the other resources like **5 Ms**—man, money, machine, materials and methods. However, the main functions of the entrepreneurs are discussed further.

1. ***Idea generation:*** This is the most important function of the entrepreneur. Idea generation can be possible through the vision, insight, observation, experience, education, training and exposure of the entrepreneur. Idea generation precisely implies product selection and project identification. Ideas can be generated through environmental scanning and market survey. It is the function of the entrepreneurs to generate as many ideas as he can for the purpose of selecting the best business opportunities which can subsequently be taken up by him as a commercially-viable business venture.
2. ***Determination of objectives:*** The next function of the entrepreneur is to determine and lay down the objectives of the business, which should be spelt out on clear terms. In other words, entrepreneur should be very much clear about the following things:

(i) The nature of business
(ii) The type of business

This implies whether the enterprise belongs to the category of a manufacturing concern or a service-oriented unit or a trading business, so that the entrepreneurs can very well carry on the venture in accordance with the objectives determined by him.

3. ***Raising of funds:*** Fund raising is the most important function of an entrepreneur. All the activities of a business depend upon the finance and its proper management. It is the responsibility of the entrepreneur to raise funds internally as well as externally. In this matter, he should be aware of the different sources of funds and the formalities to raise funds. He should have the full knowledge of different government sponsored schemes such as PMRY, SGSY, REGP, etc. by which he can get Government assistance in the form of seed capital, fixed and working capital for his business.
4. ***Procurement of raw materials:*** Another important function of the entrepreneur is to procure raw materials. Entrepreneur has to identify the cheap and regular sources of supply of raw materials, which will help him to reduce the cost of production and face the competition boldly.
5. ***Procurement of machinery:*** The next function of the entrepreneurs is to procure the machineries and equipments for establishment of the venture. While procuring the machineries, he should specify the following details:

   (a) The details of technology
   (b) Installed capacity of the machines
   (c) Names of the manufacturers and suppliers
   (d) Whether the machines are indigenously made or foreign made
   (e) After-sales service facilities
   (f) Warranty period of the machineries

   All these details are to be minutely observed by the entrepreneurs.
6. ***Market research:*** The next important function of the entrepreneur is market research and product analysis. Market research is the systematic collection of data regarding the product which the entrepreneur wants to manufacture. Entrepreneur has to undertake market research persistently in order to know the details of the intending product, i.e. the demand for the product, the supply of the product, the price of the product, the size of the customers, etc. while starting an enterprise.
7. ***Determination of form of enterprise:*** The function of an entrepreneur in determining the form of enterprise is also important. Entrepreneur has to decide the form of enterprise based upon the nature of the product, volume of investment, nature of activities, types of product, quality of product, quality of human resources, etc. The chief forms of ownership organizations are sole proprietorship, partnership, joint stock company and cooperative society. Determination of ownership right is essential on the part of the entrepreneur to acquire legal title to assets.

8. ***Recruitment of manpower:*** Entrepreneur has to perform the following activities while undertaking this function:
   (a) Estimating manpower need of the organization
   (b) Laying down of selection procedure
   (c) Devising scheme of compensation
   (d) Laying down the rules of training and development
9. ***Implementation of the project:*** Entrepreneur has to work on the implementation schedule or the action plan of the project. The identified project is to be implemented in a time-bound manner. All the activities from the conception stage to the commissioning stage are to be accomplished by him in accordance with the implementation schedule to avoid cost and time overrun, as well as competition. Thus, implementation of the project is an important function of the entrepreneur.

To conclude with, all these functions of the entrepreneur can precisely be put into the following categories:

(i) Innovation
(ii) Risk bearing
(iv) Organization and management

EXERCISES

A. Long answer type questions:

1. Briefly describe the classification of entrepreneurs as per Danhof's classification.
2. Distinguish between intrapreneur and entrepreneur.
3. What are the various types of entrepreneurs? Explain them briefly?
4. What is meant by ultrapreneur? How is ultrapreneur different from entrepreneur?
5. What are the chief functions of an entrepreneur?

B. Short answer type questions:

1. Write short notes on the following:
   (a) Imitative entrepreneur
   (b) Industrial entrepreneur
   (c) First generation entrepreneur
   (d) Forced entrepreneur
   (e) Agricultural entrepreneur
2. Distinguish between:
   (a) Fabian entrepreneur and drone entrepreneur
   (b) Innovating entrepreneur and imitative entrepreneur
   (c) Agricultural entrepreneur and corporate entrepreneur
   (d) Business entrepreneur and trading entrepreneur
   (e) Intrapreneur and ultrapreneur.

CHAPTER 3

Theories of Entrepreneurship

CHAPTER CONTENTS

Entrepreneurship is an evolved thing. With the advancement of science and technology, it has undergone metamorphosis and emerged as a critical input for socio-economic development. Various writers have developed various theories on entrepreneurship and popularized the concept among the common people. The theories propounded by them can be categorized as under:

- Sociological theories
- Economic theories
- Cultural theories
- Psychological theories

3.1 SOCIOLOGICAL THEORIES

The following theories explain how sociological factors accelerate the growth of entrepreneurship:

- Theory of religious belief—Weber
- Theory of entrepreneurial supply—Cochran
- Theory of social change—Hagen
- Theory of group level pattern—Young

3.1.1 Theory of Religious Belief—Max Weber

Max Weber has propounded the theory of religious belief. According to him, entrepreneurism is a function of religious belief and the impact of religion shapes the entrepreneurial culture. He emphasized that the entrepreneurial energies are exogenous supplied by means of religious belief. The central feature of Weberian theory of social change, therefore, consists in his treatment of the ***protestant ethic*** and the ***spirit of capitalism.*** However, the important elements of Weber's theory are discussed further.

1. ***Spirit of capitalism:*** In the Webrian theory, spirit of capitalism is highlighted. We all know that capitalism is an economic system in which economic freedom and private enterprise are glorified, so also the entrepreneurial culture. Spirit of capitalism, therefore, is the guiding factor which guides the entrepreneur to get engaged in activities that can bring about more and more profit. Thus, the profit motive character coupled with the attitude towards acquisition of money urges the individual to start new venture.
2. ***Adventurous spirit:*** Weber also made a distinction between spirit of capitalism and adventurous spirit. According to him, the former is influenced by the strict discipline whereas the latter is affected by the free force of impulse. Entrepreneurship culture is governed by both these factors. According to Max Weber, the spirit of capitalism can be grown only when mental attitude in the society is favourable to capitalism.
3. ***Protestant ethic:*** According to Max Weber, the spirit of capitalism can be grown only when mental attitude in the society is favourable to capitalism. This attitude can be provided by protestant ethic irrespective of the cultural background, personality type of the individual and the experiences in the society. According to Max Weber, Hinduism lacks this sort of mental attitude which acts as a stumbling block in their way to entrepreneurship.
4. ***Inducement of profit:*** Weber introduced the new businessmen into the picture of tranquil routine. The spirit of capitalism intertwined with the motive of profit resulted in creation of greater number of business enterprises thereby leading to a complete reorganization of industrial sector. The principle of low prices and large turnovers was the mechanism of the entrepreneurs to reap profit. So this motive of profit guided the protestant ethic to become entrepreneurial which was not found among the Hindus.

In fact, this theory suited the British rulers, who desired to encourage European entrepreneurship in India. This theory was vehemently criticized by many researchers because of the following unrealistic assumptions which **Max Weber** highlighted:

(a) There is only one system of Hindu value.
(b) The Indian community internalized those values and translated them in to daily routine.
(c) These values remained immune to and insulated against external pressures and change.

But rapid growth of entrepreneurship and emergence of a large number of entrepreneurs in the post-Independence era proved that Hinduism is neither a stumbling block nor a demotivating religious belief to the spirit of capitalism and to the sprit of adventure to start innovative enterprises.

3.1.2 Theory of Entrepreneurial Supply—Thomas Cochran

The theory, propounded by Thomas Cochran, centres round the sociological aspect of entrepreneurial supply. Beginning with the premise that fundamental problems of economic development are non-economic, he emphasizes on the cultural values, role expectation and social sanctions as the key elements that determine the supply of entrepreneurs. The basic elements of Thomas Cochran's theory are depicted further.

1. ***Entrepreneur as a society's modal personality:*** According to T. Cochran, entrepreneur is neither a supernormal individual nor a deviant person but is a role model of the society representing modal personality. This personality is a composite of the person, his skills, styles and motives.
2. ***Modal personality as a derivative of social conditioning:*** The entrepreneur, being the Chief Executive of his business, plays a social role. The role is partly shaped by the modal personality that is a derivative of ***social conditioning of his generation***. Further, ***innovation and invention*** go together with the type of conditioning in the society.
3. ***Role expectations and entrepreneurial role:*** Cochran pointed out that in corporate organizations, senior officers or the Board of Directors have well-defined expectations. They are known as ***defining groups*** and entrepreneurial role is closely defined by them. According to him, "Primary cultural factors operating on the personality of the executive and the defining of his role by those involved must accommodate to some degree to the necessities of the operation to be carried out".
4. ***The type of childrearing and schooling and its influence on intrinsic character of the executive:*** According to Cochran, the executive's 'inner character' is conditioned by the childrearing and schooling common to the cultural legacies. He contemplated, "This relatively simple framework of an entrepreneurial role defined by personality of the actor, the expectations of the groups with power to sanction deviations from expected behaviour and the operational needs of the function to be performed subsumes all the social or cultural factors".

5. ***Dynamics of entrepreneurs and thrust upon the social factors for the major changes:*** According to Cochran, the demonstration of this model of dynamics of entrepreneurs gives thrust upon the social factors for the major changes. He pointed out that the model is based upon the American Economic History which proves that American economy has experienced major changes during 19th century due to entrepreneurial dynamism. The changes are ascribed to the following factors:
   (a) Quick adoption of mechanical devices in the first half of the 19th century
   (b) Growth of professional management in the corporate sector that started in the second half of the 19th century
   (c) Widespread application of mass production techniques in the 19th century

In each of these major transformation, the social factors operating through entrepreneur appear to be well marked. Under the above backdrop, Cochran pointed out that individual's performance as entrepreneur is governed by the following elements:

(a) Attitude of the entrepreneur towards his own occupation
(b) The role expectation held by sanctioning groups
(c) The operational requirements of the job

In fact, both the first and the second elements are determined by the societal values whereas the last element is governed by the changes over a period of time in extraneous parameters such as population, technology, consumer demand, tastes and preferences of the customers, etc.

3.1.3 Theory of Social Change—E.E. Hagen

Everett E. Hagen, in his theory of social change, propounded how a traditional society becomes one in which continuing technical progress takes place. The theory exhorts the following features which presumes the entrepreneur's creativity as the key element of social transformation and economic growth.

1. ***Presentation of the general model of the society:*** The theory reveals a general model of the society which considers interrelationship among physical environment, social structure, personality and culture.
2. ***Economic growth: product of social change and political change:*** According to Hagen, most of the economic theories of underdevelopment are inadequate. He viewed entrepreneur as a creative problem-shooter who brings about economic development which is mingled with political and social changes.
3. ***Rejection of follower's syndrome:*** Hagen rejected the idea that the solution to economic development lies in imitating western technology. So the follower's syndrome on the part of the entrepreneur, is discouraged. This is because the technology is an integral part of sociocultural-complex, and super-imposition of the same into different sociocultural set-up may not deliver the goods.
4. ***Historic shift as a factor of initiating change:*** Hagen, in his book *How Economic Growth Begins*, depicts historic shift as the crucial force which has brought about

social change and technological progress thereby leading to the emergence of entrepreneurial class from different castes and communities. The historic shift caused some groups of the lesser elite, who previously held commanding position in the social hierarchy, feel that they were no longer valued and regarded. As a result of this, their inner urge was kindled to take up entrepreneurial venture through personality formation and thus they become competent enough to take up any kind of venture.

5. ***Withdrawal of status respects as the mechanism for rigorous entrepreneurial activity:*** Closely consistent with the historic shift it is the social group that plunges into rigorous entrepreneurism which experiences the status withdrawal or '***withdrawal of status respect***'. According to **Hagen,** they are a group of individuals, creative and alienated from traditional values, driven by a gnawing burning drive to prove themselves (to themselves as well as to their fellows) seeking for an area in which to do—preferably an area in which they can gain power and in some symbolic way they can vent their rage at the elites who have caused their troubles. Their inner urge will culminate into entrepreneurism disregarding their traditional values and turning to innovative entrepreneurship. The role of ***lesser Samurai*** as innovators and entrepreneur in Japan's industrial revolution is a glaring example of status withdrawal. When withdrawal of status respect occurs, it leads to four different responses and creation of four different personality types, namely:

   (i) **Retreatist**—One who constantly does his work in the society but remains indifferent to his own position.
   (ii) **Ritualist**—One who adopts a kind of defensive personality and acts in the ways accepted and approved in his society without any hope of improving his opposition.
   (iii) **Reformist**—One who initiates rebellion and attempts to establish a new order in the society.
   (iv) **Innovator**—A creative individual who converts all odds into opportunities and is likely to become an entrepreneur.

Hence, Hagen's creative personality is the admixture of **Schumpeter's** innovation and **McClelland's** high need for achievement.

But **Hagen's** analysis fails to give policy measures for backward countries which are striving for economic development as he identifies status withdrawal as the causal factor in the emergence of creative personality and withdrawal of status. **Hagen's** thesis of disadvantaged minority groups has its own limitations. There are many disadvantaged minority groups in India which have not supplied a good number of entrepreneurs.

3.1.4 Theory of Group Level Pattern: F. Young

Frank Young, in his theory, *A Micro-sociological Interpretation of Entrepreneurship*, points out that entrepreneurial initiative is a function of group level pattern. Young has elaborately analysed the shortcomings of psychogeneric interpretation of entrepreneurship and suggested a causal sequence where *transformation codes* are developed by the solidarity groups to improve their symbolic position in their larger structure and thus become entrepreneurs. The theory has the following important features:

1. ***Deficiencies in psychogenic mediation model:*** Prior to depicting a microsociological interpretation of entrepreneurship, **Young** deals with the shortcomings of psychogenic mediation model. While stating that development is an organizational phenomenon, he points out the deficiencies to explain the emergence of new kind of organization. He states, without exception, that they are mute on the question of how individual tendencies, special abilities, unusual motivation or perception of particular opportunities is transformed into emergent property that is social organization. According to Young, "Of entrepreneurs in particular, imitative time taken by the development process are some of the demerits of psychogenic interpretation of entrepreneurship".
2. ***Solidarity groups:*** **Frank Young** regarded the solidarity groups as the main agencies for building entrepreneurship. He interprets individual level entrepreneurism as the under side of group level pattern. He maintains that entrepreneurial characteristics are found in clusters, ethnic communities, occupational groups or politically-oriented factions. According to **Frank Young:** "Of these groups, those who show a certain reactiveness or solidarity define the degree to which members create, maintain a coherent definition of their situation that size upon the rhetoric of religion or politics as a vehicle for expressing their deviation view of the world".
3. ***Disregarding single-handed concept of entrepreneurship:*** Young disregards the claim that entrepreneur works single handedly or solely. According to him, entrepreneurial activity is the product of family background, experience and exposure of the individual as a member of the group and as a reflection of general values. Thus, entrepreneur as a member of a particular group does not work alone. In his own words, he is simply the most visible member from an economic point of view what is typically a cluster of families whose activity is mutually reinforcing and coordinated by a coherent outlook on the world.
4. ***Reduction of complex economic problems:*** The solidarity of entrepreneurial groups reduces a number of economic problems that crop up in case of individual entrepreneur. This effort is likely to reduce the economic problems through the device of recombination of factors related to the production, higher standards of labour, search for new resources, technology and markets and a more effective management of money and time. As such, the entrepreneur builds confidence which he derives from the concept of solidarity in a pragmatic manner by the solution of economic and social problems.

 Young conducted a Thematic Apperception Test (TAT) on a group of entrepreneurs. The following findings are derived from the test:

 (a) The test revealed the tendency to depict the situation as a problem to be solved.
 (b) An awareness of pragmatic effort required.
 (c) Confidence on their ability to solve the problems
 (d) Willingness to take the views of each individual in turn and analyse the situation as he perceives before suggesting any outcome.

 To be more clear, Young discussed the sociogenic explanation of solidarity structure of entrepreneurial supply.

5. ***Incorporation of reactive subgroups:*** In his theory, **Frank Young**, incorporated the idea of reactive subgroups which play the most important role in enterprise creation. According to **Young,** a group becomes reactive when three important conditions coincide. They are very much helpful to the entrepreneurial supply. These ***conditions*** are as follows:
   (a) When low status recognition is found in a group.
   (b) When access to important social networks is denied.
   (c) When the group has better institutional resources than other groups in the society at the same level.

In fine, Young's theory of entrepreneurial supply is a function of group level pattern which gives emphasis on the concept of solidarity clusters, ethnic communities and above all the groups.

3.2 ECONOMIC THEORIES

Entrepreneurship and economic development are interdependent. Economic development takes place when a country's real rational income increases over a period of time wherein the role of entrepreneurship is an integral part. The following theories propounded by eminent economists explain how economic development and entrepreneurship are complementary and supplementary to each other:

- Schumpeter's theory of innovation
- Leibenstein's theory X-efficiency
- Mark Casson's theory
- Papanek and Haris' theory
- Harvard School theory
- M. Kirzner's theory
- David McClelland's theory of achievement
- Knight's theory of profit
- Hayek's theory of market equilibrium

3.2.1 Schumpeter's Theory of Innovation

Schumpeter's theory of entrepreneurship is a pioneering work of economic development. Development, in his sense, implies that carrying out of new combinations of entrepreneurship is basically a creative activity. According to **Schumpeter,** an entrepreneur is one who perceives the opportunities to innovate, i.e. to carry out new combinations or enterprise. Innovation involves problem solving and the entrepreneur is a problem solver. In his views, the concept of new combination leading to innovation covers the following five cases.

(i) The introduction of ***new goods,*** that is the one with which consumers are not yet familiar, of a new quality.

(ii) The introduction of ***new method of production***, that is yet to be tested by experience in the branch of manufacture concerned which need, by no means, to be founded upon a scientifically new discovery and can also exist in a new way of handling a commodity commercially.

(iii) The opening of a ***new market***, that is a market into which the particular branch of manufacture of the country in question has not previously entered, whether or not this market has existed before.

(iv) The conquest of *a* ***new source of supply of a raw material*** or semi-manufactured goods, again irrespective of whether this source already exists or whether it has first to be created.

(v) The carrying out of ***the new organization***, of any industry like the creation of monopoly position through fructification or breaking up of a monopoly position.

The carrying out of the above-mentioned combinations, Schumpeter calls ***enterprise*** and the individual who carries them out he calls ***entrepreneur***. In view of the above, Schumpeterian theory of entrepreneurship has got the following features:

1. ***Distinction between invention and innovation:*** **Schumpeter** makes a distinction between innovation and invention. Invention means creation of new things and innovation means application of new things into practical use. An innovator is an enterprising person who applies inventions in order to make new combinations and thus manufactures new goods for better profits. An inventor is the producer or creator of ideas whereas the innovator implements these ideas. An innovator is the entrepreneur who converts these ideas into commercially-viable projects. Thus, an innovator always stands a step further than the inventor in exploiting the new ideas commercially.

   While proceeding towards economic development, each economy carries innovations. During 1967–68, the technological breakthrough in agriculture by the Government of India for introduction of HYV seeds, mechanization in agriculture are the glaring examples of innovation. Similarly e-commerce evolution of CAD, CAM and the growth of joint stock company are examples of innovation.

2. ***Emphasis on entrepreneurial functions:*** Schumpeter has given emphasis on the role of entrepreneurial functions in economic development. In his views, development means basic transformation of the economy that is brought about by entrepreneurial functions. Entrepreneurs are motivated intellectual class of people and the prime movers of economic development. They foresee the potential opportunity and constantly try to exploit it. They are distinguished from rest of the population because of their latent capacity to perceive and mobilize resources. Thus, one of the most important functions of an entrepreneur is to mobilize such resources which are known as ***5 Ms*** in modern management, i.e. Man, Material, Money, Machine and Method, etc. can be properly coordinated by the entrepreneur to maximize profit from his own venture thereby leading to economic growth.

3. ***Presentation of disequilibrium situation through entrepreneurial activity:*** The entrepreneurial activity represents a disequilibrium situation, a dynamic phenomenon and a break from the routine or a ***circular flow or a tendency towards equilibrium***.

Entrepreneurs, therefore, plunges into innovative activity to which they are new. According to **Schumpeter**: "While he swims with the stream in the circular flow which is familiar to him, he swims against stream if he wishes to change its channel. What was formerly a help becomes a hindrance. What was familiar datum becomes an unknown. Where the boundaries of routine stop, many people can go no further and the rest can only do so in a highly variable manner". This is why carrying out new combinations is an object of special kind of function.

4. ***Entrepreneurship in relation to three corresponding pairs of opposites:*** **Schumpeter** determines entrepreneurship and entrepreneurial character by three corresponding pairs of opposites:
   (i) By the opposition of two real process—the circular flow or the tendency towards equilibrium on one hand and a change in channels of economic routine or spontaneous change in the economic data arising from within the system on the other
   (ii) By the opposition of two important apparatus, statistics and dynamics
   (iii) By the opposition of two types of conduct, which following reality, we can picture as two types of individuals—mere mangers and entrepreneurs
5. ***Characteristic motives of the entrepreneurial conduct:*** In his theory, **Schumpeter** deals with the question of characteristic motives of entrepreneurial conduct. Although he tries to indicate the ***psychology of entrepreneur***, he believes that none of the results to which our analysis is intended to lead stands or falls with psychology of entrepreneur or could be vitiated by any errors in it.
6. ***Entrepreneurial dream and the will to found a private kingdom:*** Entrepreneurial motives are governed by the will power to conquer for establishing private kingdom. The motives of creating things and applying these things into practice inspire the entrepreneur to undertake innovation. According to **Schumpeter,** "Dream and the will to found a private kingdom, will to conquer and finally "***the joy of creating and getting things done or simply of exercising ones energy and ingenuity***" are the motives that inspire the innovative entrepreneur to undertake innovation.

Critical evaluation: **Schumpeter's** theory of entrepreneurship is criticized on the following grounds:

(a) The theory has broadened the scope of entrepreneurism in the sense that it has included the individual businessman along with the directors and managers of company who actually carry out new combinations known as innovative functions. It is considered narrow because individuals, though operate successful business enterprise but lacks innovation.

(b) **Schumpeter's** innovating entrepreneur represents the enterprise with R and D and innovative character. But developing countries lack these types of entrepreneurs.

(c) **Schumpeterian** theory of entrepreneurship gives too much emphasis on innovation. It excludes the risk taking and organizing aspects of entrepreneurship which are equally important from the point of view of enterprise building.

(d) **Schumpeter's** entrepreneurs are large scale businessmen who introduce new technology, methods of production, etc. But in underdeveloped countries entrepreneurs who start their business generally do not have a large scale business enterprise in the beginning. Further, they also prefer to operate on traditional technology. These countries actually need more imitative entrepreneurs than innovating entrepreneurs because of structural imperfections. That's why underdeveloped countries compel the entrepreneurs to start small sale enterprises which are already tested.

(e) **Schumpeter** remained silent about as to why some economies had more entrepreneurial talent than others. According to him an individual is an entrepreneur only when he tries new combinations to produce new things and to innovate. He ceases to be an entrepreneur the moment he establishes himself in running the business effectively. This view of **Schumpeter** is quite unrealistic and questionable.

However, despite the above criticisms, Schumpeterian theory is regarded as one of the best theories in the history of entrepreneurial development.

3.2.2 Leibenstein's Theory of X-Efficiency

Harvey Leibenstein propounded the theory of X-efficiency which is popularly called *Gap filling theory*. According to Leibenstein, entrepreneurial functions are determined by the X-efficiency which means the degree of inefficiency on the use of resources within the firm. The theory has got the following features.

1. ***Routine entrepreneurship:*** While propounding the theory, **Leibenstein** identified two broad types of entrepreneurship. First type of entrepreneurship is known as ***routine entrepreneurship***, which is intertwined with the important functions of management of the business.
2. ***New entrepreneurship:*** The second type of entrepreneurship is ***new entrepreneurship,*** which presumes innovative entrepreneurship. This entrepreneurship is characterized by aggressive assemblage of information and the analysis of results derived from sound combination of factors.
3. ***Twin roles of entrepreneur:*** Harvey Leibenstein pointed out that there always exists some deficiencies in the production function or input-output relationship. Theses deficiencies or gaps exist because all the inputs in the production function cannot be marketed. So Leibenstein highlighted the twin functions of entrepreneur, namely:

   (i) Gap filling
   (ii) Input completing

   While executing the entrepreneurial functions, the entrepreneur has to mobilize all the inputs to derive the final output. But some inputs like motivation and leadership are vague and their outputs is questionable. Thus, it is the function of the entrepreneur to marshall all the inputs to increase the efficiency of the existing methods of production to earn profit.
4. ***X-efficiency factor:*** As it is known that X-efficiency is the degree of inefficiency in the use of inputs within the firm, it is the measuring rod to know the extent of

deficiencies the firm incur in its production function. X-efficiency arises because either the resources of the firm are not properly utilized or they are wasted.

According to **Leibenstein**, the supply of entrepreneurship is governed by input completing ability and inadequate motivational state.

3.2.3 Mark Casson's Theory

Mark Casson was a renowned economist who propagated a functional definition of entrepreneur in his epoch-making book, ***The Entrepreneur—An Economic Theory***. He stated that now-a-days it is quite fashionable to be an entrepreneur. Most of the studies of entrepreneur make no attempt at proper definition. It may be said quite categorically that at the present moment, there is no established economic theory of entrepreneur. The subject area has been surrendered by economists to sociologists, psychologists and social scientists. However, his theory of entrepreneurship deals with the functional behaviour of entrepreneur and his qualities which are crucial for his success. His theory has got the following features.

1. ***Demand-supply relationship:*** He has explained the theory using the economic jargons like demand and supply. These twin market forces act as the crucial parameters for entrepreneurial activities. According to **M. Casson**, the demand for entrepreneurship stems from the need to adjust to change and the supply of entrepreneurship is limited by the scarcity of the desired personal qualities.
2. ***Identification of qualities:*** To become a successful entrepreneur, Mark Casson identified some important qualities. According to him, qualities of a person drive him to take up entrepreneurial initiative and these qualities are mostly innate. He gives example of a quality which is crucial for a successful entrepreneur—the quality of *imagination*.

The theory reveals that in the development of successful entrepreneurship the following things are to be followed:

(a) The demand for entrepreneurship need to be adjusted as per the changing needs of the time.
(b) The deficient qualities of the entrepreneur should be made good by personal care.

Thus, according to **Mark Casson**, an entrepreneur is a person, ***who specializes in taking judgemental decisions about the coordination of scarce resources***.

3.2.4 Papanek and Harris' Theory

Economists like **Papanek** and **Harris** have propounded that when certain economic conditions are favourable, entrepreneurship and economic growth will take place.

According to these two economists, economic incentives are the integral factors that have induced entrepreneurial initiatives. The main features of their theory are depicted as under:

1. ***Economic incentives:*** Entrepreneurial development is a function of economic incentives. This is one of the basic traits which drives the entrepreneur to take up entrepreneurial activities and to bring about success.

2. ***Link between economic gains and the innerurge:*** According to the above economists, the link between a person's ***inner urge*** and desired ***economic gains*** play a pivotal role for development of entrepreneurial competencies. The inner drives coupled with the hope of getting pecuniary benefits can give rise to entrepreneurial development.
3. ***Economic gain—sufficient condition:*** Theory of entrepreneurship, advocated by **Papanek** and **Harris**, reveals that entrepreneurs have got spontaneity in their willingness for undertaking diverse types of entrepreneurial activities because of economic gains. Thus, economic gain is considered as the sufficient condition for the origin of entrepreneurial initiatives in the economy.

3.2.5 Harvard School Theory

Harvard School contemplated that entrepreneurship involves any deliberate activity that initiates, maintains and grows a profit-oriented enterprise for production or distribution of economic goods or services, which is inconsistent with internal and external forces. The following points portray some important features of Harvard School theory.

1. ***Internal forces:*** These forces refer to the internal qualities of the individual such as intelligence, skill, knowledge experience, intuition, exposure etc. These forces influence the entrepreneurial activities of an individual to a great extent.
2. ***External forces:*** These forces refer to the economic, political, social, cultural and legal factors which influence origin and growth of entrepreneurship in an economy. As such, entrepreneurial activity needs an environment conducive to its growth and development.

   A.H. Cole, who had taken untiring pain in setting up Entrepreneurial Research Centre at Harvard University, speaks of the impact of the following environmental conditions which govern the emergence of entrepreneurial class:

   - Stable government
   - External security, protection from war, invasion, etc.
   - Internal security, protection from internal strife and revolution, protection of person and property under law and the assurance of legal process in disputes
3. ***Emphasis on two types of entrepreneurial activities.*** The Harvard School theory gives emphasis on two types of entrepreneurial activities, namely:

   (i) Entrepreneurial functions like organization and combination of resources for creating viable enterprises

   (ii) The responsiveness to the environmental condition that influences decision-making function

Besides, Leibenstein of Harvard School opined that the following activities are also equally important from the standpoint of entrepreneurship:

(a) To search and evaluate economic opportunities

(b) To master the process of mobilizing resources to accomplish the goal

(c) To interconnect the different market segments for creating absolutely an ideal marketing environment
(d) To create or expand the firm or the business enterprise

To conclude with **A.H. Cole:** "To study the entrepreneur is to study the central figures in modern economics".

3.2.6 M. Kirzner's Theory of Adjustment

Israel M. Kirzner, the noted economist, has coined the theory of adjustment of price. According to him, the essential entrepreneurial element is the alertness to information rather than its possession alone. He contends that those entrepreneurs who have the superior telescopic faculty keep themselves all the while alert to confront any disequilibrium in the market.

His theory has got the following features.

1. ***Adjustment of price:*** The chief role of entrepreneur is based upon the adjustment of price in the market. He contemplates that prevalence of wrong price in the market may reduce the profit of the entrepreneur. In this case, the buyer may pay higher price or seller may accept a lower price which may give rise to opportunities for profit. Further, if different prices prevail in the same market, there is the opportunity for profitable arbitrage between the two segments of the market. Thus, adjustment of price is the chief role of the entrepreneur.
2. ***Alertness To disequilibrium:*** According to **M. Kirzner**, entrepreneur possessing superior foresight are alert to disequilibrium. Alertness enables the entrepreneur to intervene in the market by changing the price. Thus, economy in purchase and profitable selling results in economic gains.

3.2.7 Theory of David McClelland's Theory of Achievement Motivation

In the late 1940s **David McClelland** and his associates developed the theory of ***achievement motivation***, which was regarded as one of the best economic theories of entrepreneurial development. They concentrated mainly on following three aspects:

- Need for achievement
- Need for power
- Need for affiliation

1. ***Need for achievement:*** A strong need for achievement 'n Ach' is found within certain individuals, groups and communities. McClelland emphasized that the need for achievement or achievement orientation is the most important factor for explaining economic behaviour. People having this need are more likely to succeed as entrepreneurs. They strive incessantly for success in getting things done in an excellent manner. They try passionately to overcome any odd that comes on their way. They are so much self-confident that they do not believe in mere luck. They look upon money as the index of their achievement but basically they are not money oriented. Therefore,

McClellland wrote: "Need for achievement is a desire to do well, not so much for the sake of social recognition of prestige, but for the sake of an ***inner feeling of personal accomplishment***."

2. ***Need for power:*** This pertains to the desire by a person to be influential in a group. People with need for power 'n Pow' believe in position of authority.

   They seek leadership in politics, business, education or arts and feel satisfied having a great number of followers. All successful managers seem to have high need for power. They derive satisfaction to influence and direct authority.

3. ***Need for affiliation:*** The persons with high need for affiliation are sensitive to social relationship. They are keen on warm and interpersonal relationship. They are associated more with popularity, social support and friendship than with decision making. They love others and wish to be loved by others. This is not predominant among managers but this 'n Aff' greatly helps them in influencing their subordinates.

Thus, the theory of achievement motivation provides a deep introspection to the human behaviour in general and entrepreneurial behavior in particular. It also glorifies the necessity of the Achievement Motivation Training (AMT) as an important tool for achievement of needs.

Keeping in view the above needs, 'n Ach', 'n Pow' and 'n Aff', **David McCelland** has pointed out that these factors, especially 'n Ach' are responsible for entrepreneurial development. The following analysis can reveal the impact of need for achievement in accelerating entrepreneurial urge among individuals.

Twin characteristics of entrepreneurship: **McClelland** pointed out the twin important characteristics of entrepreneurship that govern the economic behaviour of a person to become entrepreneurial. They are:

(i) Doing things in a novel and excellent manner
(ii) Decision making under uncertainty

Belief in personal accomplishment: According to this theory, 'n Ach' or need for achievement refers to the need for personal accomplishment by the person through excellence. This category of persons is fond of shouldering personal responsibility. They are generally moderate risk takers and try to be winners all the time. High achievers aim at personal achievement rather than the reward of success. Persons with high need for achievement behave in the entrepreneurial way.

Psychological factors for entrepreneurial motivation: Need for achievement depends upon entrepreneurial motivation. This need motivates the persons to take risk. The following psychological factors are responsible for the growth of entrepreneurial motivation:

(a) Need for achievement through performance evaluation
(b) Goal setting and problem solving
(c) Strong desire to undertake calculated risk
(d) Willingness for taking personal responsibility
(e) Spirit to achieve success

(f) Anticipating possibilities
(g) Concrete measures of task performance
(h) New instrumental activity
(i) Feeling of personal accomplishment
(j) Organizational as well as decision-making skills.

Inner concerns as the prime movers: **McClelland** opined that ***inner concerns*** or motives are the prime movers of entrepreneurship. These forces drive the individuals to take risk, plunge into uncertainty where they find opportunity, discover new ideas, save more and reinvest the savings in the enterprise. According to him: "The internal factors are the human values and motives that lead the human being to exploit opportunities, to take advantage of favourable trade conditions".

'n Ach' precursor of economic growth: McClelland applied his technique of 'n Ach' to study the relationship between achievement motivation and economic development. He founded that it was the 'n Ach' factor which was a precursor of economic growth both in socialistic and capitalistic system of economy. Entrepreneurship, thus, becomes the pivot around which need for achievement and economic growth to revolve.

Lack of ambition in less developed countries: Ambition is the basis on which **McClelland's** 'n Ach' greatly depends. In less developed countries (LDCs) achievement motivation of people is lower than that of developed countries because of low level of ambition. Lack of ambition creates a great barrier for need for achievement and consequently leads to lack of enterprise in LDCs. So in order to bring about economic development, it is necessary that the level of ambition among the people should be high enough to pressurize the need for achievement in them. Then only entrepreneurial spirit can be generated and economic growth can be accelerated.

Experience at Kakinada: According to **David McClelland,** the role of 'n Ach' is the critical factor for entrepreneurial development, which, in turn, leads to accelerate the tempo of economic development. In order to prove this fact, he conducted several experiments with different groups of businessmen in America, Mexico, Bombay and Kakinada in Andhra Pradesh. Through the experiments he tried to induce the spirit of ***achievement motivation*** in adults and urged them to take up entrepreneurial ventures. Such an inducement was, in fact, essential to increase their ***level of aspirations*** and to give rise to ***confidence building*** character in them.

In January, 1964, a full-fledged training programme was organized by **David McClelland** at Kakinada with a total intake of 52 persons. The objectives of such programme were:

(a) To instill in them the quality of imagination
(b) To encourage introspection and convert it into personal motivation and community goals.

The training was conducted at Small Industries Extension and Training Institute (SIET), Hyderabad. The Achievement Motivation Training (AMT) included the following basics which were supposed to be accomplished by the trainees:

(a) Goal setting and goal achievement
(b) Emulating the models of achievement by constant watch and alertness
(c) Attainment of concrete and frequent feedback
(d) Planning carefully the realistic goals through performance appraisal of their own
(e) Converting ideas into opportunities using the positive self-concept and controlling day dreaming.

Thus, the training helped those participants in providing high degree of motivation and subsequently the need for achievement. They displayed a more active business behaviour and took enough stress to accomplish the job. As such, Kakinada experience was considered the most successful experiment so far as the need for Achievement Motivation Training (AMT) is concerned for the benefit of the potential entrepreneurs. This AMT is regarded as a necessary tool for breaking the barrier of ***limited aspirations*** among individuals on the one hand and inducing in them high need for achievement on the other. The training also acts as a boost to the risk-taking and decision-making behaviour of the potential entrepreneurs.

To conclude with the words of V.L. Rao, a noted economist: "The n Ach factor or n achievement approach suggests promotion of achievement-oriented ways of thinking to foster economic development in the underdeveloped countries".

3.2.8 Knight's Theory of Profit

F.H. Knight, in his book ***Risk, Uncertainty and Profit*** propounded the theory of profit. He points out that entrepreneurs are a specialized group of persons who bear risk and deals with uncertainty.

Knight's theory has the following features:

1. ***Pure profit:*** Knight identified entrepreneurs as the recipient of pure profit. Pure profit refers to the reward for bearing the cost of uncertainty.
2. ***Situation of uncertainty:*** Uncertainty, according to **Knight**, is identified with a situation where the probability of alternative cannot be determined either by a prior reasoning or by statistical inference.
3. ***Risk-bearing capability:*** Risk bearing implies assuming the responsibilities of loss or gain that may occur due to unforeseen contingencies of the future. According to **Knight**, an entrepreneur is the person who willingly carries on those responsible activities which are neither insured nor salaried.
4. ***Guarantee of specified sum:*** While undertaking the responsibility of the business enterprise, entrepreneur guarantees interest to lender, wages to employees and rent to the landlord. Thus, specified sums of money are guaranteed by the entrepreneur for the assignment made to them. However, the supply of entrepreneurship depends upon the following three factors as per his opinion:

   (i) Ability of the entrepreneur
   (ii) Willingness of the entrepreneur
   (iii) The power to extend guarantees to others

5. ***Identification of socio-economic and psychological factors:*** Knight identified the social, economic and psychological factors which influence the supply of entrepreneur since entrepreneurial motivation and abilities are long-run problems. Economic, social and psychological factors should be combined to promote entrepreneurship.
6. ***Use of consolidation technique to reduce business uncertainty:*** Knight's entrepreneurs specifically commit their capital and bear the resultant risk and uncertainty. He argued that business uncertainty can be reduced by using the technique of consolidation to increase the profit. Through the help of consolidation in which individual instances are pooled, total uncertainty can be reduced.
7. ***Self-confidence:*** Self-confidence is the most important factor which is essential for the entrepreneur to undertake risk and to determine the level of profit. However, Knight felt that uncertainty defied definition as every uncertain condition was unique and depended on a number of imponderables in the market place. The elasticity of supply of self-confidence is an important factor that determined the level of profit and size of the entrepreneur.

3.2.9 Hayek's Theory of Market Equilibrium

F.A. Von Hayek propounded the theory of market equilibrium. His main contribution to entrepreneurial theory is to identify the absence of entrepreneurs in neo-classical economics which is associated with the assumption of market equilibrium.

According to **Hayek,** the services of entrepreneur can be of following types:

(a) To combine the means and resources together for production.
(b) To undertake the entrepreneurial function of planning, scheduling and decision making.
(c) To guarantee a fixed rate of income, profit and interest which will go to entrepreneur as the reward for his services.

In view of the above, the theory of market equilibrium can be depicted clearly under the following points:

1. ***Postulate of full equilibrium:*** According to **Hayek**, postulate of full equilibrium resembles the postulate of full information. Full information presupposes the fact that there is no need for further information to modify the decision.
2. ***Acquisition and communication of knowledge:*** Hayek emphasized the role of acquisition and communication of knowledge in his theory for adjustment towards equilibrium.
3. ***Market as the medium of communication:*** Markets are the crucial media which help the entrepreneurs to communicate their creative ventures or discoveries to others. Thus, they move towards the desired level of sales to arrive at equilibrium.

3.3 CULTURAL THEORIES

Advocates of cultural theories point out that entrepreneurship is the product of culture. Entrepreneurial talents come from cultural values and cultural systems embedded into the cultural environment. The following theories portray that the cultural factors are always responsible for the emergence of entrepreneurship:

- Hoselitz's theory
- Stoke's. theory

3.3.1 Hoselitz's Theory

Hoselitz explains that the supply of entrepreneurship is governed by cultural factors, and culturally minority groups are the ***spark-plugs*** of entrepreneurial and economic development. In many countries, entrepreneurs have emerged from a particular socioeconomic class. He emphasizes the role of culturally marginally groups like the Jews and the Greeks in medieval Europe, the Lebanese in West Africa, the Chinese in South Africa, the Indians in East Africa in promoting economic development. Hoselitz's theory of entrepreneurship supply can be viewed from the following standpoints which are cultural in nature:

1. ***Hypothesis of marginal men:*** Hoselitz formulated the Hypothesis of ***marginal men*** who are the important reservoir of entrepreneur development. According to Hoselitz, marginal men because of their ambiguous position from a cultural or social statement are particularly suited to make creative adjustments in situations of change and in the course of this adjustment process, they develop genuine innovations in social behaviour.
2. ***Emphasis on the functions of managerial and leadership skill:*** Entrepreneurial talents can be brought about in a society by the individuals who possess extraordinary managerial and leadership skills. Hoselitz noted that a person who is to become an industrial entrepreneur must have additional personality traits to those resulting from a drive to amass wealth. In addition to being motivated by the expectation of profit, he must also have the ability to lead.
3. ***Contribution of specific social classes:*** The theory reveals that in several countries entrepreneurial talents are found in persons having particular socio-economic background. For example, contribution of the protestant ethic of the west is significant in so far as the growth of a new class of industrialists is concerned. In Britain, the United States and Turkey, ranks of entrepreneurs were filled from commerce, Samurai in Japan, Family pattern in France, Yoruba in Nizeria, Kikiyu in Kenya, Christians in Lebanon, Halai Memon industrialists in Pakistan, Marwaris and Parsis in India are considered to be the dominant social classes in the field of entrepreneurship.

3.3.2 Stoke's Theory

Stoke's theory portrays that entrepreneurship is likely to emerge under specific social sanctions, social culture and economic action. According to Stoke, socio-cultural values channel economic action. He suggests that personal and societal opportunities and the presence of requisite psychological distributions may be seen as conditions for an individual movement to get changed into industrial entrepreneurship.

3.4 PSYCHOLOGICAL THEORIES

Psychological theories centre round the psychological characteristics of the individuals in a society. Psychological characteristics influence the supply of entrepreneurs in a society. The following theories clearly portray the emergence and supply of entrepreneurs.

- Theory of personal resourcefulness
- Theory of entrepreneurial supply

3.4.1 Theory of Personal Resourcefulness

Personal resourcefulness is a critical factor for the growth and development of entrepreneurship. The theory of personal resourcefulness has got the following implications as far as the supply of entrepreneurs is concerned in the society:

1. ***Cognitive function:*** The present theory presupposes the activities undertaken by the individuals who require cognitively mediated behaviour like emotions, sentiments, inner feelings, thoughts and actions. In these situations, entrepreneur is fully appraised of the situation and knowledge which is shaded by risk and motivational involvement.
2. ***Human aspects of psychology:*** Different authors have given their different opinions on human aspects of psychology. For example, **Bygrave** and **Hoffer** highlight the significance of human volition. **Schumpeter** pointed out entrepreneur as innovator while **Carland** gives emphasis on organization building for entrepreneurship development. In **Schumpeter's** words, entrepreneurship is influenced by the following traits:

   (a) will to power
   (b) will to conquer

Thus, studies examining non-economic factors have brought out the fact that mere provisions of economic inputs may not itself guarantee success in entrepreneurial ventures, organizational and psychological factors also still remain a subject of further investigation.

3.4.2 Theory of Entrepreneurial Supply

John H. Kunkel advocated the theory of entrepreneurship supply. According to him, psychological and sociological variables are the main determinants for the emergence of entrepreneurs. He contemplated that entrepreneurial talent can be found in minorities, religious, ethnic, migrated, displaced elites and these minorities have supplied most of the entrepreneurism in the society. Entrepreneurism can be dependent upon the following structures in the economy:

- Demand structure
- Limitation structure
- Labour structure
- Opportunity structure

1. ***Demand structure:*** It implies economic demand with relation to changes in economic development and government policies. Demand structure can be augmented with the help of material rewards which can influence entrepreneurial behaviour.
2. ***Limitation structure:*** It is originally socio-cultural in character. In this structure, entrepreneur is regarded as the most deviant individual in the society and that's why the society restricts specific activities that influence all members in the society.
3. ***Labour structure:*** It refers to the supply of skilled and willing labour. The structure is governed by a large numbers of factors such as racial stock, available job-alternatives, traditionalism, mobility of labour etc.
4. ***Opportunity structure:*** It is the most important structure governing the supply of entrepreneurs. The structure refers to the technological and managerial skills, information about techniques of production, market structure and supply of capital.

Thus, **J.H. Kunkel** in his behavioural model depicted that entrepreneurial supply is concerned with overtly expressed activities of individuals and their relations to the previously and presently surrounding social structure and physical conditions. This behavioural model is based upon the following premises.

1. ***Man's internal state—beyond objective analysis:*** Man's internal state is beyond the scope of presently available means of measurement and objective analysis and so knowledge about this is of less significance so far as the explanation and prediction of behaviour is concerned.
2. ***Conditioning procedure, determinant of individual activities:*** The behavioural model of **Kunkel** depicts that the determinant of an individual activities are to be found largely in the conditioning procedure, both deliberate and accidental to which he has been subjected in the past, and in the sets of reinforcing and discriminative stimuli which become part of his behavioural chains and are part of present social context.
3. ***Behavioural approach and human spirit:*** This model does not deny the existence of human spirit. According to **Kunkel,** "*This approach simply does not make use of these concepts in analysis of behaviour because of their ambiguities. It also does not depreciate the internal-stage of the man.*"
4. ***Model contrast with psychogenic approach:*** This behavioural model is in quite contrast with the psychogenic approaches. According to **Kunkel**, to change man's activities one need not concern oneself with altering values, one need to change only certain elements of the operant conditioning context of which all men at all times are an integral part.
5. ***Role of ambiguous and inadequate concepts:*** In his model, **Kunkel** indicates the ambiguity and inadequacy of some concepts like values, personality and attitudes. He points out that any sociological analysis will be inadequate if the above ambiguous concepts are given much importance in a society.

Keeping in view the above concepts, some writers point out that the spiritualism, philosophy of renunciation and asceticism are the stumbling blocks to the economic development of India. But **Kunkel** gives his opinion quoting **Srinivas**, **Singer** and **Lambart** who attributed India's development to existing social and political institutions rather than to the values and religious attitudes.

3.5 SPECIALISTS' VIEWS ON ENTREPRENEURSHIP

Apart from the above-stated theories, valuable views on entrepreneurship have been provided by eminent specialists as theoretical supplements to entrepreneurship. Thus, the views of these specialists/experts are as follows:

- Walker on entrepreneurship
- Harbison on entrepreneurship
- Drucker on entrepreneurship
- Peter Kilby on entrepreneurship

3.5.1 Walker on Entrepreneurship

According to **Walker,** entrepreneur is a person who organizes and coordinates the various agents of production. He points out that the true entrepreneur is one who is in possession of above average ability for organizing and coordinating the resources. But in a country, the supply of '***true entrepreneur***' is limited. Entrepreneurs are endowed with different levels of organizational skill and coordinating capacity. Thus entrepreneurs with higher level of competency are more successful and effective in earning superior rewards in terms of profit in comparison to their counterparts.

3.5.2 Harbison on Entrepreneurship

Harbison did not propound any theory of entrepreneurship but he has made very interesting observations relating to entrepreneurship as a factor of economic development. He viewed organization-building as the most critical skill needed for economic development as it facilitates the use of other innovations. He laid emphasis on the individual's organizational skill, creativity and ability to plan and initiate changes . He suggested that entrepreneurship should be treated as a resource which has both qualitative and quantitative dimensions.

Harbison categorized the functions of modern entrepreneurs in the following ways:

(a) Under-taking and managing of risk and the handling of economic activity
(b) Planning and innovation
(c) Coordination, administration, time control
(d) Routine supervision

In small enterprises, the above functions are performed by a single individual. But according to **Harbison,** all the persons who perform entrepreneurial function in a large organization are characterised as Managerial Resources. He pointed out that the efficacy of business organization depends upon the following factors:

(a) Dynamic and innovative entrepreneurs
(b) Dynamic organization with creative thinkers who can plan and initiate changes

Thus, the organization builder must be able "to harness the new ideas to select and develop persons who can properly manage enthusiasm in the accomplishment of objectives, multiply himself by efficiently delegating responsibilities."

However, **Harbison** emphasized that organization is more than a summation of particular abilities of certain individuals. It is more than the statistical aggregate of managerial personnel. Organization connotes a constellation of functions in a common undertaking.

Keeping in view the organizational importance, **Harbison** stated a few tentative hypotheses on entrepreneurship and organization. The propositions are given below:

(a) Large expenditures for equipment and machinery are likely to be quite unproductive unless there is a corresponding investment in organization.
(b) Organization is probably the principal factor determining the productivity of labour, assuming that capital and natural resources are constant.
(c) "Because of non-economic factors (managerial persons may be guided in their decision making by consideration other than profits such as power, social prestige, ability to help friends and relatives which the success brings) which determine in part the behaviour of human beings as managerial resources, all organizations are probably inefficient in effecting the optimum of combination of economic resources which is theoretically possible". All the same, the ability to build organization is perhaps the most precious of all entrepreneurial skills and thus, those who can achieve success in this very critical area, may be the ones who most nearly fulfil the role of true entrepreneur.

3.5.3 Drucker on Entrepreneurship

Peter F. Drucker opined that "an entrepreneur is one who always searches for change, responds to it and exploits it as an opportunity." He laid emphasis on two important factors—innovation and resource—that led to emergence of entrepreneurship. According to him, innovation is the real hub of entrepreneurship which creates resource. A thing is regarded as resource when its economic value is recognized. For example, mineral oil was considered worthless until the discovery of its use. Similarly, purchasing power was considered an important resource by an American innovative entrepreneur who invented instalment buying.

According to **Drucker,** successful entrepreneurship involves the following things:

(a) Value and satisfaction obtained from resources by the consumer are increased.
(b) New values are created.
(c) Material is converted into a resource or existing resources are combined in a new or more productive configuration.
(d) Entrepreneurship is the practice that has a knowledge base.
(e) Entrepreneurship is not confined to big business and economic institutions, it is equally important to small business and non-economic institutions.
(f) Entrepreneurship behaviour rather than personality trait is more important to enhance entrepreneurship.
(g) The foundation of entrepreneurship lies in concept and theory rather than in intuition.

Thus, **Drucker** has given his views that "an entrepreneur need not be a capitalist or an owner. A banker who mobilizes other's money and allocates it in areas of higher yield is very much an entrepreneur though he is not the owner of the money.

3.5.4 Peter Kilby on Entrepreneurship

Peter Kilby is a famous author on entrepreneurship. In his book *Entrepreneurship and Economic Development*, he has attempted to study the entrepreneur in greater detail and gave a comprehensive list of activities critical to entrepreneurial success in the context of an underdeveloped country.

1. ***Exchange relationship***
   (a) Perception of market opportunities
   (b) Obtaining control of scarce resources
   (c) Purchasing inputs.
   (d) Marketing the product and responding to competition.
2. ***Political administration***
   (a) Dealing with bureaucracies (concessions/licences, etc.)
   (b) Management of human relations within the firm.
   (c) Management of customer-supplier relationship management and control.
   (d) Financial management
   (e) Production management (control by written records, supervision, coordinating input flows with orders, maintenance)
3. ***Technology***
   (a) Acquiring and overseeing assembly of the factory
   (b) Industrial engineering (minimizing inputs with a given production process)
   (c) Upgrading product and product quality
   (d) Introduction of new production techniques and products'

Peter Kilby proceeds to empirically assess the differential role performance of entrepreneurs on the basis of evidence from contemporary underdeveloped countries. He draws evidence from the studies made by himself, J.J. Berna, J.J. Carole, T.C. Cochran, J.R. Harris, G.F. Papamek, A.P. Alexander, ILO missions and others. The evidence led him to the following findings. According to him: "Entrepreneurial performance in those roles involving exchange relationships and political administration is vigorous and effective. On the other hand, entrepreneurs typically do not apply themselves with equal intensity or skill to their task in the realms of management control and technology. Deficiencies in these latter areas represent, in many instances, the operational bottleneck to indigenous industrial development".

3.6 MODELS ON ENTREPRENEURSHIP

Closely consistent with the theories of entrepreneurship and views of some famous experts in this regard, the following two models contribute a great deal to the emergence as well as sustenance of entrepreneurship and entrepreneurial talents in an environment. The models are:

- A conceptual model of entrepreneurship by John J. Kao
- Integrated model of entrepreneurship by Abdul Aziz Mahmud

3.6.1 Kao's Conceptual Model

J.J. Kao in his book, *Entrepreneurship, Creativity and Organization,* has developed a conceptual model of entrepreneurship. The model is represented in Fig. 3.1. This is otherwise known as ***The ECO analysis framework*** (ECO stands for Entrepreneurship, Creativity and Organization).

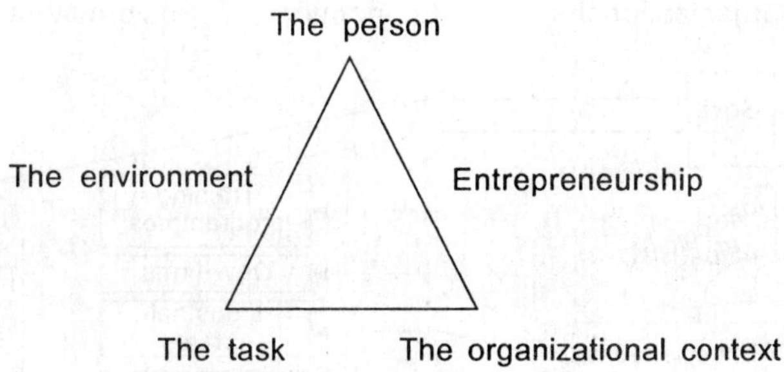

Fig. 3.1 The ECO analysis framework.

According to **Kao**, entrepreneurship and creativity result from the interrelationship of the following three elements as shown in Fig. 3.1.

- The person
- The task
- The organizational context

Element I: The most important element is the ***person***. New ideas are not generated or implemented by organization or technology but come into being through efforts of dedicated people. So, for entrepreneurial talent, it is important to understand people's personality, skills, motivation, levels of experience and psychological preferences.

Element II: The **task** is what a group of people or organization does. Tasks may be determined by an individual's personality or private vision. They are shaped by organizational strategy and influenced by the external environment. The ***task*** includes perceiving of opportunities, marshalling of resources and providing leadership qualities appropriate for entrepreneurial growth.

Element III: The ***organizational context*** is the immediate setting in which creative and entrepreneurial work rolls place. Factors like organizational structure and systems, the definition of work rolls and group culture affect significantly the nature of the creative or entrepreneurial environment.

Finally, the above elements exist in an ***environment*** which refers to the outside world surrounding the organization. Environment includes in it the available resources, infrastructure, competitive pressures, social values, rules and regulations, state of technology. Environment too can facilitate or impede creative and entrepreneurial endeavour.

As such, the environment influences the enterprise creation significantly and the most successful entrepreneur is one who adapts himself to the changing needs of the environment and makes it hospitable for the growth of his business enterprise.

3.6.2 Integrated Model of Entrepreneurship by Abdul Aziz Mahmud

This model was originally prepared by Abdul Aziz Mahmud which is presented in the chart illustrated in Fig. 3.2.

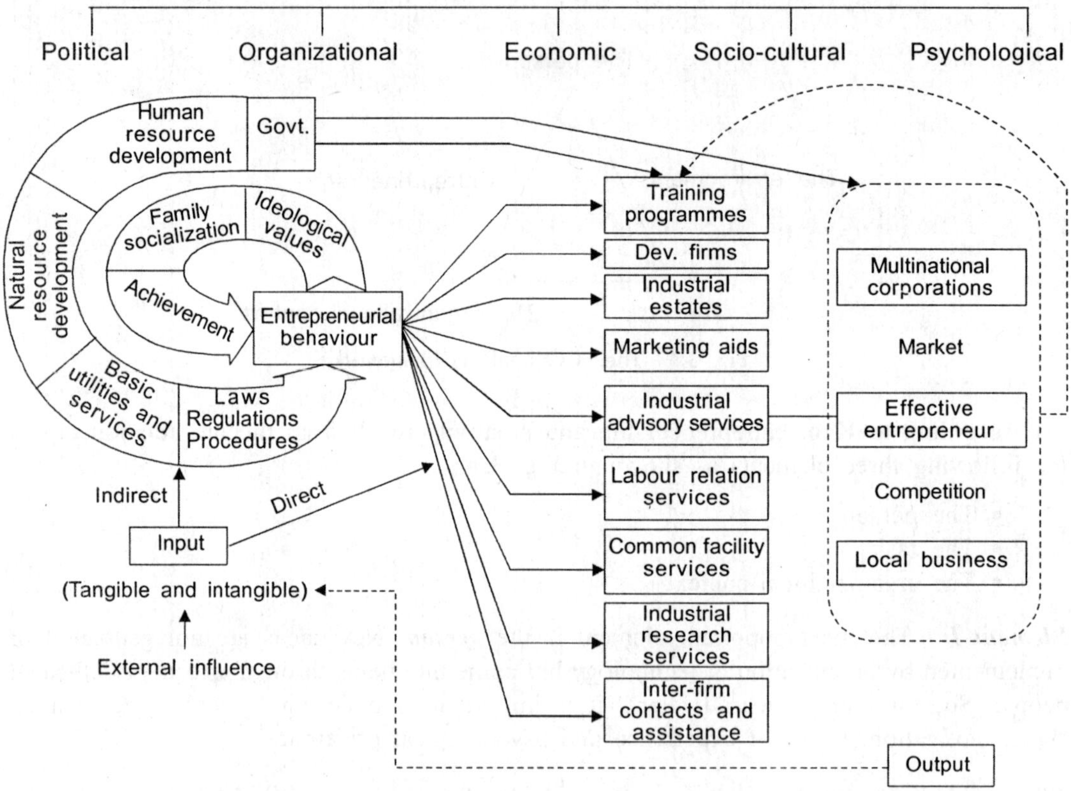

Fig. 3.2 Integrated contextual model.

Source: Adopted from Abdul Aziz Mahmud's, "Developing Effective Indigenous Entrepreneurs", *Malaysian Management Review*, April 1974, Vol. 9, No. 1.

EXERCISES

A. Long answer questions:

1. Discuss briefly economic theories of entrepreneurship.
2. Discuss briefly sociological theories of entrepreneurship.
3. Discuss briefly cultural theories of entrepreneurship.
4. Critically examine the theories of innovation propounded by J.A. Schumpeter.
5. Discuss in brief David McClelland's theory of achievement of motivation.

6. "Entrepreneurship is a product of group level pattern". Explain.
7. Discuss Peter Kilby's views on entrepreneurship.
8. Explain Harbison's views on entrepreneurship.
9. Give a comparative study of the model on entrepreneurship given by John J. Kao and Abdul Aziz Mahmud.
10. What is the integrated contextual model of entrepreneurship?

B. Short answer type questions:

1. Write short notes on the following:
   (a) Stoke's theory of entrepreneurship
   (b) Hoselitz's theory of entrepreneurship
   (c) Hagen's theory of entrepreneurship
   (d) Weber's theory
   (e) Cochran's theory of change
   (f) X-efficiency theory.
2. Define sociological theory of entrepreneurship.
3. What do you know about the theory of group level pattern ?
4. Explain in a nut shell the theory of profit.
5. What is the theory of resourcefulness?
6. Give an idea on Kao's conceptual model of entrepreneurship.
7. What is Peter Kilby's views on exchange relationship?

CHAPTER 4

Promotion of a Venture

CHAPTER CONTENTS

4.1 OPPORTUNITY ANALYSIS

Entrepreneur is an opportunity seeker. For establishing a new business unit he constantly undertakes the scanning of environment. He even goes on scanning the environment until the he finds the best of opportunities, out of several such opportunities for preparation of his business plan. The process by which an opportunity is identified is described as ***opportunity analysis*** or ***opportunity-sensing and identification***. Entrepreneur analyses the opportunities taking into account his own strengths, weaknesses, opportunities and threats, which, in management philosophy, is known as **'SWOT'** analysis. Now the question may arise that what do opportunities in business really mean. Do they differ from business ideas?

As we know, business ideas and business opportunities very often are used interchangeably. Opportunity is considered as a viable business idea which the entrepreneur selects from several ideas suited to his own capabilities and subsequently he takes it up as a good investment proposition. However, entrepreneurs identify their opportunities and select their products on the basis of the following analysis:

(a) Entrepreneurs may select their products based on their own experience or their partner's experience in the line.
(b) Entrepreneurs may select products based upon the expansion or diversification plans of their own or any other ongoing business or industry.
(c) Entrepreneurs may select products which are likely to have a ready demand either in the local or regional market.
(d) Entrepreneurs may select products whose imports are banned or controlled by the government.
(e) Entrepreneurs may select products which show high profitability.
(f) Entrepreneurs may select products based on certain specific advantages available to that product such as reservation of product line for small scale units, concessional finances or other resources being made available by the government or other incentives.
(g) Entrepreneurs may select product line guided mainly by changes in certain aspects of industrial policy, more specifically change in control and regulation of prices of raw materials.
(h) Somewhat similar to the above is the situation when entrepreneurs came to know of a product line as a result of reports by government committees. Entrepreneurs' selection of computers or electronic products is attributed to the recent approach of government policy in establishing Software Technology Park of India.
(i) Entrepreneurs may select products because a certain amount of investible savings is available to them. Small entrepreneurs and their enterprises fall in same pattern when we examine the above factors.
(j) Entrepreneurs may select products during or after undergoing entrepreneurship development programmes in ED institutes, industry associations and NGOs.

Thus, in identifying an opportunity, an intending entrepreneur will have to follow the above-mentioned factors. The major stages in which our entrepreneurs involve themselves in identifying business opportunity and selection of products can be discussed as follows:

Stage I: Scanning of business environment
Stage II: Shortlisting of opportunities
Stage III: Finalizing the selection of product

Scanning of business environment: To enter into the field of entrepreneurship, it is always wise on the part of the potential entrepreneur to try and generate as many ideas as possible which will be commercially viable. This idea generation can be possible through environment scanning. Ideas can be generated by the following ways:

(a) By discussion with friends, relatives, businessmen, industrialists and the persons associated with trade, commerce and industries.

(b) By contacting promotional agencies like District Industries Centres (DICS), Micro, Small and Medium Enterprises (MSMEs), entrepreneurship development institutes, Small Industries Corporation, chamber of commerce and industries, industry associations, etc.

(c) Generating project ideas from technical consultancy cells of commercial banks, vendor development cells of large industrial houses.

(d) Generating ideas by observing products or services required by the society.

(e) *Internet browsing:* In the present-day world, product ideas can be easily generated from the internet. A person can get enough ideas through internet by accessing different sites related to business and industry.

Shortlisting of opportunities/project ideas: As opportunities are unlimited in environment and the prospective entrepreneurs generate a good many ideas, it is necessary that these opportunities should be shortlisted to three or four for closer analysis and observation. This analysis can be done on the basis of **'SWOT'** (Strengths, Weaknesses, Opportunities and Threats) analysis whereby the entrepreneurs can arrive at the final product. The strengths for them could be educational or technical qualification, skills, trade-related knowledge, family connections, etc. while the weaknesses could be the nature of the entrepreneur, financial background, lack of market, etc.

If the entrepreneurs finalize good opportunities it is always necessary to discuss about the ideas, its pros and cons regarding the techno-economic viability with the financial institutions particularly bankers, state financial corporation and development financing institutions. If their comments and views are negative on some of the opportunities or all of them, entrepreneurs can be advised to drop such products and go for searching of new opportunities. This is because, if they are not convinced, the entrepreneurs may not be in a position to raise finance for such product line. If they are convinced, the entrepreneurs should go ahead with the best of opportunities and should not hesitate to establish the enterprise.

Before finalizing the product or opportunity, certain product-related factors should be considered. The factors may be like stability, growth, marketability, gestation period required, etc. A product whose future may not be very stable may be a risky venture. Such product idea or opportunity has to be dropped.

Finalization of opportunity or product. While finalizing the product, it is essential to assess some parameters before deciding on the product out of two or three shortlisted ones. These parameters are mainly:

(a) Total investment
(b) Return on investment
(c) Return on equity
(d) Likely volume of sales
(e) Profits and profitability

Now the final product or service which is selected by the entrepreneur will, in all probability, be accepted as the most feasible one to be taken up as a venture. Apart from this analysis, entrepreneur should collect a variety of data or information as given below for successful establishment and profitable management of the venture. These data are: (a) Total investment in plant and machinery; (b) Sources of raw materials for manufacturing the product; (c) Infrastructure facilities; (d) Size of the project; (e) Requirement and availability of skilled and unskilled manpower; (f) Total financial requirement; (g) Policy of the government; (h) Procedure adopted by the government to start enterprise; (i) Incentives, subsidies, exemptions, if any, provided by the government.

Keeping the above things in view, entrepreneur should select that opportunity which will be commercially viable and technically feasible. Further, the opportunity should be capable of giving adequate returns in a sustainable manner for long period of time and can be feasible enough to be diversified in accordance with the changing needs of the time.

4.2 ENVIRONMENT AND ENTREPRENEURSHIP

4.2.1 Role of Socio-economic Environment

Socio-economic environment plays a crucial role in governing entrepreneurial acumen among the people. A favourable socio-economic environment creates necessary conditions for the growth of entrepreneurship. In simple language, environment implies everything that is external to the organization. It is the aggregate of external factors within which the enterprise operates. External factors include in it social, economic, cultural, political, legal and technological factors. Entrepreneurs are to operate and adapt themselves to different situations in the environment in order to achieve success. Thus, the role of socio-economic environment is of much significance for the growth of entrepreneurial development.

4.2.2 Social Environment and Entrepreneurship

Entrepreneurial activities can grow manifold in a conducive and congenial social environment. Social environment presupposes a number of social factors which are critical for the growth of entrepreneurship. These factors are:

- Family background
- Social sanctions
- Kith and kin
- Social status
- Social values
- Social cost-benefit analysis
- Caste system
- Religious background
- Social mobility
- Social marginality
- Social responsibility of business

1. ***Family background:*** This is one of the most important social factors which govern the entrepreneurial environment. This includes size of family, type of family, status of family, etc. In our country, prior to Independence, zamindar families helped themselves to gain access to political power and displayed higher level of entrepreneurship. The emergence of small firms in France was due to their family pattern. In Japan, it was the ***Samurais*** who turned to business and kept their social structure intact through adoption of vigorous young businessmen or taking them

into family through marriage. In India, joint family system influences the entrepreneurial supply to a great extent.

2. ***Caste system:*** It is a well-known fact that certain castes encourage the emergence of entrepreneurship. Specific castes in the society exhibit more entrepreneurial talent than their counterparts as they have possessed latent potential and specialized culture which helps to foster entrepreneurship. For example, Parsis and Marwaris of Maharashtra, Vysyas of Andhra Pradesh have exhibited extraordinary entrepreneurial talent in enterprise building and management.
3. ***Social sanctions:*** Social sanctions and the role expectations are the key elements that determine the growth of entrepreneurs. According to **Cochran**, the sociologist, an entrepreneur is neither a supernormal individual nor a deviant person but represents a society's ***modal personality***. Thus, the growth of entrepreneurship depends upon the attitude of the person to his occupation, the role expectations held by the sanctioning groups in the society.
4. ***Religious background:*** Religion also plays an important role in influencing entrepreneurial emergence and growth. According to Max Weber, the ***protestant ethic*** provides impetus to entrepreneurial development in Europe. In our country, Jains of Rajasthan and Sikhs of Punjab have shown their enterprising character. So religion is also an important factor for entrepreneurial development.
5. ***Kith and kin:*** Entrepreneurial initiatives are very often influenced by kith and kin, friends, relatives, well-wishers, teachers and trainers. They exert considerable influence in decision-making process of starting a particular business which has significant effect on creation of entrepreneurship.
6. ***Social mobility:*** This factor greatly influences the emergence of entrepreneurship. High degree of social mobility would help in promoting entrepreneurial talents and thereby paving the path for enterprise development. **Hoselitz** viewed that the openness of a system and the flexibility in role relations reveal an imperative role mobility within a system of entrepreneurship development.
7. ***Social status:*** Social status is a contributory factor for the growth of entrepreneurship. Every human being aspires to be a man of high social esteem in the society. This aspiration drives a person to be self-propelled and entrepreneurial in his activities. He tries to be self-dependent and tries to prove his worth in the society as he is aware of the fact that only entrepreneurial initiatives can bring about high social status.
8. ***Social marginality:*** Social marginality is an important factor for the emergence of entrepreneurship. The persons from socially marginal classes often come forward and evince keen interest in choosing entrepreneurship as their career.
9. ***Social values:*** Social values and the philosophy of a country play a predominant role in the growth of entrepreneurial culture in the society. Ideologies of the society like democracy, freedom, tolerance, fair play, secularism, emancipation of weaker sections, social justice and non-violence also influence the promotion of entrepreneurship.
10. ***Social responsibility of business:*** Social responsibility of business has also considerable impact on the entrepreneurial initiative. The foremost concern in this regard is the

efficient utilization and conservation of the natural resources for the benefit of the society. The interests of various groups must be promoted in the business. Entrepreneurial initiatives should also be carried on within the framework of social rules, laws of the land and the social policies.

11. ***Social cost-benefit analysis:*** Social cost-benefit analysis is a very significant factor which influences entrepreneurial decision. It is a tool applicable to tactical decision making within the broad planning framework and contains socio-political and socio-cultural values. Hence, entrepreneurs should be aware of the social cost-benefit analysis of the business so as to enhance their contribution to the society.

4.2.3 Economic Environment and Entrepreneurship

Economic environment plays a significant role in providing inducement to entrepreneurs for specific industrial activity. Economic environment refers to those economic factors which influence the entrepreneurs in identifying the business opportunities and giving their decision to finalize the ventures out of those opportunities that are economically viable and financially feasible. The following are the most important economic factors which very often affect the entrepreneurship:

- Economic system
- Industrial policies
- Taxation
- Import duty
- Commercial policy
- Import licence
- Tariff protection and its effects
- Geographic or backward areas incentives
- Government influence on investment
- Availability of capital
- Chambers of commerce and industry
- Infrastructures
- Agricultural development
- Economic planning
- Fiscal incentives
- Rebates
- Export duty
- Foreign exchange control
- Monetary policy
- Tax holidays
- Specific industry incentives
- Market and marketing incentives
- Financial institutions
- Human capital formation
- Education, experience and training

These factors are briefly discussed further.

1. ***Economic system:*** Economic system influences economic environment as well as sociopolitical environment. Entrepreneurial environment is affected to a great extent by the economic system. Economic systems are broadly of three types—capitalistic, socialistic and mixed (capitalism, socialism and mixed economy). In capitalistic system, economic freedom, private enterprise and profit motive are glorified. Thus, the above elements of capitalism give sufficient boost to entrepreneurial environment. The United States of America (USA) has emerged as the most developed capitalistic economy in the world. In socialistic system, public sector has got the commanding height and as such entrepreneurial development rests with the hands of the government. In mixed economic system, both public and private sectors coexist and, therefore,

there is ample scope for the growth and development of entrepreneurship. Our country, India, is wedded to the mixed economic system and thus, the scope for entrepreneurial development is more here.

2. ***Economic planning:*** Economic planning aims at removal of all economic ills. It acts as an instrument for solving the problem of unemployment and poverty. In mixed economic system, it also creates necessary conditions for entrepreneurial and industrial growth. In India, Second Five Year Plan envisaged rapid industrialization and set the foundation for industrial as well as entrepreneurial development.
3. ***Industrial policies:*** Industrial polices are important for the growth of small, medium and large scale industries. In our country, Industrial Policy Resolutions (**IPRs**) have been declared by the government from time to time incorporating incentives, subsidies and exemptions of various kinds to the benefit of the entrepreneurs. Thus, **IPRs** primarily aim at promotion of enterprise in the country.
4. ***Fiscal incentives:*** Fiscal incentives influence entrepreneurial development. These incentives not only stimulate economic environment but also create favourable climate for entrepreneurial growth.
5. ***Influence of taxation:*** In a country, for convenience, tax structure is divided into mainly two categories—direct and indirect. In order to increase the investment potential and to induce entrepreneurs for industrial activities, the government adopts the policies of tax exemptions and tax holidays and helps the small scale entrepreneurs. Sometimes, exemptions are allowed for capital gains tax and wealth tax as an important incentive for entrepreneurial growth.
6. ***Rebates:*** Besides exemptions from taxes certain category of industries are declared as ***Special Category*** industries which avail rebates on raw materials purchase and import. Therefore, rebates also influence the production process of the small scale, medium scale and large scale industries.
7. ***Import duty:*** Import duty is levied as a protective cover to small scale enterprises. In underdeveloped countries, import duty is considered as a necessary instrument to help and develop nascent enterprise to a stage where it will be competitive and able to sustain amidst market pressures.
8. ***Export duty:*** Apart from custom duties, export duties are levied on a number of traditional commodities, primarily for the purpose of inducing entrepreneurs to take initiatives on innovative enterprises, like processing units to add value to the products before export. Hence, export duties stimulate entrepreneurial environment.
9. ***Commercial policy:*** Commercial policy plays a crucial role in stimulating economic environment of business. It helps the countries particularly LDCs (less developed countries) in accelerating entrepreneurial and economic development by way of maintaining balance of payments, increasing the gains from trade, enhancing the rate of capital formation and promoting entrepreneurship in the country.
10. ***Foreign exchange control:*** Foreign exchange control policy is used for regulating the flow of foreign exchange. It acts as an important instrument for entrepreneurial development because of its scarce supply. So this much-needed resource can be utilized by the entrepreneurs through effective regulatory policy for industrial development.

11. ***Import licence:*** Import licence is also a powerful tool for promotion of enterprise. This mechanism effectively allocates resources and controls the foreign exchange in such a way that the interests of the indigenous entrepreneurs is protected.
12. ***Monetary policy:*** Monetary policy acts as an important instrument for accelerating entrepreneurial development in the following three ways:

    (i) By influencing both cost and availability
    (ii) By controlling inflationary pressures
    (iii) By maintaining balance of payments equilibrium in the country

    M.L. Jhingan viewed that, "as development gains momentum, an appropriate monetary policy is all the more essential to provide an elastic credit supply to meet the requirement of growing volumes of trade, a rapidly increasing population and an expanding monetized sector." As such, monetary policy stimulates entrepreneurial development.
13. ***Tariff protection:*** In order to obtain comparative cost advantage in the country, protective tariffs are essential in LDCs. Protective tariffs lead to protective industrialization which, in turn, create conditions for the growth of entrepreneurship.
14. ***Tax holidays:*** Tax holidays act as a major incentive offered by LDCs for entrepreneurial development. This system is used to promote industries in comparatively low growth areas to bring about regional balance.
15. ***Geographic or backward area incentives:*** Besides tax holidays, backward area incentives like capital investment subsidy, land and factory-shed at lower price, exemptions from custom duty on imported machinery and equipment plus a similar exemption from indigenously fabricated capital goods are provided by the government for accelerating entrepreneurial growth.
16. ***Specific industry incentives:*** For promotion of specific industries like 100 per cent EOUs (Export-oriented Units), pioneer industries, the government declares various incentives from time to time. In this way, entrepreneurial growth is stimulated.
17. ***Government influence on investment:*** The role of government in influencing investment decision is very important. Through various employment generation schemes like PMRY (Prime Minister's Rojgar Yojana), IRDP (Integrated Rural Development Programme), SGSY (Swarnajayanti Gram Swarojgar Yojana), etc., the government takes crucial steps to promote first generation entrepreneurs by providing capital as well as training for managing the enterprise. Entrepreneurs are also guided by the officers of Industries Department in regard to the identification of viable projects, choice of technology and choice of industry.
18. ***Market and marketing incentives:*** Market is a strong mechanism of entrepreneurial growth. Small scale entrepreneurs are always encouraged by the government to produce innovative products that can create ***demand*** in the market. In order to compete with the similar product manufactured by the large and medium scale industries, the government provides a basket of incentives like sales tax exemption, price preferences and marketing through government-sponsored inlets and kiosks to the small scale industries.
19. ***Availability of capital:*** Investment decisions are generally influenced by the availability of both fixed and working capital. Economic and financial environment should be conducive so as to broaden the base of availability of capital so as to accelerate entrepreneurial development.

20. ***Financial institutions:*** Financial Institutions refer to the development financing institutions, commercial banks, state financial corporations, industrial development corporations, money market, capital market, etc., which provide financial assistance to the entrepreneurs in setting up and running their units. Provision of easy credit facilities by these institutions can enrich the small scale sector and influence the investment decisions.
21. ***Chambers of commerce and industry:*** Chambers of commerce and industry are the important organizations by which the entrepreneurial environment is greatly influenced. These chambers organize entrepreneurial training programmes, seminars and workshops on identification of viable business opportunities for the benefit of the entrepreneurs. They also constantly get in touch with the government to put forth the opinions of the small scale as well as large and medium scale entrepreneurs related to different aspects of industrial development.
22. ***Human capital formation:*** Human capital formation implies the process of acquiring and increasing the basic skill, education and experience which are critical for economic and entrepreneurial development. To quote Prof. Galbraith: "We now get larger part of our industrial growth not from more capital investment but from investment in men and improvement brought about by improved men. This physical capital becomes more productive if the country possesses adequate number of human capital which can be possible because of favourable socio-economic environment".
23. ***Infrastructures:*** Infrastructural facilities such as transportation system, railways, roads, bridges, water and airways significantly affect the entrepreneurial development. Transportation system affects the size of the market and if transportation costs fall, the entrepreneur receives a greater income for his products and the price of manufactured goods offered is equally reduced. Establishment of industrial estates with all facilities like water, electricity, road, etc. influence the growth of enterprise.
24. ***Education, experience and training:*** Education is the most important asset for the entrepreneur. Education, as a tool of entrepreneurial development, makes the entrepreneur informative as well as rational in approach. Educated entrepreneurs are more aware of the government policies and incentives provided by the government than their uneducated counterparts. Similarly, the increase in experience level is directly related to the awareness of environment. In developing countries, training is also a necessary instrument for development of entrepreneurs.
25. ***Agricultural development:*** Role of agriculture is also important for accelerating the tempo of entrepreneurial development. Agricultural development not only brings in increased food surplus but also acts as a great stimulus to industrial development. In developing countries, increased purchasing power due to increase in agricultural productivity tends to raise the demand for industrial goods and expand the size of the market. This gives rise to the expansion of industrial as well as entrepreneurial base of the country.

Thus, the role of socio-economic environment is of fundamental significance as far as the entrepreneurial and industrial development of the country is concerned.

4.3 TECHNOLOGICAL ENVIRONMENT

Technology is a means of converting scientific ideas and conceptual designs into products and process realities. Its development is a continuous process targeted towards achieving perfection on all directions, including quality, cost and environmental safety of its end products or processes. Being a continuous process, technology should make use of the state-of-the-art innovation, methods and manufacturing engineering. In short, technology is an applied science and an aid to convert basic science and research into practical end use products and processes.

With the environmental changes, many technology management concepts held in early 1990s have become part of the history. Obsolescence in management strategies have never been so rapid. A defensive strategy of import substitution has been replied by ***globalization*** which calls for a highly vigorous approach. The concept of ***appropriate technology*** has been declared as the relevant technology now—the one that imparts powerful ***competitive edge***. Production procedures were earlier ***focused*** which gave way to flexibility. Words like speed and innovation have acquired new dimensions and, of course, the list is long. Each change has its impact on the technology, but the common denominations of these changes is being shortened at the pace at which new developments taking place keeps on increasing. Thus, technology and its environment play a predominant role in entrepreneurial development. Small business is influenced greatly by the technological change that occurs continuously. Small enterprises confront competition in each sphere due to technological change and otherwise known as technical know-how. It implies the uptodate knowledge required for promoting and running the enterprise in the most efficient way. Technology also helps the entrepreneur to produce qualitative products or to deliver qualitative services. Technological environment affects the business environment in variety of ways and, therefore, due consideration is to be given to technology dimension while establishing and running an enterprise whether tiny, small, medium or large.

Under the above backdrop, it is worthwhile to discuss the impact of technological environment upon entrepreneurial decision making. It is done under the following points:

(a) Selection of proper technology is a critical element for success of the business. In a new organization, choice of product and technology of production are complementary and supplementary to each other.

(b) Management of human resources, plant and materials, capacity of the operation system, volume and quality of goods are increasingly affected by the technology and technological change.

(c) Technology also influences market competitors and the society as a whole.

(d) Technological advancement and the use of advanced technology may lead to higher productivity and reduction of costs.

(e) Technology upgradation enables the business community to cope up with the rapid improvement in manufacturing by increasing production, developing quality and reducing costs.

Thus, while promoting a venture, the entrepreneur has to take into account the entire technological environment for the purpose of taking strategic decision in choosing the technology, as technological feasibility is a critical input for the success of any kind of enterprise. Our Union Government has created a number of industrial promotion organizations and launched different schemes of modernization and upgradation of technology to encourage entrepreneurs to cope up with the changing needs of the time, to produce good quality products with competitive edge.

4.4 COMPETITIVE FACTORS

Now-a-days, entrepreneurs face numerous challenges while putting up their enterprise. But the most important challenge that drives the entrepreneur is to produce quality products. A new enterprise may confront competition from different types of firms, it may be a small scale, a medium scale or a large scale firm. In the present scenario, due to liberalization, deregulation and globalization, a new small scale firm may also compete with the products supplied by multinational companies. In this context, market demand analysis speaks of a fairly good explanation regarding the nature and extent of competition prevailing in the market. In our country, the nature of competition may vary significantly. This is due to the underdeveloped nature of our economy where there is a very large primary sector and an equally small tertiary sector. Existence of market bottlenecks, degree of responsiveness of demand to changes in price and other external factors prompt the entrepreneur to study the competitive situation with reference to the chosen market segments. In order to assess the competition or competitive situations, an entrepreneur should try to study the following key areas so that he can efficiently establish his enterprise:

(a) Prepare the profiles of customers, industry and competition
(b) Identify the size of customers
(c) Prepare the list of firms producing and marketing similar products
(d) Find out the goodwill and the image of the product in the market
(e) Examine the advantages of price, quality, warranties, service and distribution of the products
(f) Examine the operational strengths and weaknesses of the products
(g) Diagnose the market share, trends in sales and profitability
(h) Study the frequency of demand for the product
(i) Observe the pattern of demand for the product.

Keeping in view the above things and taking into consideration the SWOT analysis, the entrepreneur may select the most feasible business opportunity which can withstand competition and operate as a commercially-viable business opportunity.

4.5 SMALL SCALE INDUSTRIAL UNDERTAKINGS

Industrial undertaking in which the investment in fixed assets in plant and machinery, excluding land and building, whether held on ownership terms or on lease or on hire purchase, does not exceed Rs. 1 crore is called a Small Scale Industrial (SSI) undertaking.

4.5.1 Status of Small Scale Industrial Undertaking

1. ***Ancillary industrial undertaking:*** An industrial undertaking which is engaged or is proposed to be engaged in the manufacture or production of parts, components, sub-assemblies, tooling, intermediates or the rendering of services and undertaking supplies or proposes to supply or render not more than 50 per cent of its production or services, as the case may be, to one or more other industrial undertakings and whose investment in fixed assets in plant and machinery, whether held on ownership terms or on lease or on hire purchase, does not exceed Rs 1 crore.
2. ***Tiny industries:*** All small scale industries wherein investment on plant and machinery (excluding land and building) up to Rs 25 lakhs are classified as tiny industries.
3. ***Export-oriented units:*** All small scale units which exports more than 50 per cent of their output are classified as export-oriented units.

4.5.2 Specified Activities Eligible for SSI Registration up to Rs 5 Crores

There are certain types of industries/activities wherein investment on plant and machinery up to Rs 5 crores can also be registered under SSI category and such list of industries are available in info-help.

Note: No small scale or ancillary industrial undertaking referred here shall be subsidiary of, owned or controlled by any other industrial undertaking.

Explanation: For the purpose of this note, ***owned*** shall have the meaning as derived from the definition of the expression ***owner*** specified in Clause 1 of Section 3 of the said Act. ***Subsidiary*** shall have the same meaning as in Clause 47 of Section 2 read with Section 4 of the Companies Act (1 of 1956). ***Controlled by any other industrial undertaking*** means as under:

(i) Where two or more industrial undertakings are set up by the same person as a proprietor, each of such industrial undertaking shall be considered to be controlled by other industrial undertaking or undertakings.

(ii) Where two or more industrial undertakings are set up as partnership firms under the Indian Partnership Act 1932 (1 of 1932) and one or more partners are common partners in such firms, each such undertaking shall be considered to be controlled by any other undertaking or undertakings.

(iii) Where industrial undertakings are set up by companies under the Companies Act 1956 (1 of 1956), an industrial undertaking shall be considered to be controlled by any other industrial undertaking if:

(a) the equity holding by any other industrial undertaking in it exceeds twenty total equity or

(b) the management control of an undertaking is passed on to the other industrial undertaking by way of the Managing Director of the first mentioned undertaking being also the Managing Director or Director of any other industrial undertaking or the majority of directors on then board of the first mentioned undertaking being the equity holders in the other industrial undertakings in terms of the provisions of the following items (a) and (b) of Sub-clause (iv). The extent of equity participation by other industrial undertaking or undertakings in the undertaking as per sub-clause (iii) above shall be worked out as follows:

(a) The equity participation by any other industrial undertaking shall include both foreign and domestic equity.

(b) Equity participation by any other industrial undertaking shall mean total equity held in an industrial undertaking by any other industrial undertaking or undertakings, whether small scale or otherwise, put together as well as the equity held by persons who are directors in any other industrial undertaking or undertakings even if the person concern is a director in any other industrial undertaking or undertakings.

(c) Equity held by a person, having special technical qualification and experience, appointed as a Director in a small scale industrial undertaking, to the extent of qualification shares, if so provided in the Articles of Association, shall not be counted in computing the equity held by any other industrial undertaking or undertakings even if the person concerned is a Director in any other industrial undertaking or undertakings.

(iv) Where an industrial undertaking is a subsidiary of or is owned or controlled by any other industrial undertaking or undertakings in terms of Sub-clauses (i), (ii) or (iii) and if the total investment is fixed assets in plant and machinery of the first mentioned industrial undertaking and any other industrial undertaking or undertakings clubbed together exceeds the limit of investment specified in Paragraphs 1 or 2 of this notification, as the case may be, none of these industrial undertakings shall be considered to be a small scale or ancillary industrial undertaking.

* Excerpts from Development Commissioner (Small Scale Industries), website: http:/www.Laghu udyog.Com/SSI India/definition.htm)

4.6 MICRO, SMALL AND MEDIUM ENTERPRISES: RECENT POLICY INITIATIVE

4.6.1 Salient Features of MSMED Act 2006

There was a long standing demand from entrepreneurs, small industry associations and related stake holders for a single comprehensive legislation. The Micro, Small and Medium Enterprises Development (MSMED) Act, 2006 is the first act enacted for establishment and promotion of micro, small and medium enterprises in the country. Under the MSMED Act, 2006, the earlier, rather limited, concept of 'Industries' has been widened to that of 'Enterprises'. Enterprises have been broadly classified into two categories, viz: (a) enterprises engaged in the manufacture/production of goods pertaining to any industry, (b) enterprises engaged in providing/rendering of services. Enterprises have been defined in terms of investment in plant and machinery/equipment (excluding land and building) (Table 4.1).

MSM Enterprises

Table 4.1 Investment in plant and machinery/equipment (excluding land and building)

Categories	*Manufacturing enterprises*	*Service enterprises*
Micro	Upto Rs. 25 lakh	Upto Rs. 10 lakh
Small	More than Rs. 25 lakh and upto Rs. 5 crore	More than Rs. 10 lakh & upto Rs. 2 crore
Medium	More than Rs. 5 crore and up to Rs. 10 crore	More than Rs. 2 crore and upto Rs. 5 crore

This new Act envisages the constitution of an apex consultative body, namely, National Board for Micro, Small and Medium Enterprises, headed by the Central Minister in charge of MSMEs and will consist of members from (a) MPs; (b Representatives of central Ministries; (c) State Governments; (d) UT Administration, RBI, SIDBI, NABARD; (e) Associations of MSMEs including women; (f) Persons of eminence, and (g) Central Trade Union Organizations. The most important thing is that the National Board for Micro, Small and Medium Enterprises has a statutory status as against non-statutory SSI Board. The Act provides statutory basis to Purchase Preference Policy for goods and services provided by micro and small enterprises. This also strengthens the legal provisions to check delayed payments to MSMEs. The cumbersome two-stage registration process of SSI was substituted with an optional filing of memorandum by micro and small enterprises. The MSMED Act, 2006 was operational from October 2, 2006.

4.6.2 Functions of the Advisory Committee

The Advisory Committee is empowered to exercise the following functions:

1. To examine the matters referred to it by the national Board.
2. To advise Central Government on matters in specific clauses of MSMED Act.
3. To advise state Governments on matters specified in the rules under clause 32 of the MSMED Act, 2006.

4.6.3 Other Initiatives

The government announced the following initiatives to support the manufacturing sector:

- Formulation of *'National Manufacturing Competitiveness Programme'* (*NMCP*), particularly for the small and medium enterprise sector.
- *Announcement of Package for promotion of micro and small enterprises*: (i) legislative back up, (ii) credit support, (iii) fiscal measures, (iv) support for cluster based development, (v) technological and quality up-gradation support, (vi) Marketing support, (vii) support for managerial and entrepreneurial development, (viii) empowerment of women owned enterprises, (ix) Strengthening of PMRY Scheme, (x) Strengthening of database for MSME Sector.
- Reservation and dereservation of products *for manufacture in the small scale sector.*

4.7 STEPS IN SETTING UP A SMALL SCALE INDUSTRIAL ENTERPRISE

Promotion of a venture by a new entrepreneur is a complex job. The potential entrepreneur has to pass through a number of steps in a step-by-step approach to achieve his goal of setting up a new enterprise. In fact, deciding and motivating the self is the first bedrock upon which the establishment concept of an enterprise is entirely posited. Similarly, the identification of a viable project ensures the proposition that "well begun is half done". Hence the various steps involved in establishment of a business enterprise through which the entrepreneur may pass are the following:

1. ***Decision to be self-employed:*** This is the most crucial decision a youth has to take, shunning wage employment and opting for self-employment or entrepreneurship.
2. ***Analysing strengths, weaknesses, opportunities and threats* (SWOT analysis)*:*** The potential entrepreneur has to analyse his strengths, weaknesses, opportunities and threats, while deciding to go for entrepreneurial career. This analysis enables him to know what type and size of business would be the most suitable. This will vary from person to person.
3. ***Scanning of business environment:*** It is always essential on the part of the entrepreneur to study and understand the prevailing business environment. In order to ensure success of his enterprise, entrepreneur should scan the business opportunities and threats in the environment. He should study the administrative framework, procedures, policies, rules and regulations and other formalities implemented by the government.
4. ***Training:*** Before going to start the enterprise, the potential entrepreneur must assess his own deficiencies which he can compensate through training. He can avail the facilities of various training institutes like EDI, NIESBUD, IEDs existing in our country. These institutes are providing tailor-made **Entrepreneurship Development Programmes** (EDPs) and skill upgradation training programmes for the benefit of the new entrepreneurs, existing entrepreneurs and for the employees of the small scale industries.
5. ***Product selection:*** The most important step is to decide what business to venture into, the product or range of products that shall be selected for manufacture and in what quantity. The level of activity will help in determining the size of business and thus form of ownership. One could generate as many project ideas as one can through environment scanning and shortlisting a few of them as discussed earlier in the book. Closely examine with the help of opportunity analysis each one of them and zero on the final product or products.
6. ***Market survey:*** It is always convenient to manufacture an item but difficult to sell. So it is rational on the part of the entrepreneur to survey the market thoroughly before embarking upon production. Market survey implies systematic collection of data by the entrepreneur about the product for manufacture, demand-supply lag, extent of competition, frequency of demand, pattern and design of demand, its potential share in the market pricing, distribution policy, etc. The principle is to produce what actually people demand.

7. ***Form of organization:*** A firm can be constituted as proprietorship, partnership, limited company (public/private), cooperative society, etc. This will depend upon the type, purpose and size of entrepreneur's business. One may also decide on the form of ownership on the basis of resources at hand or from the point of view of investment.
8. ***Location:*** The next step will be to decide the location where the unit is to be established. Will it be hired or owned? The size of plot, covered and open area and the exact site will have to be decided.
9. ***Technology:*** To manufacture any item, technology is used. Information on all available technologies should be collected by the entrepreneur and the most suitable one to be identified. This will also be useful to determine the type of machinery and equipment to be installed.
10. ***Machinery and equipment:*** Having chosen the technology, the machinery and equipment required for manufacturing the chosen products have to be decided, suppliers have to be identified and their costs have to be estimated. One may have to plan well in advance for machinery and equipment especially if it has to be procured from outside the town, state or country.
11. ***Project report preparation:*** After deciding the form of the ownership, location, technology, machinery and equipment, the entrepreneur should be ready to prepare his project report or the feasibility study. The economic viability and the technical feasibility of the product selected have to be established through a project report. A project report that may now be prepared will be helpful in formulating the production, marketing, financial and management plans. It will also be useful in obtaining finance, shed, power connection, water connection, raw material quotas, etc.
12. ***Project appraisal:*** Ordinarily, project appraisal implies the assessment of a project. It is a technique for ex-ante analysis of a scheme or project. While preparing to set up an enterprise, the entrepreneur has to carefully appraise the project from the standpoint of economic, financial, technical, market, managerial and social aspects to arrive at the most socially-feasible enterprise. To avail the finance from the financial institutions and banks, a comprehensive appraisal of projects carrying technoeconomic feasibility aspects should be undertaken by the entrepreneur. Thus, a project which is selected should be technically feasible and economically viable, then only it will be bankable. For this, the following appraisals can be performed at the preliminary level: (a) Economical appraisal; (b) Financial appraisal; (c) Technical appraisal; (d) Management appraisal; (e) Organizational appraisal; (f) Operational appraisal; (g) Market appraisal.
13. ***Finance:*** Finance is the lifeblood of the enterprise. Entrepreneur has to take certain steps and follow specified norms of the financial institutions and banks to obtain it. A number of financial agencies provide capital assistance and venture capital for starting an enterprise. There are some agencies which provide financial assistance at concessional rates. Under PMRY and REGP schemes financial assistance and subsidies are being provided to the persons who want to set up their own enterprise.
14. ***Provisional registration:*** It is always worthwhile to get the unit registered with the government. The entrepreneur has to obtain the prescribed application form for provisional registration from DIC or Directorate of Industries. After having duly

filled in the application form, he has to submit the application with all relevant documents in the local DIC or Directorate of Industries. This will enable the entrepreneur to avail of various government facilities, incentives and assistance schemes including financial assistance from NSIC/SFCs/KVIC.

15. ***Technical know-how:*** In some cases, technical know-how may be arranged for setting up enterprise. This can be arranged through TCOs, NSIC, SSIDC, DIC, private consultants, SISI, ED-institutes, foreign collaborators, India Investment Centre, industry associations like FICCI, ASSOCHAM, CII, PHD Chamber of Commerce and Industry, etc. Facilities are also available to SSI for making technical know-how arrangements including turn-key jobs.
16. ***Power and water connection:*** The sites, where the enterprise will be located, should either have adequate power connections or this should be arranged. Entrepreneur can calculate the total power requirement and determine the nearest pole from which power will be given to the enterprise as it can materially affect the installation cost. Similarly, the water connection will have to be obtained or provision should be made for adequate water supply to the firm.
17. ***Installation of machinery:*** Having completed the above formalities, the next step is to procure the machinery for installation. Machinery should preferably be installed as per the plan layout.
18. ***Recruitment of manpower:*** Once machines are installed, the need for manpower arises to run them. So the quantum and type of manpower is to be decided. This presupposes the skilled, unskilled and semiskilled labour, administrative staff etc. Further, sources of getting desired labour and staff members be indented and recruited. Possibly, the labour force has to be trained either at the entrepreneur's premises or in a training establishment.
19. ***Procurement of raw materials:*** Raw materials are the important ingredients for running an enterprise. The labour will require raw materials to work upon the installed machinery. These materials may be procured indigenously or may have to be imported by the entrepreneur. Entrepreneur has to identify the cheap and assured sources of supply of raw materials for running his own enterprise. Government agencies can assist in case the raw materials are scarce or imported.
20. ***Production:*** The unit established should have an organizational set-up. To operate optimally, the organization should employ its manpower, machinery and methods effectively. There should not be any wastage of manpower, machinery and materials. If items are exported, then the product and its packaging must be attractive. Production of the proposed item should be taken up in two stages:

    (i) Trial production; (ii) Commercial production.

    Trial production will help tackling problems confronted in production and test marketing of the product. This will reduce the chances of loss in the eventuality of mistakes in project conception. Commercial production should be commenced after the ***test-marketing*** of the product.
21. ***Marketing:*** Marketing is the most important activity as far as the entrepreneurial development is concerned. Various aspects like how to reach the customer, distribution

channels, commission structure, pricing, advertising, publicity, etc. have to be decided by the entrepreneur. Like production marketing should also be attempted cautiously, that is, in two stages namely:

(i) Test stage; (ii) Commercial marketing stage.

Test marketing is necessary to save the enterprise from going into disrepute in case the product launched is not well accepted by the customers. It will also assist the entrepreneur in carrying out modifications or additions in designs and features of the product. Having successfully test marketed the product, commercial marketing can be undertaken.

22. ***Quality assurance:*** Before marketing, the product quality certification from BIS (Bureau of Indian Standards)/AGMARK, etc. should be obtained depending upon the product. If there are no quality standards specified for the products, the entrepreneur should evolve his own quality control parameters. Quality, after all, ensures long-term success.
23. ***Permanent registration:*** After the small scale unit goes into production and marketing, it becomes eligible to get permanent registration based on its provisional registration from DIC or Directorate of Industries.
24. ***Market research:*** Once the product or service is introduced in the market, there is strong need for continuous market research to assess needs and areas for modification, upgradation and growth. Market becomes waterloos for most SSI entrepreneurs as they ignore the vital day-to-day operation. Initial success should not lure the entrepreneur into a sense of complacency.
25. ***Profit generation and reinvestment:*** The next step on the part of the entrepreneur is to be vigilant about his cost of production and profit generation. Through constant monitoring, evaluation of production, quality, marketing, calculating the return on investment (ROI) and profitability ratio, the entrepreneur can be able to know where the firm actually stands. A successful entrepreneur by his business acumen and managerial efficiency can generate sufficient profit as to plough it back in the firm. The new entrepreneur should enhance his credit worthiness by meticulously adhering to the repayment schedule as prescribed by the bank or financing institution.

In fact, the steps discussed in this section are important enough for a new entrepreneur to start an enterprise. Careful observance of these steps can land the entrepreneur on a highly successful position where he can achieve his desired goal with confidence.

4.8 LEGAL REQUIREMENTS FOR ESTABLISHING A NEW UNIT

For establishment and management of a new venture or setting up of a small scale enterprise, entrepreneurs come across a number of situations to follow laws of the land. Right from the conception stage in promoting the enterprise, entrepreneurs should be careful to obey the legal formalities, procedures, policies and plans for the government so as to make themselves free from any sort of legal hassles in future.

As it has been rightly known that small scale industries are an integral part of economic development, small scale entrepreneurs should adhere to the rules of the land. Thus, an attempt has been made to elucidate some of the important laws and regulations which are common to all types of enterprises.

1. ***No Objection Certificate (NOC) from local body/panchayat/municipality:*** While promoting a new venture, the entrepreneur has to obtain No Objection Certificate from local body/NAC/panchayat or municipality as well as the requisite permission to start the SSI. This is done for the purpose of construction of industrial sheds and for land utilization as well as for the benefit which may be given to the enterprise in course of its operation by the government.
2. ***Registration of the unit in DIC:*** Small scale units are required to be registered with the District Industries Centres (DICs) which function under Directorate of Industries of the state in which the industries are established. As a rule, previously entrepreneurs are assisted with two types of registration, viz. provisional registration and permanent registration. As the name implies provisional registration is provisional in nature and the SSI unit gets a PRC (Provisional Registration Certificate) from the DIC as an incipient unit to grow for production in future normally within a period of five years. Permanent registration certificate is provided when the industry has 'gone into production'. PRC registration and Permanent registration are substituted with filing of EM1 and EM2 forms, respectively for registration of micro and small enterprises. EM form means Entrepreneur Memorandum form available at District Industries Centres for registration of micro and small enterprises after MSMED Act 2006 came into force.

   The above registration certificates are necessary to make the unit eligible to get the incentives, subsidies, exemptions provided by the government as per the benefit envisaged in the Industrial Policy Resolutions (IPRs) of the government.
3. ***Statutory licence or clearance:*** All industrial undertakings are exempted from industrial licensing except those industries which are coming under public sector or in respect of which the licensing is compulsory. The Industries Development and Regulation Act (IDRA) 1951 provides the basic framework for directing the flow of investments into different types of industries. Thus, industrial licensing is utilized as an important instrument for the above purpose. In our country, a number of administrative bodies in government are established for considering the proposal for the issue of industrial licence and a time limit exists for issue of the licence. In general, a letter of intent is issued initially with prescribed condition subject to which licence is issued after fulfilment of these conditions. However, after the announcement of New Industrial Policy in July 1991, industrial licensing is abolished for all projects except for eighteen industries related to security and strategic concern, social reasons, hazardous chemicals and overriding environmental reasons and items of elitist consumption. Thus, the process of liberalization has played a significant role in abolition of industrial licensing for a large number of industrial items of manufacturing.

Table 4.2 depicts the product line/activity and services and their corresponding competent authorities from which the entrepreneur can avail clearance certificates.

Table 4.2 Authorities to Contact for Various Clearance Certificates

1. Starting a MSME unit	1. Registration certificate, EM1 and EM2 to be obtained from District Industries Centre (DICs) under Directorate of Industries
2. For units operating in places other than industrial estate	2. NOC from Panchayat/NAC/Municipal Corporation
3. Pollution control	3. State Pollution Control Board
4. Registration under the State Sales Tax Act	4. Local sales tax authorities
5. Manufacturing of drugs	5. State drug controller
6. Registration under Central Excise Act	6. Superintendent of Central Excise of the area
7. Manufacturing of fruit and vegetable based products (under fruit products order)	7. Deputy Director, Fruit and Vegetable Preservation, Ministry of Agriculture, Government of India
8. Registration of the unit under partnership	8. Registration of partnership firms
9. Registration of manufacturing of electronic items under decentralized category	9. State level technical committee under Directorate of Industries
10. Electronic items other than decentralized items	10. Development Commissioner, Small Scale Industries through State Directorate of Industries
11. Certificate of quality/standardization	11. Bureau of Indian Standards
12. Licence for export of products	12. Chief Controller of Imports and Exports, New Delhi/Directorate of Export Promotion, Udyog Bhavan, New Delhi
13. Power connection	13. State Grid/Electricity Board
14. Registration under Factories Act for the units employing 10 workers or more with power or 20 workers or more without power	14. Chief Inspector of Factories
15. 100% export-oriented units (EOUs), other than free trade zones and export processing zones	15. Secretariat for Industrial Approvals (SIA), Department of Industrial Development, Government of India
16. Industries using water and involving effluent disposal gaseous wastes, etc.	16. Directorate of Public Health of the State Government, District Health Officer of the particular district

(Contd.)

Table 4.1 (Contd.)

17. For production and sale of fire crackers, explosives and related goods	17. Licence from District Collector under Explosive Act
18. For benefit of purchases made for government office	18. Registrations with Director General of Supplies and Disposal (DGS&D) or National Small Industries Corporation (NSIC)

Table 4.3 provides a number of state and national level sources to contact for various types of assistance.

Table 4.3 Whom to Contact for What Information

S.No.	*Area of assistance*	*State level sources*	*National level sources*
1.	For selectionof a project	MSME-DI, DIC, IDCS, TCOs, SFCs, SIC, IC, IEB OR PTC	CB, SIDO, CSIR, DEP, IFCI, IPB, NRDC
2.	Registration and licences	CIF, DDCA, DIC, GMD, SIC, SPCB, IC, IA, STC, TC	CECD, CCIE, ISI IDC, NSIC, RC, PT, SC, DGI
3.	Finance	DIC, banks, SIC, IICs, IDCs	CB, CEC, CSIR, IIC, IIT, NSIC, RT, SBI, MSME-DI, ICMR.
4.	Technical	DDCA, DIC, DJCII, TCOs, GMD	CIPET, CSIR, IIC IIT, NSIC, RT, SBI, SISI, ICMR
5.	Training	MSME-DI, TCOs, DICs, IEDs	SBI, EDI, CB, CIPET, IPL, IITS, NIESBTD, INISIET
6.	Infrastructure facilities	DIC, EB, IDC, LA	
7.	Raw materials	DIC, MID, MDC, MSME-DI, IC, STC	CCIE, MMTC, MDC
8.	Plant and machinery	DIC, IIC, SPC, SEC, IC	CCIE, NSIC, MSME-DI
9.	Marketing information	DIC, TCOs, SEC, SIC, RINCO	DEP, DGSD, CCIE, MIC, ICMR, IIPT, ICAR

4.9 IMPORTANT ACTS

The Consumer Protection Act

The Consumer Protection Act 1986 envisages to provide protection of interest of consumers and for the settlement of consumers' disputes. The Act shall apply to all goods and services except those not notified by the Central Government. As per the Section 1 of the Act, any person who

(i) buys or
(ii) hires or avails of any services on payment, either in full or in instalment or under hire purchase system and
(iii) any person who used goods or is benefited from services without making any payment. However, any person who obtains such goods for resale or for any commercial purpose is not regarded as a consumer.

For hearing the complaints of the consumer, the following redressal agencies have been formed by the government at various levels:

1. ***District forum:*** A district forum is set up in each district having the jurisdiction to entertain complaints where the value of goods and services and compensation claimed does not exceed Rs 5 lakhs.
2. ***State commission:*** A state commission is set up by the state government for the respective state. The state commission entertains complaints where the value of goods and services and compensation, claimed, if any, exceeds Rs 5 lakhs but is less than Rs 20 lakhs and shall also hear appeals against the order of the district forum.
3. ***National Commission:*** A National Commission is set up by the Union Government. It has the jurisdiction to hear the complaints where the value of goods or services and compensation claimed, if any, exceeds Rs 20 lakhs and shall also hear appeals against the orders of any state commission.

The time limit within which the complaint may be filed is two years from the date on which the cause of action has arisen. However, the authority in the district forum or state commission or National Commission for their respective complaint may condone the delay on being satisfied by the complainant and after recording the reason for the same. All appeals are required to be filled within those days from the date of the order appealed against.

The Essential Commodities Act

This Act has been enacted for regulating production, distribution, storage and pricing of certain items of mass consumption. This Act keeps in its purview as many as sixty six items of essential commodities. The control orders ordinarily provide for licensing of production, storage, transport, distribution, and use or consumption of any essential commodity, price controls, prohibitions on hoarding of any essential commodity kept for sale, compulsory sale of a part of the production to the government. On the basis of the restrictions provided in the control orders, the orders may be classified into the following categories: (a) Price control orders; (b) Quality control orders; (c) Movement control orders; (d) Packaging control orders; (e) Licensing control orders; (f) Stock and storage orders; (g) Usage control orders; (h) Distribution control orders; (i) Production control orders.

Penal Provision under the Act

(a) Where there is a contravention of any control order in relation to an essential commodity, the essential commodity may be seized or confiscated.

(b) Any person who contravenes any control order, shall be punishable with imprisonment up to seven years (minimum three months) and also be liable to fine.

(c) Any person who fails to carry on an undertaking in accordance with the directions of the authorized controller shall be punishable with imprisonment up to seven years (minimum three months) and also be liable to fine. Any person who attempts to contravene or bets a contravention of any order shall be deemed to have contravened that order.

The Prevention of Food Adulteration Act

The Prevention of Food Adulteration Act aims at making provisions for the prevention of adulteration of food. The standards of quality of various food articles have been specified in Appendix B to the Prevention of Food Adulteration Rules 1955. Any food article which does not conform to the standards specified in Appendix B will be said to be adulterated.

Manufacture, sale, stocking, distribution or exhibition for sale of any article of food, including prepared food or ready-to-serve food, cannot be done by any person except under a licence called food licence.

For the offences committed in contravention of the provisions made in the Act will lead to imprisonment of minimum six months up to life and minimum fine of Rs 1 lakh.

The Sale of Goods Act

The Sale of Goods Act 1930 governs the contracts relating to sale of movable property. The contract for sale of goods is on subjects such as transfer of ownership of goods, delivery of goods, rights and duties of the buyer and seller, remedies for the breach of contract, conditions and warranties implied under a contract for sale of goods, etc.

The remedial measures against the breach of contracts are:

(a) Suit for damages for non-delivery; (b) Suit for price; (c) Suit for specific performance; (d) Suit for breach of warranty; (e) Suit for damages for repudiation of contract before due date and (f) Suit for interest.

The Negotiable Instruments Act

Negotiable instruments are documents commonly used in commercial transaction and monetary dealings. A negotiable implement represents a special kind of contract which entitles a person to a sum of money and to transfer the instrument (and the right theirin) to another person by mere delivery or by an endorsement and delivery.

As defined in the Act, a negotiable instrument means a promissory note, bill of exchange or cheque payable either to order or bearer.

Promissory note: A promissory note is an unconditional written undertaking, signed by the maker, to pay a certain sum of money only to or to the order of a certain person or to the bearer of the instrument.

Bill of exchange: A bill of exchange is an instrument in writing containing an unconditional order, signed by the maker, directing a certain person to pay a specific sum of money only to or to the order of a specific person, or to the bearer of the instrument.

Cheque: A cheque is a bill of exchange drawn on a special field banker and not expressed to be payable otherwise on demand. To be more clear, a cheque is a bill of exchange drawn by specified bank payable on demand. In case of dishonour of cheque for insufficiency of funds drawee will liable to be punished with imprisonment.

Factories Act 1948

Section 2 m defines a factory as follows:

Any place wherein ten or more persons are working and where a manufacturing process is carried on with the aid of power supplied by steamroller or electricity is termed as a factory. If twenty or more persons are working in premises in which power is not used, it can also be treated as a factory.

Factories Act 1948 prohibits a person to work in a factory, if he is below 14 years. The Act reduces the hours of work for children between the age 14–17 from 5 hours to $4^{1}/_{2}$ hours per day and also prohibits them to work at night. Women are also not allowed to work from 6 pm to 7 am under the provision of the Act and the working hours are reduced from 5–4 hours to 48 hours per week, i.e., 9 hours to 8 hours per week.

The Act also lays down that there should be proper clean light in the factory with proper ventilation and temperature in every workroom. It is the duty of the management to maintain sufficient lighting, sufficient supply of wholesome drinking water, safety provisions, welfare provisions, first aid appliances for the benefit of the workers.

For any contravention of the provisions of the Act, the owner and the manager of a factory shall each be guilty of an offence and be entitled for imprisonment for a term not exceeding three months or with a fine up to Rs five hundred or with both. If any person again found to be guilty for the same offence involving contravention of the same provision within a period of two years from the date of conviction he shall be entitled for imprisonment up to six months or with a fine of up to Rs 1 thousand as per the Act.

The Industrial Disputes Act 1947

The Industrial Disputes Act 1947 is an important Act which aims at promoting harmonious industrial relation between the workers and the employers. The Act applies to all industrial and commercial establishments employing one or more workers except those who are employed in administrative and managerial positions.

The important provisions of the Industrial Disputes Act are the following:

(i) In case of any industrial dispute, the appropriate government may refer the dispute to (a) a board for promoting settlement, or (b) to a court of enquiry, or (c) to a tribunal for an arbitration.

(ii) In case the dispute has been referred to a board or a tribunal, the government may prohibit the continuance of strike or lockout in connection with such dispute.

(iii) A conciliation proceeding is drawn and a settlement arrived under the Act.
(iv) Protection of workmen during presence of proceedings.
(v) Workers employed in public utility industries shall not continue the strike and the employers shall not resort to lockouts.
(vi) No person shall knowingly apply any money in direct support to legal strike or lockout.
(vii) As per the 1982 Amendment, this Act encourages that an employer should establish a Grievance Settlement Authority in his establishment if 50 or more workers have been employed in the preceding twelve months. Industrial disputes relating to a workman should have to be settled there.

The Workmen's Compensation Act 1923

The Act aims at securing the payment of compensation by employers and personal inquiry caused to a workman by an accident arising out of and in the course of his employment. Main provisions of the Act cover the following four categories of injuries:

(i) Death
(ii) Permanent total disablement
(iii) Permanent partial disablement
(iv) Temporary disablement—partial or total.

The Act also provides compensation for occupational diseases which are given in the Schedule III of the Act. The Act provides compensation for those categories of injuries as envisaged in Schedules I to V of the Act.

There are also provisions in the Act regarding the model of payment of compensation, provision for appeal and obligations and rights of workmen and employees.

The Employees Provident Fund Act 1952

The Act is a piece of welfare legislation which aims at making provisions for securing in old age after the employee retires or for his dependant in case of his early death.

The Act covers all facilities and establishments employing 20 or more employees. For government establishments, if the member is less than 20, the Act can also be applicable if the employees desire so.

The important provisions of the Act relate to the contribution to EPF by the employer and the employee. The contribution varies from 8.33% to 10% of basic salary for different types of industries.

The Payment of Bonus Act 1985

The objective of the Act is to provide statutory obligation for the payment of bonus to the employees in certain establishments on the bearing profit. The Act applies to the establishments employing 20 or more persons on any day during a year. All workers getting salary up to Rs 2500 per month are covered under this Act. The Act also provides the payment of maximum and minimum bonus, timely and non-eligibility to get bonus. Any employee who has worked at least 30 days in accounting year in the establishment shall be eligible for the bonus.

The Minimum Wages Act 1948

The main objective of the Act is to fix the minimum wages in the specified industries and trading concerns for the employees/workmen where labour organization are nonexistent and defunct. The Act covers all employees, skilled as well as unskilled, working in any type of establishment. The chief provision of the Act envisages determining and revising the minimum wages and ensuring the right of the employees working in the organization.

Tax Consideration

Tax is a compulsory contribution from the public to the government. Its main objectives are to raise revenue, reduce inequalities of wealth and income and support the developmental activities. It also facilitates the promotion of the interests of industrial sector of the country. In the initial stages of the small scale substantial unit, it is found that many small industries lack shock-absorbing capability as they confront large number of problems. In order to safeguard the interests of these small units, the government can provide them benefits and preferences such as tax holidays, concession in tax liability, etc. The benefits may be in the following forms:

(a) Exemption of excise duties was produced on a turnover of Rs 50 lakhs for small scale industries implemented in 1998-99. Small scale industrial units may also have the option of going for MODVAT (Modified Value Added Tax) with concession in normal vote of duty.
(b) Small scale industrial units manufacturing products under another brand name in rural areas are also provided the benefit of duty exemption as per 1998–99 Union Budget.

Income Tax

New industrial undertakings including small scale industries are exempted from the payment of income tax on their profit subject to a maximum of 6 per cent annually of their capital employed in accordance with Section 80 J of the Income Tax Act. The exemption is allowed for a period of five years from the day the industry goes into production. This is termed as tax holidays.

Sales Tax

Sales tax exemption is given to small scale units by the State Government to encourage entrepreneur to set up more number of small scale units. Sales tax exemption can be granted to small scale units for a period of three to fifteen years by the State Government. So far the states providing this benefit are Uttar Pradesh, Jammu and Kashmir, Haryana, Punjab, Gujarat, Maharashtra, Rajasthan, Nagaland and Sikkim. 100 per cent Export-Oriented Units (EOUs) are exempted from import licensing and they can import raw materials and capital goods, consumables, etc. under Open General Licence (OGL). In view of the above, the new entrepreneur has to abide the rules of taxation and at the same time, procedure of registration from appropriate authority so as to avail concessions and benefits provided by the government for promotion of the enterprise.

4.10 POLICIES OF THE GOVERNMENT

4.10.1 Industrial Policy Resolutions (IPRs)

The policy support of the Union Government is always directed towards consistent socioeconomic development, identified thrust areas and investment criteria adopted in the five year plans. Industrial policies are intertwined with economic development perspective enunciated in plan document. A step-by-step approach was taken in the formulation and implementation of the industrial policies formulated during more than five decades of planned development from the announcement of Industrial Policy Resolution (IPR) 1948.

IPR 1948

IPR 1948 was aimed at post-Independent national reconstruction through industrialization in providing basic minimum needs, justice and equality to the people by improving the standard of living. Prime industries such as coal, steel, aircraft, ship manufacturing, telecom, mineral oil and fertilizer were kept in central sector. Manufacture of arms, atomic energy and rail transport was the monopoly of the Central Government. The policy also envisaged the importance of cottage and small enterprises in the national economy due to the following potentialities:

(a) Employment creation and (b) Utilization of local resources and skill.

Thus, the main thrust of IPR 1948, as far as the small sector was concerned, centred round ***protection.***

IPR 1956

Industrial Policy Resolution propounded in 1956 provided a clear and emphatic policy and procedural as well as incentive support to the small scale and cottage industries incorporating the Gandhian thought for the all-round development of the economy. Privately-owned production and manufacturing activities were encouraged by this policy. IPR 1956 has ushered in an era of industrial development in India. As regards SSI sector, the resolution envisaged two important roles—manufacturing of consumer goods such as cloth and manufacturing of component for the newly-established industry as part of the programme for long-term industrial development. Thus, IPR 1956 aimed at ***protection plus development*** for small scale industrial sector.

IPR 1977

The next IPR was announced after the lapse of two decades. The establishment of District Industries Centre (DIC) focusing on the regional growth of industries and utilizing the local resources and skill was the main thrust of Industrial Policy Resolution (IPR) 1977. Removal of disparities between urban and rural sector and fulfilment of genuine aspiration of the people through linkage between agriculture and industries were ingrained in the policy. Financial support to small scale sector was given priority by establishment of a separate wing of Industrial Development Bank of India (IDBI) and Khadi and Village Industries Board (KVIB). Commissions were strengthened for the growth of village and cottage industries. This IPR had assigned a positive role to small scale industries in terms of wage employment and self-employment. Thus, to the earlier emphasis of protection plus development, this resolution added *promotion*. The small scale sector, therefore, was to be protected, developed and promoted.

IPR 1980

The policy support of IPR 1980 was initiated to re-emphasize a boost to the industrial take-off envisaged in IPR 1956. The thrust areas of IPR 1980 were industrial infrastructure, optimum utilization of installed capacity, higher productivity promotion of agro-based industries, promotion of export-oriented and import-substitute industries, consumer protection and quality services. Investment limit in plant and machineries for tiny units was raised from Rs 1 lakh to Rs 2 lakhs and for small scale sector from Rs 10 lakhs to Rs 20 lakhs. Small Scale Industrial (SSI) sector was again treated as the most important sector for generation of wage employment and development of entrepreneurial spirit among the people of India.

IPR 1990

The basic objective of IPR 1990 was to introduce the policy of economic liberalization and to simplify the procedures and formalities, rules and regulations with a view to widening the technological base of industry to raise the level of output. The investment limit for SSI in plant and machineries was increased to Rs 60 lakhs, greater emphasis was given to training of youth and women under entrepreneurship. Development programme and an apex bank namely Small Industries Development Bank of India (SIDBI) was established in 1990 to assist the entrepreneurs in the small scale sector.

4.10.2 New Small Enterprise Policy 1991

The Government of India has also brought out a New Small Enterprise Policy (NSEP) with adequate support to tiny and micro-enterprises. The thrust areas of this policy were:

(a) Single window and composite loan scheme
(b) Financial support to the entrepreneurs by allowing equity participation up to 24 per cent of share
(c) Liberalization by a Limited Partnership Act and solution of the problem of delayed payment

(d) Integrated infrastructure development system with the participation from State Government and financial institutions
(e) Technology development and equitable distribution of local and imported raw materials
(f) Improvement in incentive delivery system
(g) Marketing and export support modernization
(h) Quality upgradation and procedural simplification
(i) Increase in investment limit in plant and machineries of tiny industrial units from Rs 2 lakhs to Rs 5 lakhs.

In the context of globalization and competitiveness, the NSEP is the step in right direction to accept challenges providing quality services to the consumers.

EXERCISES

A. Long answer type questions:

1. What are the steps involved in promotion of a venture?
2. Briefly discuss the opportunity analysis for promotion of a venture.
3. Define environment. Discuss in brief the various environmental factors affecting entrepreneurship.
4. What is economic environment of business? What are the economic factors affecting the development of entrepreneurship? Explain the social factors which govern the development of entrepreneurship.
5. Discuss in brief the psychological factors that influence the development of entrepreneurship.
6. Briefly discuss the technological environment which influence the development of an enterprise.
7. What is PRC? What are the advantages of PRC for a new entrepreneurship?
8. Discuss briefly the legal requirements of establishing a new enterprise.

B. Short answer type questions:

1. Define statutory licence.
2. Write short notes on the following:
   (a) Consumers Protection Act
   (b) Negotiable Instrument Act
   (c) Industrial Disputes Act 1947
   (d) The Payment of Bonus Act 1985
   (e) Food Adulteration Act
   (f) Export-oriented Units
   (g) Permanent registration.

CHAPTER 5

Raising of Funds

CHAPTER CONTENTS

5.1 RAISING OF FUNDS: INTERNAL AND EXTERNAL

Finance is the life-blood of an enterprise. In fact, it is the finance which pools together the other resources like man, machine, material and method to start and run the enterprise. According to **R. Cameron** and **H.T. Patric**: "The significance of finance in production is elucidated like a lubricant to the process of production". As such, raising of finance for an enterprise is the most important function of an entrepreneur.

Generally funds can be raised from two important sources:

- Internal sources
- External sources

Internal sources: Internal sources refer to the owner's own funds which can be invested as equity. In case of a small scale industry, owner's contribution in shape of equity is low. So large chunk of money is raised from external sources.

External sources: External sources refer to the funds raised from different financial institutions like development banks, commercial banks, financial corporations, etc. by the entrepreneur.

However, funds required by an enterprise are primarily known as fixed capital and working capital.

Fixed capital and working capital: The money invested in fixed assets like land and building, plant and machinery, furniture and fixture, etc. which are fixed for a long period of time, is called fixed capital. Similarly, the money invested in current assets like raw materials, finished goods, etc. and used for day-to-day operation of the business is called working capital.

Besides, on the basis of utilization of funds according to time period, funds raised by the entrepreneur can be categorized into the following types:

1. ***Short-term capital:*** The money whose repayment period is one year or less is called short-term capital. Borrowings from commercial banks for working capital are treated as short-term capital.
2. ***Medium-term capital:*** The money whose repayment period ranges from one to five years and is usually required for permanent working capital, small expansion, replacements and modification of industrial units is known as medium term capital.
3. ***Long-term capital:*** The money whose repayment exceeds a period of five years is called long-term capital and is usually required for installation of plant and machinery.

Commercial bills: Commercial bills are short-term credit provided by banks and private discounting agencies. It is generally made available to firms and enterprises with high credit rating which carries low interest rate also.

Bridge finance: This is an internal form of finance secured to land or building and against sanctioned loans. This is a short period loan but the interest rate is higher than usual short- or medium-term loan. This type of loan can be obtained from banks, state financial corporation and finance companies.

Overdrafts: This is also a short period finance, especially used for meeting working capital requirements in order to cope with the seasonal fluctuation. Banks are the major sources of this type of finance. It should not be used for long term purposes.

Leasing finance: This type of finance is usually available to entrepreneurs for leasing of plant and machinery. Banks, leasing companies and financial institutions are the major sources of leasing finance. It carries higher rates of interest even more than the short- and medium-term loans. In this case, the borrower normally furnishes collateral securities.

5.2 SOURCES OF FINANCE TO ENTREPRENEURS

Internal sources of financing: Entrepreneur can raise financial assistance internally from the following sources:

(a) Owner's own investment such as equity
(b) Deposits and loans given by the owner
(c) Personal loan from provident fund, life Insurance policy, etc.
(d) In case of running enterprise, funds can be raised through retention of profits
(e) Ploughing back of profits into one's own enterprise

External sources of financing: Entrepreneurs can raise funds externally from the following sources:

(a) Borrowings from friends and relatives
(b) Borrowings from the commercial banks for working capital
(c) Term loans from development financing institutions like IDBI, SIDBI, IFCI Ltd., ICICI Ltd., etc.
(d) Hire-purchase or leasing facilities from national small industries corporations, state small industries development corporations, etc.
(e) Seed capital loan from the financial institutions or the government
(f) Credit facilities provided by different financial institutions as well as commercial banks.

As such, in order to set up small scale enterprise, the entrepreneur mostly depends upon institutional finance for initial capital investment. A small number of entrepreneurs rely upon their friends and relatives and that too as a last resort. Further, in our country, institutional finances especially from commercial banks and development banks are attractive because of low rate of interest being charged by them in comparison to other forms of loans raised by the entrepreneur. The sources used for raising funds determine capital structure of the enterprise which presupposes the relation between debt and equity capital, otherwise called debt-equity ratio. Table 5.1 depicts various sources of finance to entrepreneurs.

Table 5.1 Sources of Finance to Entrepreneurs

Short term	*Medium term*	*Long term*
1. Bank credit	1. Issue of shares	1. Issue of shares
2. Trade credit	2. Issue of debentures	2. Issue of debentures
3. Instalment credit advance	3. Loans from banks and financial institutions	3. Loans and advances
4. Customer advances	4. Public department for running concern	4. Ploughing back of profit from existing enterprise
5. Factoring	5. Ploughing back of profit for running enterprise	
6. Public deposits		
7. Discounting bills exchange		
8. Bank overdraft		
9. Accrued accounts		

5.3 CAPITAL STRUCTURE

The term ***capital*** means the total investment in the form of money, tangible assets like land, building plant and machinery, etc., and even the goodwill of a firm or company. The composition of equity and debt in overall capital of an enterprise is called ***capital structure***. Thus, capital structure of an enterprise involves the ratio of capital invested by the owner from his own sources to the credit capital, between short-term and long-term capital and the ratio among different sources of finance for capital which includes loans, bonds, share issues and reserves. The maintenance of proper ratios between different types of securities is known as ***capital gearing***.

Optional Capital Structure

This depends upon the overall business condition of an enterprise. As a rule, for a successful enterprise, debt capital may be twice or even more than equity capital. But for a business incurring loss and not in a healthy condition, the proportion of debt capitalized should be as low as possible. This is because due to unfavourable conditions, the enterprise may not be in a position to pay off the interest and the amount of loan. Optional capital structure may be defined as a financing mix increasing the least cost but yielding the maximum returns. It is obtained when the market value for equity share is the maximum. However, capital structure depends upon the following factors:

(a) Trading on equity
(b) Nature of an enterprise
(c) Retaining contrast of a company
(d) Size of the enterprise
(e) Cash flows
(f) Purpose of financing
(g) Provision for future

An optimum capital structure bears the following important features:

(a) The optimum capital structure should involve the minimum costs and the maximum yields.
(b) Adopted capital structure should be flexible
(c) The use of debts should be within the repaying capital of the enterprise.
(d) The capital structure should ensure the effective control over the affairs of the enterprise.

5.4 CAPITALIZATION

Capitalization refers to the sum total of all long-term securities issued by a firm or enterprise and the surplus not meant for distribution; it covers only term loans and retained profits. In a broad sense, ***capitalization*** means the determination of the quantity of finance and also the quality of finance.

In case an enterprise raises more capital than that warranted by the proper figure of capitalization or its earning power, it is called overcapitalization. If it is lower than the actual earning power, it is said to be undercapitalization.

Overcapitalization: Overcapitalization portrays a situation when an enterprise possesses excess of capital than warranted by its earning capacity. In this case, the actual earnings are lower than the expected ones. The following are the evil effects caused by overcapitalization.

(a) There is a significant fall in the rate of dividend on equity shares.
(b) Due to the decline of market value of shares, investors lose confidence upon the enterprise.
(c) Overcapitalized enterprises often come to societal rejection.
(d) Company or the enterprise loses its goodwill.

Undercapitalization: Undercapitalization portrays a situation when capital utilized by an enterprise is lower than that warranted by its earning capacity. In case of undercapitalization the market value of shares is higher than that of shares of similar enterprise. The effects of undercapitalization can be depicted as under:

(a) It leads to cut-throat competition in the market.
(b) Higher rate of dividend given to the shareholders encourages the workers to demand for higher wages.
(c) It encourages the management to manoeuvre the value of shares.
(d) Higher taxation is charged by the government.

5.5 EXPORT FINANCE: PRE-SHIPMENT AND POST-SHIPMENT

The term ***export finance*** refers to the credit facilities offered to the exporters at the pre-shipment and post-shipment stages. The export credit is provided by the Indian and foreign commercial banks. The RBI, IDBI and EXIM banks provide financing facilities.

Pre-shipment finance: Pre-shipment finance reveals the financial assistance provided to the exporters before actual shipment of goods. Credit for packaging, advances against incentives and duty drawbacks are available as pre-shipment finance.

Post-shipment finance: Post-shipment finance refers to the loans or credit provided by a bank or financial institution to an exporter of goods from India from the date of extending the finance after the shipment of goods to the date of realization of export proceeds. Such a loan can be availed by the exporter for a period of 6 months only. This finance functions as a bridge loan for a period between shipment of goods and realization of proceeds. The Export Credit and Guarantee Corporation provides export assistance in the form of insurance cover and guarantee. The risk involved in export sector is reduced by the Export Credit and Guarantee Corporation. Export Inspection Council of India has also been established to assist the exporters in quality control of exportable items.

5.6 VENTURE CAPITAL: ORIGIN AND EVOLUTION

The concept of venture capital is a relatively new phenomenon in the Indian industrial scenario. It is a new financial service which facilitated the development of new breed of entrepreneurs to start high-risk and high-technology projects for higher returns. As the name suggests, it implies capital provided to start a new venture.

The origin of venture capital may be traced back to General Doriot who set up the American Research and Development Fund (AR and D) at Massachusetts Institute of Technology in 1946 to finance the commercial exploitation of new technologies developed in universities in USA. This organization financed about 100 companies nearly for 11 long years and made its investment 35 times.

Allured by the performance of the AR and D, large companies in the USA like Xerox, 3M and General Electric entered into the field of venture capital. The Japanese suddenly followed the Americans and started venture capital division in their country. The beginning of 1950 marked the growth of venture capital companies in different countries. The origin of venture capital in UK is also traceable during the 19th century when European Merchant Bankers helped the growth of industry in their dominions like South Africa, India and USA. Inspired by the success of venture capital abroad, many companies in India came forward to promote venture capital. The Tata Group's Investment Corporation of India successfully developed a number of companies like Associated Bearings, Ceat Tyres during the Independence period. In the post-Independence period, venture capital financing was first started by IFCI which sponsored the Risk Capital Foundation in 1975.

5.7 CONCEPT, AIMS AND FEATURES OF VENTURE CAPITAL

Venture capital is a form of equity financing especially designed for funding high-risk, high-technology and high-reward projects. It is equity finance based upon the fact that a partnership can be formed between the entrepreneur and the venture capitalist or the investors and thus, represents an attempt to innovative entrepreneurship which goes beyond the conventional projects and project financing. Venture capital implies investment in such types of enterprise where the uncertainties have yet to be reduced to risks. This type of capital is provided to the entrepreneurs who have conceived good business ideas have sound knowledge of the particular business but lack financial resources to implement them. Venture capital can open new avenues for such entrepreneurs.

Thus, venture capital can be defined as *equity support to fund new concepts that involve a high risk and at the same time, have high growth and profit potential*. Venture capital is important enough to help the small and medium entrepreneurs to launch innovative enterprises. It is closely linked with creativity, innovation, high growth and high profit. It is regarded as the launching pad to innovative entrepreneurship by which adequate boost is given to convert novel business ideas to commercially-viable ventures.

Aims of venture capital: Venture capital aims at the following things:

(a) It fulfils the ambition of entrepreneurs.
(b) It breathes life into promising business initiative.
(c) It provides telescopic faculty with a free sense of direction.
(d) It helps in building enterprise vision.
(e) It partners enterprises on to thrilling success.

Features of venture capital: The following are the salient features of venture capital arrangement:

(a) It assumes a high degree of risks in the expectation of earning a high return.
(b) It finances high-technology projects.
(c) It takes active interest in guiding the assisted enterprise.
(d) The gestation period is usually high. It takes generally 4 to 5 years to yield the desired level of profit.
(e) It is basically long-term investment and the returns are in the form of capital gains.
(f) Venture capitalists normally liquidate their investment in the assisted company when it reaches a certain stage of profitability.
(g) It has provisions to have conditional financial assistance, which, unlike the traditional loans, does not carry interest charges. Instead, it carries a royalty linked to sales generated by the company after commercialization.

5.8 VENTURE CAPITAL: FINANCING STEPS

First step—Seed money finance: Small amount of financing needed to prove a concept or to create a product. Marketing is not included in this stage.

Second step—Start-up: Financing for a firm that started up in the past one year. Funds are utilised to pay for marketing and product development.

Third step—First round financing: Additional money to start sales and manufacturing after a firm has spent its start-up capital.

Fourth step—Second round financing: Finance kept for working capital for a firm that is selling its product, but is still losing money.

Fifth step—Third round financing: Financing for a firm that reaches breakeven point and is contemplating an expansion project.

Sixth step—Fourth round financing: Money provided for firms that are likely to go public soon. This is also known as bridge finance.

5.9 SOURCES OF VENTURE CAPITAL AND CRITERIA TO PROVIDE VENTURE CAPITAL FINANCE

Venture capital is a transitory start up financing in the form of equity capital or loans, with return linked to profits and managerial control measures. For starting a high-risk and high-return project, venture capital is instrumental and thus, entrepreneurs search for the sources from which venture capital can be obtained. Due to liberalization and privatization in the economy, a number of companies have established venture capital divisions to assist the entrepreneurs. Though initially the major players in this field were financial institutions all over India, subsequently others also have followed them. The important funds and the schemes by which the venture capitalists in our country provide financial assistance can be depicted as follows:

1. ***Programme for Advancement of Commercial Technology (PACT):*** The first venture capital funding in India was USAID's Programme for Advancement of Commercial Technology which started in 1955 to provide finance to Indian firms in commercializing the innovative technologies by Indo-US joint ventures.
2. ***Technology Development and Investment Corporation of India (TDICI):*** This was the first venture capital company of India and was promoted by ICICI in 1986. The following are the salient features of its scheme:
   (a) TDICI invests in companies with high earning and growth potential with a view to achieve long-term capital gains.
   (b) The scheme spearheads towards assisting entrepreneurs involved in manufacturing products which are commercially viable by indigenously developed or ultramodern yet untested technologies on commercial scale.
   (c) The financial assistance may be up to Rs 2 crores in the form of equity or conditional loan and the equity would be held for a period of 5–8 years and then either sold to the promoter or disposed in the secondary market.
   (d) The most important aspect of this type of assistance is in the developmental phase, the conditional loan would carry no interest, but after this period, the interest rate would depend upon the effectiveness of the project.
3. ***Risk Capital and Technology Finance Corporation (RCTFC):*** This institution is an independent body launched by Industrial Finance Corporation of India (IFCI) to enhance the purview of venture-capital operations. It assists the entrepreneurs especially those who engage themselves in technological development.
4. ***Venture capital scheme of IDBI:*** IDBI's venture capital fund has been set up with an initial corpus of Rs 10 crores. This scheme of IDBI has been emerging as major source of venture-capital funding. Its aims are the following:
   (a) It is designed especially to assist projects which promote new and untested technologies in Indian conditions.
   (b) The funding amount may vary between Rs 5 lakhs and Rs 250 lakhs which includes both capital and operating expenses.
   (c) This part of funding is usually 80 to 90 per cent of the total project cost.

(d) The assistance may be in the form of equity or loan.
(e) The equity component carries a service charge of 1 per cent while the loan component carries an interest of 6 per cent in the developmental phase and 14 per cent thereafter.
(f) It enjoys a 3-year moratorium period and is repayable in about 10 years.
(g) If the project does not succeed, IDBI can insist on transfer of technology to some other promoter or the entrepreneur who is interested to take over the firm on mutually agreeable terms.

Apart from the above organizations, the following are some of the players in the venture capital finance in the country:

(a) ANZ Grindlays Bank
(b) Credit Capital Venture Fund (India) Ltd
(c) 20th Century Venture Capital Corporation
(d) APIDC Venture Capital Ltd
(e) Canbank Venture Capital Fund
(f) Gujarat Venture Finance Ltd
(g) Industrial Development Bank of India
(h) IL and FS Venture Corporation
(i) SBI Capital Venture Fund
(j) SIDBI Venture Capital Fund
(k) Pardeshiya Industrial and Investment Corporation of Uttar Pradesh Ltd (PICUP)

Criteria adopted by venture capitalists to provide venture capital finance: The following criteria are adhered to by the venture capitalists while making investment decisions:

(a) The integrity, business acumen and the entrepreneurial spirit of the management team as the most important factors
(b) The track record of the entrepreneur and his management team
(c) The technical feasibility and commercial viability of the project, process or service
(d) Large and rapidly-growing market opportunity
(e) Competitive advantage in terms of price or cost
(f) Potential for adequate profitability and attractive returns over a period of four to seven years

Therefore, risk capital is the cutting edge with which entrepreneurs exploit opportunities to put together apparently neutral or sterile resources to create firms with capitalized earning power or market value well in excess of the cost of invested funds.

In the west, particularly in USA, this form of financing is very popular and it enjoys considerable tax incentives. Venture capital gives an opportunity to the small entrepreneurs for starting innovative enterprises.

Merits of venture capital: The following are the merits of venture capital:

(a) Venture capital helps in accelerating the pace of industrialization in the country.
(b) It helps in developing new technologies and new methods of production.

(c) It helps the first-generation entrepreneurs in both small and medium scale to translate their ideas into reality.
(d) It generates employment opportunities.
(e) It promises entrepreneurship in the country.

Hire-purchase scheme: The type of loan which is advanced for the purchase of plant and machinery on hire-purchase basis is known as hire-purchase scheme. The organizations which provide hire-purchase loans are usually national small industries corporations, state small industries corporations, private finance companies and other financial institutions. The ownership of the plant and machinery is vested with the lender until the final payments are made. The interest is generally charged at a flat rate and the borrower has to furnish collateral security.

EXERCISES

A. Long answer type questions:

1. Briefly explain the various sources of finance to a small scale enterprise.
2. What are the internal sources of finance to a SSI unit?
3. What is meant by venture capital? What are the various venture capital sources to raise funds?
4. Define capital structure? What are the factors governing optimum capital structure?
5. Define capitalization. Distinguish between overcapitalization and undercapitalization.

B. Short answer type questions:

1. What do you mean by export finance?
2. Write shorts notes on the following:
   (a) Venture capital
   (b) Export finance
   (c) Overcapitalization
   (d) Undercapitalization
   (e) Capital structure
   (f) Fixed capital

CHAPTER 6

Entrepreneurial Behaviour

CHAPTER CONTENTS

6.1 INNOVATION AND ENTREPRENEUR

Innovation and entrepreneur are two sides of the same coin. Both are intimately interrelated and correlated to each other. Innovation is the crux of entrepreneurship. It helps in developing entrepreneurial base of the country through application of newly-created things into practical use. According to **Schumpeter**, entrepreneurship is a creative activity and entrepreneur is essentially an innovator. Innovation manifests itself in problem-solving activities wherein entrepreneur acts as a problem solver. He is the person who converts the problems into opportunities. His role is to do the things in a novel and better way. He goes beyond the traditional ways of thinking and starts the activity in an innovative way. It is a fact that a businessman who behaves in traditional ways hardly becomes an entrepreneur. Thus, in **Schumpeter's** opinion, the dream and the will to establish a private kingdom, will to conquer and finally the joy of creating, getting things done or simply exercising one's energy and ingenuity are the motives that inspire the innovative entrepreneur to undertake innovation.

6.2 SCHUMPETER'S AND DRUCKER'S THEORIES

Joseph A. Schumpeter and **Peter F. Drucker** have stressed on the role of entrepreneurial function in economic development. They have emphasized that entrepreneurs innovate and innovation is the ***spark-plug*** of entrepreneurship. For detailed study of the theories propounded by **J.A. Schumpter** and **P.F. Drucker,** refer to Chapter 3 of this book.

6.3 ENTREPRENEURIAL BEHAVIOUR AND PSYCHOLOGICAL THEORIES

Among the theories put forth by experts in the field of behavioural sciences, the following theories are very much relevant with regard to the entrepreneurial behaviour.

- Maslow's need hierarchy theory
- McClelland's need achievement theory

6.3.1 Maslow's Need Hierarchy Theory

Abraham H. Maslow, an eminent American psychologist, propounded a general theory of motivation named ***Need Hierarchy Theory***. This theory is important enough to influence the human behaviour in many aspects as per the satisfaction of human needs. According to him, human needs are complex, inter-related and everchanging in nature and thus, there exists stratification or hierarchy of needs. The main features of this theory can be depicted as follows:

(a) The ***inner urge*** to fulfil needs is the fundamental factor in entrepreneurial motivation.
(b) Human needs form a particular structure of hierarchy starting with physiological needs ending with self-actualization needs via other needs.
(c) Higher-level needs do not become an active motivating force unless and until the preceding lower-order needs are satisfied.
(d) As soon as one need is satisfied, another need crops up and this process continues.
(e) The unsatisfied needs are the basic ingredients which regulate the human behaviour.
(f) Various needs are interdependent and overlapping. Higher-level need emerges before the lower-level need is fully satisfied.

In view of these features, the needs can be categorized into the following five categories:

(i) Physiological
(ii) Safety and security
(iii) Social affiliation
(iv) Ego or esteem
(v) Self-actualization

Figure 6.1 displays the hierarchical structure of the needs.

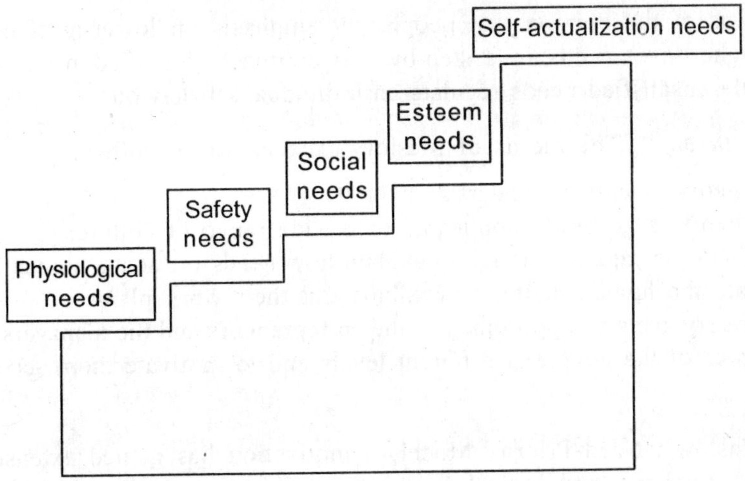

Fig. 6.1 Hierarchical structure of the needs.

Table 6.1 describes various types of needs under Maslow's need hierarchy theory.

Table 6.1 Maslow's Need Hierarchy

Nature of need	*Description*
Physiological needs	Biological needs to pressure human life. These needs include food, clothing, shelter, drink, sleep, etc. These are the basic needs which are recurring in nature. They must be satisfied repeatedly on priority basis.
Safety needs	Human beings search for a protected environment. Safety and security needs kindle the urge for freedom from present and future physical and economic hazards. Though these needs are finite, still they may serve as motivators in case of arbitrary and unpredictable management action. Therefore people put by money in form of insurance, provident fund, etc.
Social needs	Man is a social animal and his desire to be loved and accepted by his near and dear ones is enormous. Thus, he seeks social affiliation and interaction with the people with whom he works together. In the home front, family members and the neighbours fulfil these needs.
Ego (esteem) needs	These needs arise after physiological, safety and social needs are fulfilled. Self-esteem, self-confidence, self-respect, competence, independence and achievement are vital elements in this process. They determine the entrepreneurial action of the human beings. A person desires to gain reputation, respect, status and appreciation from others.
Self-actualization needs	This desire arises after other needs are fulfilled. These are the needs for realizing one's full potential for continued self-development for being creative. Theses are aesthetic needs to attain moral maturity, contentment, authority, etc. it is an infinite growth need. This presumes man's inner urge for making the best use of his potentialities.

Maslow was of the opinion that people put emphasis on lower-level needs and then proceed to higher-level needs in a step-by-step approach. Satisfied need ceases to be a motivator while unsatisfied needs regulate an individual's behaviour.

Merits of the theory: The merits of Maslow's theory are as follows:

(a) This theory is easy to understand.
(b) This theory is generally applicable to a wide range of culture.
(c) This theory is capable enough to explain how needs influence human behaviour and motivate the human beings to chalking out their work plans.
(d) This theory gives an opportunity to the entrepreneurs and the managers to understand the needs of the people at different levels and to motivate them according to their needs.

Criticism: Maslow's Need Priority Model of motivation has gained extensive popularity because of its simplicity and logical explanation. This theory also explains how human behaviour differs in two similar situations. Nevertheless, there is little impartial support for it because its proposition could not be vigorously tested through empirical research. However, the theory is widely criticized for the following reasons:

(a) The theory does not give any scientific explanation or tool for measuring needs.
(b) The theory gives an oversimplification of human needs and motivation.
(c) Not everyone strives for higher-level needs.
(d) The hierarchy of needs is not always fixed. It varies from person to person, place to place and time to time. For example, in case of creative people like singers, artistes, etc., self-actualization need may be a dominant force even before the lower-order needs are fulfilled. Similarly, the need priorities of the same individual may change over a period of time.
(e) Motivation and needs are not directly linked. The same need may lead to different types of behaviour in different individuals.
(f) Deprivation of needs may not necessarily motivate, it may cause depression also.

Inspite of the criticism, Maslow's theory has a commonsense appeal for all managers and entrepreneurs. The theory provides a deep insight into the concept of need and its relation to human behaviour.

6.3.2 McClelland's Need Achievement Theory

The most important theory that influences the entrepreneurial behaviour is the theory of need achievement developed by David McClelland in late 1940s. According to him, an individual's need for achievement (n Ach) is the triggering factor which drives the individual to excel and take risks on a different way. This type of behaviour for accomplishment of goals is the entrepreneurial way that is stimulated by the need for achievement.

A number of psychological factors influence the entrepreneurial motivation. These are stated as under:

(a) Need for achievement through goal setting

(b) Moderate risk-taking intuition
(c) High desire to take personal responsibility
(d) Concrete measures of task performance
(e) Possibility thinking
(f) High level of aspirations
(g) Non-traditional instrumental activity
(h) Organizing skills etc.
(i) Decision making and swift execution policies
(j) Strong inner spirits to attain a measurable variable arising from a need

Thus, McClelland considers the need for achievement to be the most critical factor for entrepreneurial motivation. This theory has been vividly discussed in this book in Chapter 3.

6.4 SOCIAL RESPONSIBILITY

Entrepreneurial development is the key to achieve all-round economic development through acceleration of industrial and entrepreneurial activities. Entrepreneurship, therefore, will flourish in an atmosphere which is favourable for enterprise building—politically, economically and socially. In the context of new economic scenario where liberalization, privatization and globalization are glorified, the responsibilities of business have undergone radical changes. Ethical discipline plays a great role in the changing environmental conditions. Entrepreneurs have to follow the ethical norms of the business in the society. As such, social responsibility implies responsibility of the entrepreneur towards smooth operation of the society by efficient utilization of national resources for greater interest of the people.

To remain in business on a sustainable basis, an entrepreneur has to exercise his responsibilities to the society in the following ways:

1. ***Responsibility of the entrepreneur towards conservation of national resources:*** The first and foremost social responsibility of an entrepreneur is to efficiently conserve and utilize national resources for the public good.
2. ***Responsibility towards owners/shareholders:*** An entrepreneur is responsible to safeguard the capital invested by the shareholders and the owners of the enterprise. He should ensure that they get adequate dividend from their investment.
3. ***Responsibility towards customers:*** An entrepreneur has to satisfy his customers by the following two ways:

   (i) Providing quality products to the customers
   (ii) Charging reasonable and affordable price for the product

4. ***Responsibility towards employees:*** Social responsibility of an entrepreneur is to provide adequate measures to make the employees contented in all respects so as to encourage them to contribute their best. The responsibility of an entrepreneur towards the employees may include the following:

   (a) Providing at least minimum wages to the employees
   (b) Providing conducive working environment for good work culture

(c) Provision of social security measures
(d) Granting weekly holidays
(e) Settling employees grievances
(f) Giving opportunity to employees participation and management

5. ***Responsibility towards creditor/banker:*** One of the most important social responsibilities of an entrepreneur is responsibility towards creditors and bankers who provide financial assistance. This responsibility includes the following:

(a) Regular repayment of principal and interest
(b) Effective utilization of funds
(c) Adhering to the repayment schedule without any default.
(d) Restricting diversion of loans to the uses other than the specific purpose for which it has been advanced

6. ***Responsibility towards community:*** An entrepreneur should have the concern for the community where the enterprise is located. The following are the responsibilities of the entrepreneur towards the community:

(a) Generation of employment opportunities for local youth
(b) Prevention of environmental pollution
(c) Restricting the problem of congestion housing and crime in the community where the enterprise is located
(d) Creating awareness about population pressure and the family welfare measures
(e) Reducing the deleterious effects of industrial products on human health and environmental balance
(f) Reduction of illiteracy among the people, both for men and women.

7. ***Responsibility towards government:*** India is considered the largest democracy in the world. Its policies aim at public welfare. In the country, the responsibility of the entrepreneur towards the government includes the following:

(a) To pay taxes, duties in time and discourage tax evasion
(b) To comply with the government rules, procedures and legal requirements
(c) To support the socio-economic development policies of the government
(d) To work in close association with the government for social welfare.

8. ***Responsibility to uphold general values and philosophy of the country:*** In Indian context, this includes:

(a) Respect towards ideologies of the society like democracy, freedom and tolerance
(b) Fair play in marketing and establishing enterprises
(c) Due respect towards secularism
(d) Emancipation of weaker sections of the society
(e) Empowerment of women in the society
(f) Highlighting technological dynamism

The following factors in the Indian socio-economic environment have got much significance in this context.

(a) Socialistic and secular pattern of society
(b) Removal of poverty
(c) Development of trade union for the benefit of the workers
(d) Development of professional management in industries
(e) Pressure from financial institution exerted on the borrowing companies to stick to the norms of the government
(f) The need for developing the knowledge expertise in the country

The following are the arguments cited against social responsibility:

(a) The concept of social responsibility is vague. It is difficult to distinguish it from economic responsibility.
(b) Entrepreneurs and business managers are familiar with economic aspects of the activities. They are not social scientists and, therefore, lack social skills.
(c) It would be unjust to overburden the businessmen since they have several economic responsibilities like payment of tax, payment of tariff, etc.
(d) A social responsibility approach may not always be viable and hence be suicidal in the long run.
(e) Business enterprises have hardly any social power. No responsibility can be accepted without the necessary power.
(f) Private entrepreneurs are essentially responsible only to their shareholders.
(g) Social responsibility influences the decision-making process and would involve additional cost.
(h) It would entail certain division of resources meant for economic activities.

EXERCISES

A. Long answer type questions:

1. What is innovation? Discuss in brief the theory of innovation by Schumpeter.
2. Explain Drucker's theory of innovation.
3. Critically examine the Maslow's theory of hierarchy of needs.
4. Explain the need achievement theory and its applicability to entrepreneurship development.
5. Discuss the social responsibility of an entrepreneur to various sections of the society.

B. Short answer type questions:

1. Distinguish between:
   (a) Invention and Innovation
   (b) Need for power and need for achievement
   (c) Schumpeter's theory and Drucker's theory
   (d) Esteem needs and self-actualization needs

CHAPTER 7

Entrepreneurship Development Programme

CHAPTER CONTENTS

7.1 ENTREPRENEURSHIP DEVELOPMENT PROGRAMMES (EDPs): MEANING AND OBJECTIVES

Entrepreneurs play a predominant role in accelerating the socio-economic development of a country. They are regarded as the nation builders and wealth creators. They are the change agents who initiate economic activities to create wealth. They undertake the business initiative, employ themselves in that business and open up employment avenues for others. Therefore, the role of entrepreneur is of fundamental importance to a country like India where the twin problems of poverty and unemployment coexist.

During early sixties, the small scale sector was considered as exclusively an employment-generating sector, but gradually this sector began to be recognized as the crucial tool for tapping latent entrepreneurial talent and now in the post-liberation period, there seems to be ample opportunities for entrepreneurship and entrepreneurial growth.

Considering the importance of small scale industries in employment creation and economic development, the Government of India envisaged promotional packages to facilitate setting up of new enterprises. In order to bring about entrepreneurial growth, the policy makers and financial institutions started thinking in terms of imbibing entrepreneurship culture through training interventions. Thus, Entrepreneurship Development Programmes (EDPs) emerged and the pioneering effort in this regard was taken up by Gujarat Industrial Investment Corporation (GIIC) and other agencies who have organized a three-month entrepreneurship development programme in late sixties. The programme was conducted for a selective group of energetic and potential entrepreneurs who had the willingness and desire to achieve the goal set by them. The objectives laid down for the above programme were as follows:

(i) To set up small scale ventures
(ii) To manage them effectively
(iii) To earn adequate profit from these ventures
(iv) To undertake personal responsibility of the business

It has been found out that the 'n Ach' factor developed by **David McClelland**, the renowned behavioural scientist, is the most important quality for entrepreneurial development. In order to prove that the need for achievement could be induced, he conducted an experiment in collaboration with the erstwhile Small Industries Extension and Training Institute (SIET) of Hyderabad at Kakinada, Andhra Pradesh. Young persons were selected and put through rigorous training for a period of three months to guide them to set new goals. The achievement motivation has a positive impact upon their task performance. The Kakinada experiment could be treated as an important basis for the present-day EDP inputs on behavioural aspects.

In later stage, Achievement Motivation Training (AMT) has become an integral part of EDP course curriculum. Institutes like MSME, NIMSME, SIDO and TCOs came forward to conduct EDPs and national level organizations like Entrepreneurship Development Institute (EDI) of India, Ahmedabad and National Institute for Entrepreneurship and Small Business Development (NIESBUD), Delhi were established to coordinate Entrepreneurship Development Programmes. According to a study conducted by NIESBUD, at present, as many as 686 odd organizations, including the state level organizations like IEDs/CEDs, are organizing EDPs in the country.

Objectives of EDPs: The important objectives of Entrepreneurship Development Programmes (EDPs) can be stated as follows:

(a) Accelerating industrial development by enlarging the supply of entrepreneurs
(b) Developing entrepreneurial qualities and motivating the prospective entrepreneurs to achieve the goal
(c) Enhancing the growth of small- and medium-scale enterprise sectors which offer better potential for employment generation and dispersal of industrial unit
(d) Providing productive self-employment avenues to a large number of educated and low educated young men and women coming out of schools and colleges

(e) Improving performance of small- and medium-scale industries by the supply of carefully-selected and trained entrepreneurs and diversifying sources of entrepreneurship
(f) Enterprise development in rural and no-industry areas where local entrepreneurship is not really available and entrepreneurs from nearby towns are not easily lured

7.2 THE INDIAN EDP MODEL

There is a saying that entrepreneurs are the products of nature, nurture and culture. Of course, this is very much true in Indian context. Apart from the nature and the culture, the role of ***nurture*** is very much significant for human resource development. The myth that entrepreneurs are born and not made has no longer been accepted. Ordinary persons can be turned into successful entrepreneurs through well-designed training programmes conducted by the ED institutes. The term ***nurture*** here implies the ***training intervention*** which is a real endeavour towards human resource development, especially entrepreneurial development. The Entrepreneurial Development Programmes, therefore, are based upon well-designed and integrated modular packages to suit to the needs of the budding entrepreneurs. The training institutions like EDI, NIESBUD, MSME and NIMSME at national level and IEDs, CEDs at state level follow more or less the same principle in organizing Entrepreneurial Development Programmes. In the present context, EDPs are usually conducted for four to six weeks and the curriculum adopted by the above institutes for imparting training is also apparently uniform.

7.3 PHASES OF EDPs

The EDPs normally pass through following three important phases:

- Pre-training phase
- Training phase
- Post-training or follow-up phase

Pre-training phase: This phase is the preparatory phase for launching the programmes. It includes a number of activities, which are as follows:

(i) Identification of operationally-promising area, normally a district
(ii) Selection of a project leader /course coordinator to coordinate the programme
(iii) Arrangement of infrastructural facilities for the programme
(iv) Undertaking potential industrial survey/environmental scanning for identification of good business opportunities
(v) Planning the programmes on various fronts such as:

(a) Promotional campaigns through publicity either with the help of print or electronic media, leaflets, posters, etc.
(b) Establishing contacts with business personalities, NGOs and related agencies which can contribute to the programme both directly and indirectly

(c) Getting the application forms printed and making them available at different centres alongwith instructions.
(d) Forming selection committee for selecting the trainees
(e) Preparing the budget, obtaining administrative sanctions and organizing other activities which form a part of EDP
(f) Preparing and finalizing the need-based inputs in training syllabus and to tie up with guest faculties to impart training

(vi) Contacting the support agencies like DICs, SFCs, MSME, banks, NSIC, District Magistrate, etc. to receive support in implementing the programme

(vii) Organizing industrial motivational campaigns to mobilise as many number of applications as possible.

In fine, pre-training stage involves selection of potential entrepreneur and arrangement of facilities for imparting training to the participants in the best possible manner.

Training phase: Training potential entrepreneurs and providing them proper guidance for setting up enterprise constitute the cornerstone of EDP. Most of the ED institutes generally conduct training programmes of 4–6 weeks duration on full time basis. The programmes design in terms of objectives, training inputs and their focus is described in Table 7.1.

Table 7.1 Training Phase: Programme Design

Objectives	*Focus*	*Inputs*
Motivation and reinforcement of entrepreneurial traits, confidence building	Entrepreneur	Behavioural inputs
Facilitating decision-making process to set up a new venture	Enterprise establishment	Business opportunity guidance, information and project planning inputs, technical inputs
Successful and profitable operation of enterprise. Industrial exposure	Enterprise management, first-hand knowledge of factory layout, business sites, etc.	Management inputs, plant visit/ in-plant training

Post-training phase: Post-training phase is otherwise known as the phase of follow-up support. During this phase, post-training support services are rendered to the participants who have successfully completed the Entrepreneurship Development Programme (EDP). This is because of the fact that, very often, the potential entrepreneur after undergoing the training confronts a number of problems while implementing the action plan for grounding the project. So during this phase, the training organization helps the entrepreneur in sorting out the problems through counselling support. A committee is formed consisting of members generally drafted from the leading bank of the district, State Financial Corporation, training organization and above all, the District Industries Centre to help the entrepreneurs with the following objectives during the follow-up:

(i) To provide a meaningful direction to the trainees in grounding their enterprise
(ii) To review the progress made by the trainees in implementation of the project
(iii) To review the post-training approach
(iv) To provide escort services to the trainees by involving financial institutions and promotional agencies.

Usually, follow-up action meetings are organized thrice a year after the completion of training and the following methods are generally used for follow-up:

(a) Postal questionnaire
(b) Telephonic follow-up
(c) Personal contact by the trainer
(d) Group meetings

7.4 EDP CURRICULUM

The ED institutes usually follow a uniform course curriculum for the EDPs conducted in the country. The duration of the training is normally four to six weeks and the ideal intake in a group is 30–35. The following inputs are covered during the period of training which are sufficient for a person to gain fundamental knowledge of entrepreneurship and enterprise during launching and management.

- Introduction to fundamentals of entrepreneurship
- Motivational inputs
- Management inputs
- Support system services
- Project feasibility study
- Plant visits/industrial exposure

1. ***Introduction to fundamentals of entrepreneurship:*** This unit is devoted to give an exposure to the trainees on fundamentals of small scale enterprises and small business sector, the characteristics of economy the role of entrepreneurs in economic development, charms of being an entrepreneur, history of entrepreneurship, entrepreneurial qualities and the facilities available for starting small scale enterprise.
2. ***Motivational inputs:*** In order to develop competencies of entrepreneur, entrepreneurial traits and motivational inputs are included in the course curriculum. In training parlance, these inputs are termed as Achievement Motivation Training (AMT). The aim of AMT is to strengthen the achievement need, self awareness, confidence building, creativity and other entrepreneurial qualities with the help of various methods of behavioural psychology.
3. ***Management inputs:*** The potential trainee entrepreneurs are required to be equipped with sound management techniques to start their business venture and make them profitable. The EDP trainees are, therefore, introduced to the basics of functional areas of management like production, financial, marketing and labour management.

4. ***Support system and procedure:*** The participants have to be exposed to the role and functions of promotional agencies which support the entrepreneur for setting up and running the enterprise. The main objective of including it in the curriculum is to make the participants aware of the policies and procedures laid down by the government, industrial services agencies and financial support system institutions for the promotion of small scale enterprise in the country.
5. ***Project feasibility study:*** The trainees are given information and counseling about the various business opportunities in the area where EDP is conducted. After the trainees select the business opportunities of their choice, they are guided to prepare project (feasibility) reports for submission to banks or other financial institutions. Inputs on feasibility study, market survey, technical and commercial viability analysis, project appraisal, etc. are imparted to the trainees.
6. ***Field visits/industrial exposure:*** Industrial exposure or field visits are inbuilt into the course curriculum. This is done to familiarize the trainees with real-life situation of the entrepreneurs in small business. Further, field visits give first-hand knowledge and exposure to the participants regarding the problems and prospects of an industrial enterprise.

The successful entrepreneurs are invited to the training programme to share their experiences even with the trainees as "role models".

In fine, the training inputs are designed in course curriculum in such a manner that the trainee entrepreneur can be well groomed to shoulder the responsibility of the business venture effectively and can stand to challenges, odds and adversities that may crop up during his enterprise creation and management.

Model Six weeks (EDP) Schedule

Programme Schedule

1st Day	I	Registration of participants
	II	Inauguration of training programme
	III	Interaction with the participants and
	IV	sharing their expectation
2nd Day		
3rd Day		Achievement Motivation Training (AMT)
4th Day		
5th Day	I	Interaction among the entrepreneurs
	II	Enterprise, entrepreneurs and entrepreneurship (3 Es)
	III	Characteristics of an entrepreneur
	IV	Sum up of the session
6th Day	I	Experience sharing with a successful entrepreneur
	II	Women entrepreneur
	III	Experience sharing with an unsuccessful entrepreneur
	IV	Video presentation of a case study
7th Day	I	Role of District Industries Centre
	II	Role of State Financial Corporation

	III	Role of commercial banks
	IV	Sum up of the session/sources of information
8th Day	I	Small scale industries and the items included therein
	II	The steps for setting up of SSI/tiny/micro-units
	III	Role of IDBI and SIDBI
	IV	Sum up of the session, whom to contact for what
9th Day	I	Role of Pollution Control Board
	II	Role of KVIB, KVIC and Directorate of Handicraft and Cottage Industries
	III	Role of NABARD/role of insurance company
	IV	Sum up of the assignment/session and views
10th Day	I	Industrial Policy Resolutions (IPRs)
	II	Environmental scanning
	III	Business Opportunity Guidance (BOG), Identifying good business opportunities
	IV	Sum up of the session of the day
11th Day		Business Opportunity Guidance (BOG), group discussions by the bankers
12th Day		Factory visit to industrial estate
13th Day		How to maintain Books of Accounts
14th Day	I	How to study balance sheet and profit and loss account
	II	Do
	III	Case study and summing up of the session
15th Day	I	Cost of production
	II	Case study on cost of production
	III	Cost control and its justification
	IV	Summing up of the session
16th Day	I	Break-even analysis, marginal costing
	II	Case study and summing up of the session
17th Day	I	Taxation/income tax
	II	Sales tax/octroi duties
	III	Funds flow/cash flow and budgeting
	IV	Forms of business organization
18th Day	I	Basic managerial skills
	II	Business communication skill
	III	Personal management/procedure of recruitment and job enrichment
	IV	Summing up of the session
19th Day	I&II	Labour laws and its applicability
	III	Decision making and problem solving
	IV	Summing up of the session
20th Day	I	Production management and layout
	II	PERT/CPM
	III&IV	Inventory control and summing up of the session
21th Day	I	Quality control and its needs
	II	Purchase management and its necessity
	III&IV	Procedure of procurement of fixed assets and summing up

Day	Session	Topic
22nd Day		
	I,II&III	Preparation of project report, case study
	IV	Summing up of the session
23rd Day	I	Working capital management
	II	Effects of wrong assessment
	III&IV	Case study and summing up of the session
24nd Day	I	Submission of loan proposal for term loan and
	II	for working capital loan
	III	How to keep good relation with bankers/financial institutions
	IV	Summing up of the session
25th Day	I	Marketing management
	II	Sales management
	III&IV	How to study market reports and summing up of the session
26th Day	I&II	How to fill up PRC application form
	III&IV	Causes of industrial sickness and remedies and summing up of the session
27th Day	I&II	Rehabilitation of sick units
	III&IV	Video presentation and summing up of the session
28th Day		How to conduct market survey and prepare market survey report
29th Day		Presentation of market survey report and sharing of experience of participants
30th to 41st Day		Market survey and factory visit
42th Day		Certificate distribution and valediction

Besides theoretical inputs, in plant training or plant visit also constitutes an integral part of training. Industrial exposure helps the trainees in gaining experience and first-hand knowledge on the business site, factory layout as well as on different departments of industrial units like production, quality control, marketing, HRD, etc. Moreover, the trainees can also avail the opportunities of direct interaction with the entrepreneurs and the staff members of the industrial units.

7.5 EVALUATION OF EDP

Entrepreneurship Development Programme at first began as an experiment in 1970 in Gujarat. This gradually captured the attention of politicians, scientists, economists management experts and has now become a national movement. Hundreds of EDPs are conducted each year in our country by 686 odd organizations to impart entrepreneurial training to thousands of participants. But the important question before all these organizations is what are the results. The most recent evaluation study on EDPs has been conducted by EDI, Ahmedabad. According to the findings of the study, it has been proved that the performance of EDPs across the states is not uniform. The actual start-up rate as a result of EDP varies between 9 and 50 per cent leading to the national start-up rate of about 26 per cent which is not at all impressive.

Problems of EDPs: The low level of performance is usually attributed to the following problems involved in organizing and conducting EDP trainings:

(a) Shortage of adequate number of specialized and committed organizations
(b) Insufficient trainer motivators to motivate people for undergoing EDPs and to impart training
(c) Identification and selection of wrong projects
(d) Lack of entrepreneurial environment and culture
(e) Apathetic attitude of the support agencies like banks and financial institutions to support entrepreneurs
(f) Lack of forward and backward linkages
(g) Selection of wrong person for training
(h) Improper identification of projects
(i) Inadequate counseling support after training
(j) Lack of continuous follow-up action or post-training support services for grounding the project

Criteria for assessment or evaluation of EDPs: Following criteria are being used by the behavioural scientists to assess the effectiveness of EDPs in the country.

(i) New enterprise creation
(ii) Employment generation in quantifiable terms
(iii) Creation of job opportunities both directly and indirectly
(iv) Increase in sales and profit
(v) Enterprise expansion
(vi) Enterprise transformation
(vii) Improvement in quality of product or services
(viii) Repayment of loans

7.6 COMMON DENOMINATORS OF SUCCESS OF EDPs

It is worthwhile to discuss some lessons from the experience of Entrepreneurship Development Programme in India so as to educate the people on how to tackle a few important problems and issues involved in coordination and implementation of EDPs in the country. The following lessons in this context are known as the common denominators of success of EDPs.

1. ***Comprehensive approach:*** In order to make EDP meaningful and successful, easy temptation to take a quick view and partial approach must be avoided. More specifically, an aggregate view of EDP strategy covering all stages must be taken and within each stage, a similar comprehensive approach needs to be followed.
2. ***Integrated approach:*** Each element of EDP activity must be intertwined with each other so as to make it a complete integrated whole. The three specific stages—pre-training, training and post-training—need to be interwoven into one single "fabric". This can be possible if common underlying purpose will be followed which will result in establishment of new and commercially-viable ventures.

3. ***Goal-oriented involvement:*** The entire process of EDP should have an implicit goal-oriented concern right from the conceptual date. The goal should be clear cut and oriented towards enterprise creation. So the ED institutes should create complete awareness about the objectives of the EDPs and instil a sense of "inner-spirit" in the minds of the participants to be successful in their endeavour. The goal which the EDPs aim at is identification of an appropriate bankable project suitable for each trainee. The project should be technically feasible and commercially viable for enterprise creation.
4. ***Individual counselling support:*** In addition to the formal classroom training, emphasis must be given on the need for individual counselling. In a hostile business environment, individual counselling is as important as the AMT input. This will ensure a morale-boosting effect and help the trainee to build further confidence and hope in grounding his projects.
5. ***Need-based flexibility approach:*** A rigid and similar curriculum will not hold good for developing entrepreneurs at all places. There are target groups and individuals within groups whose special needs must also be recognized, if potential entrepreneurs are to be converted into successful captains of industry. Therefore, the responsibility of the training organization is to give emphasis upon the importance of matching product with the entrepreneur. This calls for imagination, innovation and flexibility.
6. ***Introspective view:*** For the success of EDP activity, programmes should be strategically modified, updated and developed to suit the needs of the circumstances. An introspective view is of fundamental importance in this regard. Validation of tools or techniques used in EDP and also evaluation of performance at regular intervals are the important manifestations of such a critical spirit which necessitates self-improvement.

To be effective, entrepreneurship development programmes need the support of promotional agencies, financial institutions, infrastructural agencies and all those support system agencies which ultimately help the enterprise. In Indian context, entrepreneurship development training programmes undertaken by the ED organizations in isolation of the support system cannot be effective.

7.7 ROLE, RELEVANCE AND ACHIEVEMENTS OF EDPs

7.7.1 Role of EDP

The Entrepreneurship Development Programme (EDP) is an important innovative breakthrough in the strategy for developing human resource and promoting economic development of the country. According to A.N. Oza: "The EDP is an innovation in which those persons who possess certain identifiable qualities of entrepreneurship are counselled, motivated and trained to strengthen their self-confidence, seize a business opportunity, initiate an enterprise and be the master of their destiny, i.e. to become ***entrepreneurs*** instead of passively waiting for suitable employment or continue suffering from frustration in their current jobs. Under the above backdrop, the role of EDP can be discussed as the most important instrument to tackle the problem of poverty and widespread chronic unemployment through rapid growth of small scale industrial sector in India". Dr M.M.P. Akhouri, formerly Executive Director of NIESBUD, New Delhi, has stated that entrepreneurship development follows a cycle consisting of stimulatory, support and sustaining activities. A balanced emphasis on all these three activities ensures accelerated and healthy environment for creation and proper management of enterprise on a sustainable basis. Entrepreneurship Development Programmes primarily play the following roles:

- Stimulatory role
- Supportive role
- Sustaining role
- Socio-economic role

1. ***Stimulatory role:*** This role refers to all such efforts that stimulate emergence of entrepreneurship in a society. These are mainly:
   (a) Entrepreneurial education
   (b) Planned publicity for entrepreneurial opportunities
   (c) Identification of potential entrepreneurs through scientific methods
   (d) Motivational training to new entrepreneurs
   (e) Help and guidance in selecting products and preparing project reports
   (f) Making available technoeconomic information and project reports
   (g) Evolving local suitable new product and process
   (h) Availability of local agencies with trained personnel for entrepreneurial counselling and promotion
   (i) Creating entrepreneurial forum
   (j) Recognition of entrepreneurs
2. ***Supportive role:*** This role helps the entrepreneurs in establishing and running enterprises by group support activities. These include:
   (a) Registration of unit
   (b) Arranging finance
   (c) Providing land, shed, power, water etc.
   (d) Guidance for selecting and obtaining machinery
   (e) Supply of scarce raw materials
   (f) Providing common facilities
   (g) Granting tax relief and other subsidy
   (h) Offering management consultancy
   (i) Help marketing products
   (j) Providing information
3. ***Sustaining role:*** Sustaining role of EDPs presupposes the activities which help the entrepreneurs in running their enterprise on a sustained basis amidst competitive market conditions. The activities include:
   (a) Helping modernization
   (b) Helping diversification/expansion/substitute production

(c) Additional financing for full-capacity utilization
(d) Deferring repayment/interest
(e) Diagnostic industrial extension consultancy services
(f) Production units legislation, policy change
(g) Product reservation/creating new avenues for marketing
(h) Quality testing and improving services
(i) Need-based common facilities centre

4. ***Socio-economic role:*** Socio-economic role of EDPs is important for promotion of industries as well as socio-economic status of the people. It includes

(a) Augmenting latent qualities of the persons to become entrepreneurs in thoughts and actions
(b) Utilizing the latent and unutilized resources like hoarded wealth for enterprise building
(c) Helping dispersal of industries to promote balanced regional development
(d) Creating immediate employment opportunities in small enterprises and business sector
(e) Ensuring more equitable distribution of national income and wealth

7.7.2 Relevance of EDP

The relevance of entrepreneurial resource as the most critical input for economic development has been widely recognized by economists, policy makers, planners and political scientists in recent years. In our country, continuous emphasis has been put upon the role of small and medium scale enterprises in view of their contribution to employment generation, balanced regional development, dispersal of industries in both rural and urban areas, import substitution, export promotion and economic growth.

Under different five year plans in India, a number of schemes such as IRDP, ERRP, SGSY, PMRY, REGP, etc. were introduced in the economy from time to time to tackle the twin problems of poverty and unemployment by inducing people to take up self-employment activities or entrepreneurship as an alternative to wage employment. But it has been found out that potential entrepreneurs being ordinary people of the country do not respond spontaneously to available opportunities despite various incentives and benefits envisaged in these schemes. An effective mechanism is, therefore, the felt need to enlarge the base of new entrepreneurs who will be assisted to face risks and uncertainties boldly while establishing and managing their new business enterprise. Here arises the relevance of Entrepreneurship Development Programme to motivate, groom and develop ordinary persons to be the owners of business enterprises by equipping them with tailor-made entrepreneurial inputs. In the above backdrop, the relevance of Entrepreneurship Development Programmes (EDPs) can be summarized as under:

(a) EDPs have proved that entrepreneurs can be made and they are not born
(b) EDPs are expected to bring about economic and social change in the entrepreneur's behaviour

(c) Entrepreneurial training can convert ordinary persons into risk takers, innovators, employers, visionaries and above all, the leaders of business and industries
(d) Entrepreneurship development training can develop individuals to be the economic emancipators upon whom the economic well-being of the society depends
(e) Entrepreneurial training can instil in people the sense of innovativeness and as a result of which the trainees are expected to produce things which the people have not previously dreamt of. Thus, they will become innovators
(f) EDPs are relevant from the point of view of assisting the trainee entrepreneurs in converting their idle saving into productive investment. Thus, additional wealth is created leading to capital formation of the economy
(g) EDPs help the entrepreneurs to create condition for environmental improvement rather than degradation
(h) EDPs are expected to create the sense of ***social responsibility*** in the minds of the budding entrepreneurs leading to the observance of ethical discipline of business for socioeconomic development
(i) According to David McClelland, people with inclination for achievement motivation can be developed to become entrepreneurs. For this, Achievement Motivation Training (AMT) is necessary which is the part and parcel of entrepreneurial development programme inputs
(j) Entrepreneurship Development Programmes are expected to create such emancipated souls who always work for the benefit of the society or environment, constantly keeping in mind the economic well-being of the business

Apart from these observations, relevance of EDP can also be viewed from the standpoint of training benefits accrued to the trainees. The benefits are in the forms of improvement of knowledge and efficiency, systematic approach to problem solving, better planning technique, better financial management, better marketing skills, proper canalization of managerial skills and professional approach in managing the business/enterprise.

7.7.3 Achievements of EDPs

In our country, as many as 686 organizations are engaged in organizing entrepreneurship development training programmes and thousands of candidates are being trained by these agencies. So far, the national average of start-ups in programmes focusing on industrial projects and services is around 30 per cent, i.e. only 30 out of 100 EDP trained entrepreneurs put up their enterprise. Studies conducted by Department of Science and Technology and EDI state that the success rate is closer to 20 per cent only.

The performance of EDPs across the states and across the ED institutes have not been uniform. The actual grounding of the projects are observed to be revolving between 9 to 56 per cent bringing down the national start-up rate to about 26 per cent which is obviously not an impressive achievement. Not only there is substantial wastage of resources and effort when 74 out of 100 trainees do not establish enterprise, but also the credibility of the whole effort is further affected discouraging newcomers and the support agencies who share the cost of EDPs. In fact, there can be no fixed percentage as the minimum satisfactory level, where it is recognized that in rural areas or in dealing with underprivileged groups, rural poor, tribal people and women, initial effort yielding 26 per cent results is not bad, we must raise our expectation in terms of for all other target groups. This is especially so when poor results are due to poor training inputs and support.

So the first opportunity for the future, therefore, is to ensure that with the same resources and efforts, at least 50 out of 100 trainees set up their enterprises. The self-employment and employment impact of this increase is obvious. In this way, the whole effort will become cost-effective. Better results can be achieved by the institutions which come forward to carry out the programmes in the following ways:

(a) In a committed fashion
(b) With adequate professional staff
(c) Better conceived selection and training inputs
(d) With well-organised institutional support for project selection
(e) Timely funding support from the government and the development financing institutions.
(f) Joint and effective follow-up by the ED institutions and promotional agencies of the government and proper coordination with banks

7.8 ROLE OF GOVERNMENT IN ORGANIZING EDPs

Entrepreneurship Development Programmes are the Human Resource Development Programmes of the highest order which basically deal with human motivation, skills, competencies, creativity, social and economic risks and investment of financial and physical resources of the state. Therefore, the role of government in organizing EDPs is of much significance in a country like ours which requires the conversion of surplus labour force into real entrepreneurs to tackle the problems of unemployment and poverty by means of the EDP mechanism. Efforts so far put in by union and state governments in this regard are really commendable. For organizing EDPs on a sustained manner, the following activities have been undertaken by the Union and State governments right from the beginning of the EDP movement in Gujarat since 1970:

7.8.1 Establishment of Specialized Institutions at National Level

Specialized EDP organizations have been set up by the Government of India to promote entrepreneurship in the country. The details of these organizations are given below:

1. ***National Institute for Entrepreneurship and Small Business Developedment (NIESBUD):*** Apex organization for oganizing and conducting EDP under Ministry of Industry, Government of India and located at Noida (UP)
2. ***Micro, Small and Medium Enterprise Development Institute (MSME-DI):*** Set up by Government of India, having its network of branches in many states in India
3. ***National Institute for Micro, Small and Medium Enterprises (NIMSME):*** Under Ministry of Small Scale Industries, Government of India and located at Yousufguda, Hyderabad

4. ***Entrepreneurship Development Institute of India (EDI):*** The apex resource agency for promotion of entrepreneurship and small scale sector, promoted by development financing institutions like IDBI, IFCI, ICICI, SBI and located at Ahmedabad
5. ***National Science and Technology Entrepreneurship Development Board (NSTEDB):*** In order to focus on special target groups like science and technology personnel, the Union Government has established the NSTEDB, operating under the Department of Science and Technology, Government of India. It has strived to spread the message of entrepreneurship among science and technology personnel by organizing EDPs.
6. ***IEDs and CEDs in different states of India***

   IEDs

   (a) Institute of Entrepreneurship Development, Bhubaneswar (Orissa)
   (b) Institute of Entrepreneurship Development, Lucknow, (UP)
   (c) Institute of Entrepreneurship Development, Patna (Bihar)
   (d) Indian Institute of Entrepreneurship Development (national level institute), Guwahati (Assam)

   CEDs

   (a) Centre for Entrepreneurship Development, Hyderabad (Andhra Pradesh)
   (b) Centre for Entrepreneurship Development, Gandhi Nagar (Gujarat)
   (c) Centre for Entrepreneurship Development, Shimla (Himachal Pradesh)
   (d) Centre for Entrepreneurship Development, Dharward (Karnataka)
   (e) Centre for Entrepreneurship Development, Bhopal (Madhya Pradesh)
   (f) Centre for Entrepreneurship Development, Aurangabad (Maharashtra)
   (g) Entrepreneurship and Management Development Institute, Jaipur (Rajasthan)
   (h) Centre for Entrepreneurship Development, Madurai (Tamil Nadu)
   (i) Centre for Entrepreneurship Development, Madurai (Tamil Nadu)

The objective of these specialized institutions is to equip the ordinary person with basics of entrepreneurial and managerial skills so as to enable him to be an effective entrepreneur. The schemes which include EDP concept are:

(i) Prime Minister's Rojgar Yojana (PMRY) scheme
(ii) Swarnajayanti Gram Swarojgar Yojana (SGSY) scheme
(iii) Rural Employment Generation Programme (REGP) scheme

7.8.2 Establishment of District Industries Centres (DICs)

District Industries Centres have been established in every district of almost all the states of India to primarily focus on entrepreneurship awareness programmes and tiny and small scale sector projects.

7.8.3 Introduction of Entrepreneurship Courses

Several universities, IITs, management institutes have introduced the course of entrepreneurship in their curriculum to induce the students to choose entrepreneurial career instead of job employment. The recent trend in introducing entrepreneurship courses in commerce stream at undergraduate level is a welcome beginning. This must spread to arts and science streams also. It has been rightly pointed out by the government and their agencies that an early cultivation of entrepreneurial spirit can help the youths start assessing self-employment options.

7.8.4 Financial Support Provided by the Government, Development Banks and Nationalized Public Sector Banks

For organizing EDPs in a sustainable basis, financial support is being provided by Union and State governments, development financing institutions like IDBI, IFCI, ICICI, SIDBI and public sector commercial banks have been continuously assisting the EDP conducting organizations. Target covered under EDPs are groups like unemployed youths, science and technology graduates, women target group, scheduled caste and scheduled tribe candidates, etc.

Further, infrastructure and grants for purchase of modern training gadgets like OHP/LCDs/audio-visuals/computers, etc., are being provided to the ED institutes by the government to make the EDPs more comprehensive and meaningful.

7.8.5 Funding Support by the Government/Development Bankers to Conduct Seminars/Workshops and Industrial Potential Survey

In order to aware the entrepreneurs of the various incentives and benefits envisaged by the government in IPRs (Industrial Policy Resolutions), funding support has been provided by the government to organize seminars and workshops. Further, financial assistance is also given to the organizations conducting industrial potential survey of different areas to identify the projects to be taken up by the entrepreneurs as per resource availability in the respective areas. Trainee entrepreneurs are benefited to a great deal from the industrial potential survey while identifying their projects and selecting their products. In the above ways, government plays the most important role in organizing EDPs in the country. Without the help and assistance of the government and the promotional agencies established by the government, it is impossible on the part of the ED institutions to organise the EDPs in an effective manner. So government support is a necessary adjunct to the organization of Entrepreneurship Development Programmes in India for human resource development on one hand and creation of enterprise on the other.

7.8.6 Institutional Support System for Entrepreneurial Development and Need for Institutional Support

Small scale enterprises are important for generation of employment, utilization of available resources, creation of infrastructure facilities and acceleration of economic development. Now-a-days, due to Liberalization, Privatization and Globalization (LPG), significant changes have occurred in the small business sector all over the world. Technological development, particularly in the sphere of Information Technology (IT), has provided access to different products/services enabling the customers to get the information of his desired products/services in a twinkling of an eye. Competition among the producers is also rampant high. In order to cater to the demands of the people, need for innovative products at competitive market prices is imperatively needed. Further, entrepreneurs are required to be capable enough to produce/deliver the goods and services so as to compete with the goods/services of global quality. Thus the need for support service organizations in our country is of much significance. That's why a number of important organizations have been set up in the government as well as in the non-government sector to cater to the needs of the entrepreneurs in various aspects like finance, technology, marketing, market research, quality control and in entrepreneurial and management training. Some of the institutions which support entrepreneurs in our country are discussed here.

Small Industries Development Organization (SIDO)

Small Industries Development Organization (SIDO) is functioning under Department of SSI and ARI, Government of India, New Delhi. It acts as a policy-making, coordinating and monitoring agency for the development of small scale industries in India. The main functions of SIDO are classified as follows:

(i) Framing of policy
(ii) Coordination
(iii) Monitoring
(iv) Industrial development and
(v) Extension

It is the nodal agency for the development of small scale industries and its above-mentioned functions are performed through a large number of field outfits and subordinate formations providing a wide-ranging technoeconomic consultancy, services and support. All small scale industries, except those falling under specialized boards and agencies like KVIC, Coir Boards, Central Silk Board, fall under the purview of the SIDO.

SIDO has got 27 offices, 31 small industries service institutes and 37 extension centres. Four regional testing centres and field testing stations, 6 process-cum-product development centres, 10 tool rooms and tool design institutes, 3 footwear training centres and 5 production centres.

National Small Industries Corporation Ltd

The NSIC was established in 1955 as a Government of India enterprise to promote small scale industries in the country. The corporation's head office is at Delhi and it has as many as four regional offices and 11 branch offices in different states. The main functions of NSIC are the following:

(i) To provide machinery on hire-purchase basis.
(ii) To assist small scale industries bringing forth a large number of viable SSEs with its support under various schemes all over the country.

The NSIC has adopted 310 focused sectoral approach for competence building and making a tangible contribution and facilitating the entrepreneurial growth in small scale sector with following objectives:

(a) To help in development and upgradation of technology
(b) To assist in modernization programme of small scale industries
(c) To distribute basic raw materials through their depots
(d) To help in export marketing of SSIs
(e) To import and distribute components and parts to actual small scale users in specific industries
(f) To set up industrial estates
(g) To organize trade fairs/exhibitions of small scale industries products, machineries, tools, equipments, etc.
(h) To impart training on various industrial trades
(i) To provide info-mediary services

State Small Scale Industries Development Corporations (SSIDCs)

Most of the state governments have set up Small Scale Industries Corporation in order to undertake a variety of commercial and industrial activities. The main functions of State Small Scale Industries Corporation are:

(a) To undertake the distribution of scarce raw materials
(b) To assist the entrepreneurs in supply of machinery
(c) To provide assistance for marketing of products of SSEs
(d) To undertake construction of sheds/industrial estates
(e) To provide allied infrastructure facilities and their maintenance
(f) To extend seed capital assistance on behalf of the state government concerned
(g) To provide management assistance to production units

Small Scale Industries Board (SSIB)

In pursuance of the recommendations provided by an international team of experts, constituted by the Government of India, to study the problem of small scale industries in the country, a Small Scale Industries Board was set up in 1954. The prime function of SSIB was to give advice on development of small scale industries. The SSIB is also known as Central Small Industries Board (CSIB). The Union Minister of Industries is the Chairman of the Board. A Standing Committee of the Board was set up in 1957, which meets once in two months. For implementation of the recommendations and policies laid down by the Small Scale Industries Board, a separate officer of the rank of Joint Secretary has been appointed in the Ministry of Commerce and Industry.

India Investment Centre (IIC)

India Investment Centre was set up as a non-profit making autonomous organization funded and supported by the Government of India. The main functions of IIC are as follows:

(a) It undertakes the task of promoting mutually-rewarding joint venture projects between Indian and foreign entrepreneurs.
(b) It acts as a nodal point of dissemination of information relating to economic condition, laws, opportunities procedures and formalities for investment in India.
(c) It provides linkage between Indian and foreign entrepreneurs and assist them in coming together for fruitful collaborations.
(d) It offers objective advice on investment condition in the light of industrial priorities and policies of the Government of India.
(e) It also helps in locating suitable Indian partners for prospective foreign investors.
(f) Its services are mainly related to industrial development and as such it brings the problems and reactions of the entrepreneurs to the notice of the Government of India.

MSME—Development Institute (MSME–DI)

Micro, Small & Medium Enterprises (MSMEs) are set up by the Government of India to provide consultancy and training to small entrepreneurs. There are 28 offices and 30 branch offices set up in state capitals and other places all over the country. In Orissa, SISI is situated at Cuttack. The main functions of MSMEs include:

(a) To undertake economic consultancy/information/EDP consultancy
(b) To provide trade and market information
(c) To prepare, project profiles for small scale industries
(d) To undertake state industrial potential survey and district industrial potential survey
(e) To undertake modernization and in-plant studies
(f) To conduct training in various trades/activities
(g) To organize Entrepreneurship Development Programmes of various types such as product/process-oriented EDP, EDP for women target groups and general target groups, management development programmes, workshops and seminars, etc.

District Industries Centres (DICs)

The District Industries Centres (DICs) programme was started on 8 May, 1978 with a view to provide integrated administrative framework at the district level for promotion of small scale industries in rural areas. The organizational structure of DICs consists of General Manager, functional managers and project managers to provide technical services in the areas relevant to the needs of district concerned. Management of DICs is done by the State Government. The main functions of DICs are:

(a) To undertake industrial potential survey and to identify the types of feasible ventures which can be taken up in ISB sector, i.e., Industrial Sector, Service Sector and Business Sector
(b) To prepare and keep model project profiles for reference of the entrepreneurs
(c) To prepare action plan to effectively implement the schemes already identified
(d) To guide entrepreneurs in matters relating to selecting the most appropriate machinery and equipment, sources of it supply and procedure for importing machineries
(e) To provide guidance for appropriate loan amount and documentation
(f) To assist entrepreneurs for availing land and shed, equipment and tools, furniture and fixtures
(g) To appraise the worthiness of the project-proposals received from entrepreneurs
(h) To help the entrepreneurs in obtaining required licences/permits/clearance
(i) To assist the entrepreneurs in marketing their products and assess the possibilities of ancillarization
(j) To conduct product development work appropriate to small industry
(k) To help the entrepreneurs in clarifying their doubts about the matters of operation of bank accounts, submission of monthly, quarterly and annual returns to government departments
(l) To conduct artisan training programme
(m) To act as the nodal agency for the district for implementing PMRY (Prime Minister Rojgar Yojana)
(n) To function as the technical consultant of DRDA in administering IRDP and TRYSEM programme
(o) To help the specialized training organizations to conduct Entrepreneurship Development Programmes

In fine, DICs function as the ***torch-bearer*** to the beneficiaries/entrepreneurs in setting up and running the business enterprise right from the concept to commissioning. So the role of DICs in enterprise building and developing small scale sector is of much significance.

Industrial Estates

Industrial estates are considered instrumental in promotion of small and medium scale industries in the country. In the opinion of **William Bredo**: "An industrial estate is a tract of land which is subdivided and developed according to a comprehensive plan for the use of a community of industrial enterprises". It is a place where required facilities and accommodation for factory/industry are provided to the entrepreneurs to establish their industries. In Orissa, Infrastructure Development Corporation Orissa (IDCO) was established to provide industrial infrastructure to the entrepreneurs. The following are the important objectives behind the establishment of industrial estates:

(a) To provide infrastructure and accommodation facilities along with electricity, water transportation, etc. to the entrepreneurs
(b) To encourage ancillarization and downstream industrial facilities around a major industrial unit

(c) To help in development of small and medium scale enterprises in the country
(d) To help in dispersal of industries to rural and backward areas
(e) To develop entrepreneurship by creating a conducive atmosphere to run the industries in the industrial estates

However, the first and foremost industrial estate was established at Rajkot in Gujarat in 1955. By now, the number of industrial estates had gone up to more than 650, making it the largest project in the country.

Specialized Support Institutions

1. ***National Institute for Entrepreneurship and Small Business Development (NIESBUD), New Delhi:*** It is an apex body established by Ministry of Industry, Government of India for coordinating and overseeing the activities of various institutes, agencies involved in entrepreneurship development in small industry as well as in small business. The activities of the institute include:

   (a) Evolving model syllabus for training various groups
   (b) Providing effective training strategies, methodology, manuals, tools, etc.
   (c) Facilitating and supporting Central and State Government institutions in executing programmes for entrepreneurship and small business development
   (d) Conducting training programmes for trainers, motivators and entrepreneurs
   (e) Developing entrepreneurial culture in the society

   The institute is also the Secretariat for National Entrepreneurship Development Board in the country and presently located at A-23, Sector-62 Institutional Area–II, Noida-20/30.

2. ***Central Institute of Tool Design (CITD), Hyderabad:*** The Institute has been set up by Central Government in 1968 with the help of ILO and UNDP to assist small scale sector by imparting specialized training to the personnel working in the manufacture of tools, jigs, fixtures, dies and moulds. The main functions of CITD are:

   (a) To offer advisory and consultancy services including assistance in the design and development of tools
   (b) To recommend measures to improve the standard of tools, tooling element and component etc.
   (c) To organise different types of training on tool design

3. ***Central Toolroom and Training Centres (CTTC):*** These centres have been set up by the government to provide toolroom services and facilities in designs, manufacture and training. These centres are located at Delhi, Bangalore, Kolkata and Bhubaneswar.

4. ***Central Institute of Handtools (CIHT):*** This Institute is located at Jalandhar. The main functions of the Institute are:

   (a) To provide improved technology to the small scale entrepreneurs
   (b) To help the entrepreneurs in getting raw materials
   (c) To provide services with regard to designing and testing for handtools industry

5. ***Institute for Design of Electrical Measuring Instruments (IDEMI), Mumbai:*** This Institute was set up in 1969 with assistance from UNDP at Mumbai. This Institute has got the provision of technical consultancy in the design and development of electrical and electronic instrument, calibration and testing, tool design, tool fabrication, prototype fabrication and training.

6. ***National Institute of Micro, Small and Medium Enterprises (NIMSME):*** This Institute is a premier institute in development of small industries and small business training. The Institute was set up in 1956 to develop the required manpower for running small scale industries in the country. The following functions are being undertaken by NIMSME.

   (a) To impart training to the persons engaged in SSI sector
   (b) To undertake Entrepreneurship Development Training Programme (EDP)/ Management Development Training Programme (MDP) for the entrepreneurs
   (c) To undertake research studies relating to small scale sector
   (d) To provide consultancy services to the small and medium scale entrepreneurs

   The Institute also conducts short-term courses in business management, industrial management and export management for the benefit of the entrepreneurs as well as officers and managerial personnel of small and medium scale industries. The Institute is located at Yousufguda, Hyderabad.

7. ***Technical Consultancy Organizations (TCOs):*** Technical consultancy organizations were established by the All India Financial Institutions in collaboration with state level financial, development institution and in many cayses with commercial banks to cater to consultancy needs of small industries and new entrepreneurs. Functions of the TCOs are as follows:

   (a) To prepare project profiles and feasibility studies
   (b) To undertake industrial potential survey
   (c) To undertake market research and survey for specific product
   (d) To provide consultancy services to the new entrepreneurs
   (e) To offer merchant banking facilities
   (f) To conduct entrepreneurship development programme

   At present, the following TCOs are working in different states and some of them also work in more than one state:

   (i) Andhra Pradesh Industrial and Technical Consultancy Organization Ltd (APITCO)
   (ii) Bihar Industrial and Technical Consultancy Organization Ltd (BITCO)
   (iii) Gujarat Industrial and Technical Consultancy Organization (GITCO)
   (iv) Himachal Consultancy Organization (HIMCO)
   (v) Industrial Technical Consultancy Organization of Tamil Nadu Ltd. (ITCOT)
   (vi) Haryana-Delhi Industrial Consultants Ltd. (HARDICON)
   (vii) Jammu and Kashmir Industrial and Technical Consultancy Organization Ltd (JKITCO)
   (viii) Karnataka Industrial and Technical Consultancy Organization Ltd (KITCO)

(ix) Madhya Pradesh Consultancy Organization Ltd (MPCON)
(x) Maharashtra Industrial and Technical Consultancy Organization Ltd (MITCON)
(xi) North-Eastern Industrial Consultants Ltd (NECON)
(xii) North-Eastern Industrial and Technical Consultancy Organization Ltd (NEITCO)
(xiii) North India Technical Consultancy Organization Ltd (NITCON)
(xiv) Orissa Industrial and Technical Consultancy Organization Ltd (ORITCO)
(xv) Rajasthan Consultancy Organization Ltd (RAJCON)
(xvi) UP Industrial Consultants Ltd (UPICO)
(xvii) West Bengal Consultancy Organization Ltd (WEBCON)

8. ***Institutes of Entrepreneurship Development (IEDs)/Centres for Entrepreneurship Development (CEDs):*** In order to give special attention to entrepreneurship development and industrial development needs of the backward states, IDBI in association with other development financial institutions and banks and the state governments set up Institutes of Entrepreneurship Development (IEDs) in Uttar Pradesh, Bihar, Orissa and Madhya Pradesh. In Orissa, the IED has been established in the year 1987 by the joint effort of IDBI, IFCI Ltd, ICICI, SBI, Allahabad Bank and the State Government of Orissa.

   The various functions which the IEDs exercise are given below:

   (a) To act as the nodal centre for entrepreneurial development activities in the state
   (b) To organize and conduct EDPs, MDPs, EACs, TOTs (Training of Trainers) and training programme for PMRY beneficiaries
   (c) To identify, train and assist potential entrepreneurs amongst technical and non-technical personnel in setting up ventures for self-employment in both industries and service-oriented business
   (d) To undertake industrial potential survey
   (e) To undertake documentation and research in the field of entrepreneurship and small business development
   (f) To conduct workshops, seminars and conferences for promotion and development of entrepreneurship
   (g) To provide consultancy services to the entrepreneurs for setting up small enterprise
   (h) To publish magazines, newsletters for furtherance of entrepreneurship development
   (i) To provide escort services to the potential entrepreneurs to start their own enterprise
   (j) To provide a forum for interaction and exchange of views with agencies engaged in entrepreneurial activities and small business development

   A number of CEDs were established as specialized training organizations to provide training to various target groups such as general target group, technical graduates, women, educated unemployed persons, etc. These centres are akin to IEDs and their functions are similar to the functions of IEDs.

9. ***Central Silk Board:*** Central Silk Board is engaged in various types of activities required for promotion of silk industries in the country. India is fortunately the only country in the world which produces all varieties of natural silk. In terms of

employment, sericulture provides employment to about 4 million people. Central Silk Board, therefore, functions as a nodal agency for providing adequate promotional measures for silk industry. The following functions are chiefly undertaken by the Central Silk Board:

(a) Providing training to the entrepreneurs to take up sericulture
(b) Undertaking research in various connected areas fulfilling the basic needs of silk industry
(c) Promoting price stabilization and undertaking a host of other activities assisting the development of sericulture

Despite various promotional measures, per hectare output of mulberry silk in our country is low as compared to that in Japan and the cost of production is also high. Therefore, appropriate measures are to be undertaken to improve the production of silk and launch a movement for getting sericulture accepted as a source of income and employment generation by the people of this country.

10. ***The Coir Board:*** Coir Board is a statutory body established under Coir Industry Act 1953. Coir and its products are important exportable items of India. Following are the functions of the Coir Board:

(a) To promote coir products in the market
(b) To innovate new designs and new products made of coir
(c) To provide training to the entrepreneurs to set up ventures in coir and coir training and design centres

The Board has its own research institutes, training and design centres across the country. Coir industry is well developed in the southern states like Kerala and a lot of cooperatives are organized in the state.

11. ***Entrepreneurship Development Institute of India (EDI), Ahmedabad:*** Entrepreneurship Development Institute of India (EDI) is the principal resource centre with special responsibility for promotion of entrepreneurial movement in the country. It was established as an autonomous, non-profit institution sponsored by all India financial institutions namely IDBI, IFCI Ltd, ICICI Ltd, SBI at Ahmedabad in 1983. The major functions of EDI are:

(a) To accelerate the process of entrepreneurship development ensuring its impact throughout the length and breadth of the country
(b) To conduct Training for Trainers for the officers of promotional agencies, banks and the trainer-motivators of IEDs, CEDs and NGOs
(c) To conduct EDPs, REDPs, Product Process EDPs, etc.
(d) To provide professional assistance to various institutions for their entrepreneurial development activities such as ICICI Ltd. and SBI
(e) To conduct workshops, seminars, conferences etc. To promote entrepreneurship development
(f) To act as the national resource institution committed to investment promotion, entrepreneurship education training and research

(g) To interact with developing countries and help them in capacity-building programmes for industrial development
(h) To organize economic cross-cultural programmes to promote entrepreneurship among the Small and Medium Enterprises of India and Europe
(i) To conduct entrepreneurship development programmes through ***open learning programme***, i.e., distance education system.

The Institute has received support from the World Bank, ILO, UNIDO, Commonwealth Secretariat, Friedrich Nauman Stiftung (FNST), European Union and several international agencies. Its international activities cover a range of entrepreneurship and investment promotion related training programmes, seminars and workshops. The EDI is the partner institution for the implementation of the European Union economic cross-cultural programme ENTRIXIE (Entrepreneurship Training and Information Exchange for Small Business in India and Europe), a project especially established to promote entrepreneurship among the SMEs of India and Europe.

12. ***Rural Development and Self-Employment Training Institute (RUDSETI):*** It was established at Ujre, a small village of Karnataka, in 1982. Two leading banks, Syndicate Bank and Canara Bank, took the initiative in alleviating unemployment problem under the leadership of Dr Veerendra Heggade, a great visionary and religion head of Sreekshetra Dharmasthal, Karnataka. The collective thinking gave shape in providing an institutional framework to RUDSETI. So far, RUDSETI is having a network of 18 branches all over the country covering 10 states. The objectives of RUDSETI are as follows:

(a) To provide free training to the unemployed youths in entrepreneurship development
(b) To build up the potential to provide escort services to these trainees to set up their micro-enterprise
(c) To create a resource centre for business ideas
(d) To promote networking between existing and potential micro-entrepreneurs

The different training programmes imparted by the Institute are as follows:

(i) *Agricultural EDPs:* Agriculture and allied activities, dairy, sheep-rearing, poultry, beekeeping, horticulture, sericulture, piggery, mushroom cultivation, etc.
(ii) *Product EDPs:* Dress design for men and women, agarbatti manufacturing, wool knitting, bag making, cane chair making, Bakery product, etc.
(iii) *Process EDPs:* Two-wheeler repairs, pump set repairs, radio/TV repairs, Beautician, Motor winding, etc.
(iv) *General EDPs:* Rural Entrepreneurship Development Programme, Entrepreneurship Development Programme for women, PMRY training, etc.
(v) *Skill upgradation programme for existing entrepreneurs:* Escort services and follow-up support to the trainees to sustain motivation level and overcome teething problems of new entrepreneurs. This is achieved by the following activities:

(a) Facilitating credit linkage with financial institutions for setting up of micro-enterprises

(b) Post-training follow-up for 2–3 years through regular correspondence, individual contact and unit visit

(vi) *Rural development and human resources development training Programmes for development workers of NGOs:* Training self-help group management, training bank staff, social animators, etc., in rural development activities.

(vii) *Technology transfer programmes for introduction of cost-efficient, environment friendly technology:* Some of the technologies transferred are:

(a) Palm tree climber appliances and ASTRA *chulla*
(b) Stabilized mudbricks and microdot tiles
(c) Construction of gobar gas, vermi-composting and palmgur making

13. ***Integrated Training Centre, Nilokheri:*** This training centre has been set up by the government to impart technical training to artisans and workers. Industries promotion officers and extension officers of the state government are sponsored to undergo training at this centre so as to make them equipped with modern training inputs for the benefits of the entrepreneurs and astisans of respective states.

Institutional Finance to Entrepreneurs

Finance is the lifeblood of any enterprise. An entrepreneur has to assess his actual financial requirement before the establishment of his enterprise. As the small scale entrepreneurs do not have adequate amount of funds for establishing and running the enterprise, the Government of India has set up a number of institutions to provide financial assistance to small scale entrepreneurs. The various financial institutions which provide finance with the types of assistance to the entrepreneurs in the country are listed below:

- Industrial Development Bank of India (IDBI)
- Industrial Finance Corporation of India Ltd (IFCI)
- Industrial Credit and Investment Corporation of India Ltd (ICICI)
- Life Insurance Corporation of India (LIC)
- Unit Trust of India (UTI)
- Small Industries Development Bank of India (SIDBI)
- Industrial Reconstruction Bank of India (IRBI)
- State Financial Corporations (SFCs)
- National Bank for Agriculture and Rural Development (NABARD)
- Export-Import Bank of India (EXIM bank)
- Regional Rural Banks
- National Industrial Development Corporation Ltd. (NIDC)
- Commercial Banks
- Khadi and Village Industries Commission (KVIC)

These institutions are discussed as follows:

1. ***Industrial Development Bank of India*:** The IDBI was established on July 1, 1964 by the Government of India under the Act of Parliament as the principal financial institution in the country. Initially, it was a wholly-owned subsidiary of Reserve Bank of India and in February 1976, the IDBI was made an autonomous organization and its ownership passed on to the Government of India from the RBI. The main functions of IDBI are as follows:

(a) The IDBI provides assistance to the small scale sector through its scheme of refinance and bills rediscounting scheme.
(b) The financial assistance has been indirect in the form of refinancing of loans granted by the commercial banks and the state financial corporations (SFCs).
(c) In order to assist the small scale sector, IDBI has set up Small Industries Development Fund (SIDF) in May 1986. This fund basically aims at providing a focal point to coordinate financial and non-financial inputs required for growth of small industries sector.
(d) In association with Government of India, IDBI has constituted National Equity Fund (NEF) to prevail equity type of support to tiny and small scale units which are engaged in manufacturing activities. The scheme is administered by IDBI through nationalized banks.
(e) The IDBI has also introduced the single window assistance scheme for grant of term loans and working capital assistance to small, tiny and medium scale enterprises.
(f) The IDBI has also set up a Voluntary Executive Corporation Cell (VECI) to utilize the services of experts, professionals for counselling small units and for providing consultancy support in specified areas.

2. ***Industrial Finance Corporation of India Ltd:*** The Government of India set up the Industrial Finance Corporation of India (IFCI) under IFCI Act in July 1948. It has been brought under Companies Act, 1956. It is an important financial institution which extends financial assistance to the entrepreneurs through rupee and foreign currency loans, underwriting, direct subscriptions to shares, debentures and guarantees. It also extends other financial facilities like equipment procurement, equipment finance, buyer's and supplier's credit, equipment leasing and finance to leasing and hire-purchase companies.
The IFCI has devised new promotional schemes such as:

(a) Consultancy fees, subsidy schemes for assisting small scale entrepreneurs in marketing sector
(b) Interest subsidy schemes for women entrepreneurs
(c) Pollution control in small and medium scale enterprises (SMEs)
(d) Encouraging the modernization of tiny, small and medium scale industries

Though IFCI Ltd has performed in the best possible manner over the years, due to lack of control over the defaulting borrowers, it is facing many problems in recent years.

3. ***Industrial Credit and Investment Corporation of India Ltd (ICICI):*** The Industrial Credit and Investment Corporation of India Ltd (ICICI) was established by the Government of India under the Indian Companies Act in 1955. It was established

with the objective of providing financial assistance to the small and medium scale sectors. The main functions of ICICI can be described as under:

(a) Financial assistance is extended by way of rupee and foreign currency loans, underwriting and direct subscriptions to shares, debentures and guarantees.
(b) Financial facilities such as deferred credit, leasing credit, instalment sale, asset credit and venture capital are extended by ICICI Ltd.
(c) It also guarantees loans from other private investment sources. small scale units are the major beneficiary of the ICICI assistance.

4. ***Life Insurance Corporation of India (LIC):*** The Life Insurance Corporation of India (LIC) was established under the LIC Act in 1956. It offers multitude of insurance policies to extend social security to various segments of society.

   As per its investment policy, LIC invests 75 per cent and above in Central and State Government's securities including government-guaranteed marketable securities and in the socially-oriented sector.

   The LIC extends loans for the following activities also:

   (a) Housing
   (b) Rural electrification
   (c) Water supply and sanitation
   (d) Expansion, diversification of industrial ventures
   (e) Modernisation of industry, etc.

5. ***Unit Trust of India:*** The Unit Trust of India (UTI) was set up by the Government of India in 1964 under an Act of Parliament. The chief objectives of Unit Trust of India are:

   (i) To mobilize savings of small investors through sale of units
   (ii) To channelize these savings towards corporate investment.

   The UTI has introduced many schemes which aimed at common investors. These schemes are mainly Primary Equity Fund, Retirement Benefit Plan, Grihalaxmi Unit Plan, Unit Scheme 1995 and Columbus India Fund. The UTI also provides financial assistance to corporate sector in the form of term loans and underwriting direct subscriptions to shares and debentures.

6. ***Small Industries Development Bank of India:*** The Small Industries Development Bank of India (SIDBI) was established in the year 1989 as a subsidiary of IDBI under a special Act. The chief functions of SIDBI are the promotion and development of small scale industries by way of financing. It commenced its operation from April 2, 1980 with its Head Office at Lucknow. The initial authorized capital of SIDBI was Rs 250 crores which can be extended up to Rs 1000 crores.

   The following functions are undertaken by SIDBI:

   (a) To promote small scale industries in semiurban areas to create more employment opportunities
   (b) To undertake technological upgradation and modernization of existing small scale industries

(c) To expand the channels for marketing the products of SSI sector on both domestic and international markets
(d) To extend seed capital or soft loan assistance under National Equity Fund Scheme/*Mahila Udyam Nidhi Scheme*
(e) To grant direct assistance and refinance for exports of small scale sector
(f) To provide financial assistance to SFCs, SIDCs, commercial banks, RRBs through existing credit delivery system
(g) To provide factoring and leasing service
(h) To provide financial assistance to the institutes, organizations for undertaking Entrepreneurship Development Programmes
(i) The most important feature of SIDBI is the special emphasis and the new schemes of assistance for marketing support to the small scale sector.

7. ***Industrial Reconstruction Bank of India:*** Industrial Reconstruction Corporation of India (IRCI) was set up in 1971 under the Indian Companies Act to act as an agency to rehabilitate the sick units. But in the year 1984, the Government of India renamed the IRCI as Industrial Reconstruction Bank of India (IRBI) by an Act of Parliament. Thereafter, it acts as a reconstruction agency to revive, reconstruct and rehabilitate the sick industrial concerns.

   The IRBI undertakes the following functions:

   (a) It provides financial assistance to industrial concerns.
   (b) It acts as an agency of State Government as well as Union Government and also of other financial institutions as per the authorization of the government.
   (c) It provides consultancy and merchant-banking services for reconstruction and development of industrial units.
   (d) It also helps in providing infrastructural facilities, raw materials, machineries and other tools on the basis of hire-purchase and lease schemes.

   Therefore, the IRBI plays a significant role in promoting entrepreneurial and industrial development in the country.

8. ***State Financial Corporations:*** Financial assistance provided by the Industrial Finance Corporation of India is limited to large sized industrial undertakings only. In order to cater to the needs of the small scale units, the Government of India passed the State Financial Corporations Act in 1951 under which the State Financial Corporations (SFCs) were set up. The first and foremost State Financial Corporation was set up at Punjab in 1953. Today, there are 18 SFCs functioning in the country. State Financial Corporations are managed by a Managing Director, Board of Directors and the Executive Committee which is headed by a Chairman.

   The functions of the SFCs are as follows:

   (a) The chief function of SFCs is to advance term loans to small scale and medium scale industrial units.
   (b) It underwrites the issue of stocks, shares, bonds and debentures of industrial units.

(c) It grants loans to the industrial concerns which is repayable within a period not exceeding twenty years.
(d) It subscribes to debentures floated by industrial concerns.
(e) It also provides financial assistance to small road transport operators, tour operators, hoteliers, hospitals and nursing homes, etc.

In Orissa, the State Financial Corporation has been operating along with its branch network throughout Orissa.

9. ***National Bank for Agriculture and Rural Development (NABARD):*** In pursuance of the recommendations of the committee for reviewing arrangements for financing institutional credit for agriculture and rural development (CRAFICARD), NABARD was set up to operate as an apex bank in agriculture. NABARD's resources were initially contributed by the central government and the Reserve Bank of India. To meet its loan requirement, it draws funds from the central government, the World Bank and other agencies. NABARD is empowered to raise funds from the market also.

The main functions of NABARD are as follows:

(a) It acts as a refinancing institution and advances loans to agriculture, small scale industries, cottage and village industries.
(b) It also provides financial assistance to handicrafts sector, rural artisans, agriculturists, farmers and entrepreneurs engaged in allied non-farm sector activities.
(c) It provides short-term, medium-term and long-term credit to the RRBs, cooperative banks and other financial institutions to promote integrated rural development.
(d) NABARD is entrusted with the responsibility of coordination among Union and State governments, the Planning Commission and other state level institutions engaged in promotion and establishment of small scale, village and cottage industries, rural art and crafts and micro-enterprises.
(e) It undertakes entrepreneurship development programmes, skill upgradation programmes for tiny, small and medium scale entrepreneurs, workshops and seminars to promote integrated rural development both in agricultural and industrial sectors.

The following are the innovative initiatives of NABARD:

(a) Micro-finance programme
(b) Natural resources management initiatives
(c) Empowerment of rural women through micro-credit, micro-enterprise and Self Help Group (SHG) programmes
(d) Creation of special funds to support innovations in neglected areas
(e) Creation of millions of rural employment opportunities through initiatives like cluster development and rural entrepreneurship development programmes
(f) Construction of infrastructure like roads, bridges and rural hats, etc.

Over a period of time; NABARD has ensured transfer of funds from urban India to rejuvenate rural India. A Rs. 4519.00 crore institution has grown into a dynamic organization worth Rs. 62,000 crores helping the rural masses in upliftment of their economic conditions and physical quality of life.

10. ***The Export-Import Bank of India:*** The Export-Import Bank of India (EXIM Bank) was established in the year 1982 by an Act of Parliament. The export loans and guarantee portfolio of IDBI was taken over by EXIM Bank. The important functions of EXIM Bank are as follows:

(a) To advance financial assistance to exporters and importers
(b) To give a boost to India's export promotion strategy
(c) To provide finance for joint ventures in foreign countries
(d) To undertake merchant-banking services of companies engaged in export-import business
(e) To offer buyer's credit to the foreign government and banks
(f) To rediscount export bills

The Export-Import Bank has introduced ***clusters of excellence*** for quality upgradation. It has also introduced the following programmes:

(i) Export bills rediscounting
(ii) Technology and consultancy
(iii) Financing and relending facility to banks abroad

Thus, EXIM Bank plays a very important role in boosting the export promotion in the country.

11. ***Regional Rural Banks (RRBs):*** A rural bank scheme has been inaugurated in India on October 2, 1975 with the objective of establishing regional rural banks to finance credit needs of the small and marginal farmers, rural artisans, agricultural labourers, small and tiny entrepreneurs.

These banks came into existence with the sponsorship of central government, state government and a specific commercial banks. The ratio of share capital contributed by the above agencies for formation of RRB is 50:15:55 respectively. Though the RRBs resemble commercial banks in many respects, they virtually differ from commercial banks in certain aspects, viz:

(a) The area of operation of RRB is confined to a specific region consisting of generally one or more districts in a state.
(b) These banks advances financial assistance to small and marginal farmers, agricultural labourers, small entrepreneurs and persons of small means.
(c) The interest charges of RRBs should not be higher than those of the cooperative societies.

The functions of RRBs are as follows:

(a) To provide loans and advances to small and marginal farmers, agricultural labourers, artisans, etc.
(b) To advance financial assistince to small entrepreneurs for establishing small and tiny enterprises

(c) To assist entrepreneurs in handicrafts and cottage sector
(d) To provide financial assistance to small entrepreneurs for development of trade, commerce, industries, agriculture and other allied economic activities in rural areas.

12. ***National Industrial Development Corporation Ltd:*** The National Industrial Development Corporation (NIDC) was established in the year 1954 to bring about a balanced development of industries both in private and public sectors. Its main objective is to promote small and medium scale industries. The following functions are being undertaken by the NIDC:

(a) It gives emphasis on manufacture of capital goods and machine tools.
(b) It undertakes industrial potential survey and seeks cooperation from private entrepreneurs to establish more industries in private sector.
(c) It extends financial assistance for rehabilitation and modernization of industries like cotton textiles, jute industry and machine tools industry.
(d) It also can supply machinery, technical counselling and any other facility which the industrial units need from time to time.
(e) The most important function of NIDC is to assist that type of industrial units which are conducive to the economic development of the country.

13. ***Commercial Banks:*** Commercial banks assist in providing finance to the entrepreneurs. Financial assistance may take the form of term loan or working capital loan. In general, commercial banks provide short-term loans in the shape of working capital to the small entrepreneurs but with the development of industrialization, these banks have become more and more interested to advance long-term finance to the entrepreneurs.

An important feature in financing SSIs has been Lead Bank Scheme under which each district was allotted one schedule bank to intensify development activities. Further, the introduction of ***Credit Guarantee Scheme*** in the year 1960 was a big step in the field of commercial bank financing to SSIs. After nationalization in 1969, the commercial banks have extended their activities to help small borrower an access to bank credit. These banks have extended liberal credit facilities to the priority sectors such as agriculture and agro-based industries, small scale industries. One of the key features is that timely and adequate credit at low rate of interest is increasingly awaited by the small scale entrepreneurs.

14. ***Khadi and Village Industries Commission:*** The Khadi and Village Industries Commission (KVIC) is a statutory body established by an Act of parliament (No. 61 of 1956 and as amended by an Act No. 12 of 1987) in April 1957. It took over the work of former All India Khadi and Village Industries Board.

The broad objectives that the KVIC has set for it are:

(a) To generate employment avenues for rural unemployed people through its different schemes such as Gramodyog Rojgar Yojana
(b) To develop entrepreneurship ability among the rural unemployed youths
(c) To achieve the goal of rural industrialization

(d) To mobilize bank finance for the entrepreneurs looking to the limited resources of KVIC
(e) To bring about regional balance in assisting cottage and village industries
(f) To assist the artisans by way of providing machinery, procuring raw materials, etc.

Financial support system in the State of Orissa: The following institutiions provide financial support of the entrepreneur in the state of Orissa.

(i) Industrial Promotion and Investment Corporation of Orissa (IPICOL)
(ii) Agricultural Promotion and Investment Corporation Ltd (APICOL)
(iii) Khadi and Village Industries Board (KVIB)
(iv) Orissa State Financial Corporation (OSFC)

EXERCISES

A. Long answer type questions:

1. What is entrepreneurship development? Discuss the need for entrepreneurship development.
2. Explain the need for and objectives of EDP.
3. Explain the various phases of EDP.
4. Discuss the course curriculum of EDP in detail.
5. What are the objectives of EDP? How can it be evaluated?
6. "Entrepreneurs are made, not born". Comment.
7. Discuss the need for entrepreneurship development in India.
8. Discuss briefly the role of government in organizing EDPs.
9. Discuss briefly the role of promotional agencies in entrepreneurship development in India.
10. Explain the role, relevance and achievements of EDPs in Indian context.
11. State the need for institutional finance for small scale enterprises.
12. Give an account of the institutions providing institutional support to small scale entrepreneurs?
13. What are the main functions of SIDBI?
14. Discuss the functions of EXIM Bank.

B. Short answer type questions:

1. Write short notes on the following:

(a) SIDBI	(b) IFCI Ltd
(c) UTI	(d) ICICI Ltd
(e) IDBI	(f) SFCs
(g) NIESBUD	(h) SISI
(i) IEDs	(j) EDI
(k) NISIET	(l) NSIC
(m) DICs	(n) Industrial estates
(o) NABARD	(p) Regional rural banks

2. Describe the following in five lines only:
   (a) Support system institutions
   (b) Training-intervention
   (c) Pre-training stage
   (d) Follow-up stage
   (e) Indian EDP model

CHAPTER 8

Women Entrepreneurship

CHAPTER CONTENTS

8.1 INTRODUCTION

Women constitute almost half of the total population of the world. Similarly, in India also, women constitute fifty per cent of the total population. Till the turn of the century, man has enjoyed a dominant position and woman has been relegated to a subservient level. Despite all protection granted to women in the Constitution of India, they have been often quoted as the second sex. This status of women is in vogue in many countries even today, though in a lesser scale. Moreover, the position a woman enjoys varies from country to country according to the prevailing conditions and socio-cultural environment which prevails. It is true that age-old practices cannot be eradicated overnight. But change in attitude, technological innovation and modern ways of thinking can reduce the disparity between man and woman and bring about equality and equity between them. So the need of the hour is women empowerment both through provision of employment and enterprise creation. Typologically, the former leads to endogenous empowerment (enterprise absorbing women) and the latter gives rise to exogenous empowerment (women creating enterprise).

However, with the march of economic reforms—liberalization, privatization and globalization—employment in the government agencies is reduced whereas it is increasing in private sector enterprises. On the flip side of the reform process are the vast emerging opportunities for entrepreneurial ventures. Through appropriate intervention, if women are attracted to make use of these opportunities of enterprise promotion, they will not only come to the mainstream of the nation but also contribute to the shift from welfare approach to empowerment. Informed opinion also suggests that women enterprises create reasonable levels of employment for women.

8.2 CONCEPT OF WOMEN ENTREPRENEURS

Women entrepreneurs may be defined as the woman or a group of women who take initiative to set up a business enterprise and to run it smoothly. According to the Government of India, a woman entrepreneur is defined as "an enterprise owned and controlled by a woman and having a minimum financial interest of 51 per cent of the employment generated in the enterprise to women." This definition has been criticized by many on the ground that the condition of employing more than 50 per cent women workers in the enterprises owned and run by the woman is discriminatory.

In fine, women entrepreneurs are those women who generate business ideas or select the best opportunity, mobilize resources, combine the factors of production, undertake risks and operate the enterprise in the most effective manner with a view to earning profit.

8.3 EMPOWERMENT OF WOMEN THROUGH ENTERPRISE

The verb ***empower*** means to bestow power. So empowerment of women implies creating conditions for enabling the women to be motivated for task accomplishment by taking personal responsibility. In the context of empowerment through enterprise, empowerment of women involves access to resources and markets, actual ownership and active control. These three factors act as the bullwork for empowering women through enterprise.

The essence of self-development and empowerment of women lies in self-concept of women which can be developed through the following competency-development exercises:

(i) Self-concept which implies discovering one's potential.
(ii) Self-identity which relates to the exercise "Who am I".
(iii) Self-evaluation which indicates self-confidence and self-respect, i.e. "What am I worth".
(iv) Self-ideal which reveals "What should I be" and What could I become".

The above-mentioned competency-development exercises are illustrated in Fig. 8.1.

In the process of empowerment, women should consider their strengths, weaknesses, opportunities and threats and move forward to unfold their own potential to achieve their goals through self-development. In our country, empowering women through enterprise

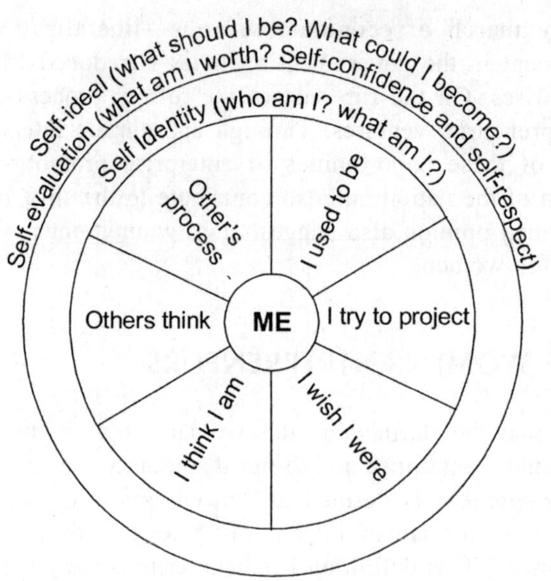

Fig. 8.1 Competency-development exercises for empowerment of women.

development has become an integral part of our development efforts because of the three important advantages:

(i) Women development
(ii) Economic growth
(iii) Social stability

The future of small enterprises depends on enabling women to become entrepreneurs and their participation in the entrepreneurial process.

8.4 FACTORS GOVERNING WOMEN ENTREPRENEURSHIP

Women entrepreneurship is governed by four spheres—psycho-sphere, socio-sphere, techno-sphere and econo-sphere. These above spheres are illustrated in Fig. 8.2.

The constraints faced by women entrepreneurs in differnt domains are given below:

Constraints in psychological domain:

(a) Lack of self-motivation.
(b) Conflicts due to dual responsibility
(c) Poor risk-taking ability

Constraints in social domain:

(a) Lack of social contacts
(b) Male dominance
(c) Not in tune with social norms

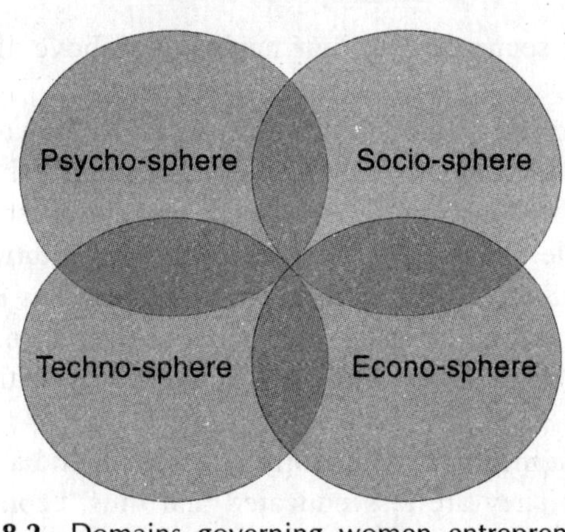

Fig. 8.2 Domains governing women entrepreneurship.

Constraints in technical domain:

(a) Lack of project ideas
(b) Lack of process know-how
(c) Lack do-how (implementation capacity)

Constraints in economic domain:

(a) Economic support not forthcoming from family
(b) Inadequate amount advanced through financing agencies.
(c) Lack of of economic ownership and control

Problems faced by women entrepreneurs

In India, women entrepreneurs generally face a large number of problems. Due to these problems, entrepreneurship development among women has not been satisfactory. These barriers can be elaborated as follows:

- Lack of self-confidence
- Male-dominated society
- Low risk-bearing capacity
- lack of encouragement from family
- Discrimination in upbringing
- Role conflict
- Lack of education
- Low mobility
- Problem of access to finance
- Stiff competition

1. ***Lack of self-confidence:*** Women lack self-confidence in their own abilities which is partly due to cultural environment. This is because of family's reluctance to provide them funds for their venture. Banker's reluctance to fund their project due

to lack of collateral securities on their names and above all, very few development agencies come forward to extend them assistance.

2. ***Male-dominated society:*** Important barrier to the empowerment of women through enterprise is the male chauvinism. Prevalent sociocultural attitudes and beliefs are not conducive to the blossoming of women as entrepreneurs. Male child is still preferred to a female child right from the birth. Constitution of India speaks about equality of sexes but till today women are considered as ***abala*** i.e., weak, passive and home-oriented and as a result, less capable than men. This consideration acts as a stumbling block in their strife for equal status with men in the pursuit of economic activity.
3. ***Low risk-bearing capability:*** Generally, women in India are confined to the four walls of the house. They are less educated and thus, economically backward. This reduces their risk-bearing capability in running the enterprise.
4. ***Lack of encouragement from family:*** Very few women get encouragement from their family to start a business. In India, it is mainly a woman's duty to look after the children and other members of the family. Consequently, family bonding spares a little time for the woman to take up entrepreneurial activity. Studies have found out that women brought up in homes which are not restrictive in their outlook tend to be innovative, independent and dynamic and are likely to become successful entrepreneurs.
5. ***Discrimination in upbringing:*** Right from early childhood, girl child is taught not to be aggressive or independent. They are discouraged to move out of the family and take up their business. Conservative attitude of the family members makes the women weak and passive in their approach. Decisions are taken for them by others.
6. ***Role conflict:*** Entrepreneurship needs a high level of commitment, devotion and dedication. Women taking on the mantle of entrepreneurship suffer from stress and strain caused by role overload and role conflict as they strive simultaneously to cope with their multiple roles of being a mother, wife, homemaker, etc.
7. ***Lack of education:*** The greatest barrier to entrepreneurial career among women is the lack of education. In India 60 per cent of women are still illiterate and illiteracy is the major problem of socio-economic backwardness. Lack of education restricts the innerurge of the women to accomplish jobs through personal risk-taking capability.
8. ***Low mobility:*** Women, in general, are less mobile due to sociocultural barriers. The dual responsibility that women entrepreneurs have to cope with is making a success of their enterprise as well as looking after the home and hearth place restrictions on their mobility.
9. ***Problem of access to finance:*** Women entrepreneurs are lacking access to institutional finance due to absence of tangible security and credit in the market. Women do not have property in their names. Most of the women enterprises suffer from sickness due to lack of financing.
10. ***Stiff competition:*** Women enterprises face stiff competition from organized industries due to the absence of any kind of organizational set-up by women entrepreneurs. As a result of this, such a competition leads to the closure of women enterprises.

Other constraints faced by women entrepreneurs are:

(a) Negative attitude of banks and financial institutions
(b) Lack of managerial efficiency
(c) Red tapism
(d) Lack of business experiences
(e) Inefficient arrangement for marketing, i.e. through middlemen
(f) Difficulty to procure raw materials

8.5 SCHEMES FOR WOMEN ENTREPRENEURS

Commercial banks and other financial institutions have come forward to introduce different schemes for women entrepreneurs. Some of the important schemes to provide financial assistance to women enterprises are briefly described here:

1. ***SBI Stree Shakti Package:*** The SBI introduced ***Stree Shakti Package*** in the year 1989 to develop women entrepreneurs. Highlights of the package are as follows:
   (a) Under this scheme, Entrepreneurship Development Programmes (EDPs), exclusively designed for women entrepreneurs, are conducted. The programmes are organized with the help of SBI staff training college and the local branches.
   (b) The branch managers and the field officers of the banks would provide necessary support and assistance to women who want to set up enterprise.
   (c) In this scheme, financial assistance to the extent of Rs 25000 can be provided to the women entrepreneurs without keeping collateral security or guarantee.
   (d) Further, a discount of half per cent is allowed on the interest charged.
   (e) Loan proposals can be sanctioned within a period of 30 days from the date of receipt of the application form from the women entrepreneur. But in case of high value proposal and when there is the involvement of more than one financial institution, this stipulation is ignored.

2. ***IDBI's Mahila Udyam Nidhi (MUN) scheme:*** The IDBI has set up a special fund, Mahila Udyam Nidhi with a corpus of Rs 5 crore to provide seed capital assistance to women entrepreneurs intending to set up projects in SSI sectors. The scheme is implemented by SIDBI. Women entrepreneurs who can start and manage an enterprise with a minimum financial status of 51 per cent of the equity are eligible for assistance, provided the project cost excluding working capital is less than Rs 10 lakhs. In this case, the following norms are followed by SIDBI.
   (i) Debt equity ratio should be 3:1.
   (ii) Seed capital assistance is proved in the form of soft loan upto a maximum of 15 per cent of the fixed cost.
   (iii) Minimum promoter's contribution is 10 per cent of the fixed cost.
   (iv) Service charge of 1 per cent per annum is charged.
   (v) Repayment period is 10 years including an initial moratorium period of 5 years.
   (vi) Seed capital assistance is provided without insisting on security.

3. ***SIDBI's assistance for women entrepreneurs:*** The Small Industries Development Bank of India (SIDBI) has special schemes for financial assistance to women entrepreneurs. These schemes aim at the following objectives:
   (i) Training and extension services according to their small socio-economic status
   (ii) Financial assistance at concessional terms to help them in setting up tiny and small units

   These schemes are basically operated through State Financial Corporations (SFCs), State Industrial Development Corporations (SIDCs), etc.
4. ***Bank of India's Priyadarshini Yojana:*** The scheme aims at providing financial assistance to the women entrepreneurs who come under the following categories.
   (i) Small business, e.g. beauty parlour, laundry, lending library, etc.
   (ii) Retail traders, e.g. fair price shops, general stores, etc.
   (iii) Road transport operators, e.g. autorickshaws
   (iv) Professional and self-employed, e.g. chartered accountants, lawyers and doctors
   (v) Allied agricultural activities

In this case, the maximum unit of loan amount is up to Rs 2 lakhs for term loans and up to Rs 1 lakh for working capital. The assets acquired with bank finance will need to be hypothecated to the banks as security. Repayment period is normally for a span of three to five years. The margin money to be departed by the promoter is usually 20 per cnet depending upon the type of activity. Apart from this the following schemes are in operation to help the women entrepreneur in obtaining financial assistance.

(i) Prime Minister's Employment Generation Programme (PMEGP)
(ii) Self-Employment Programme for Urban Poor (SEPUP)
(iii) Swarnajayanti Gram Swarojgar Yojana (SGSY)
(iv) Integrated Rural Development Programme (IRDP)
(v) Micro-finance through Rastriya Mahila Kosh (RMK).

EXERCISES

A. Long answer type questions:

1. Define women entrepreneurship. Discuss the problems faced by women entrepreneurs.
2. What is meant by women entrepreneurs ? What are the promotional schemes available in India for the development of women entrepreneurship?
3. What are the factors governing the development of women entrepreneurs?
4. What is empowerment? Discuss briefly the empowerment of women through enterprise.

B. Short answer type questions:

1. Write short notes on the following:
   (a) Functions of women entrepreneurs

(b) Empowerment of women through enterprise
(c) Domains governing women entrepreneurship
(d) Problems of women entrepreneurs
(e) Schemes of financial assistance for women entrepreneurs

2. Describe the following questions in 5 lines only:
(a) Socio-economic background of women entrepreneurs in India
(b) Role of rural women entrepreneur
(c) Identification of projects for women entrepreneur
(d) Growth of women entrepreneurship in India
(e) Financial consistance to women entrepreneurs in India.

CHAPTER 9

Rural Entrepreneurship

CHAPTER CONTENTS

9.1 INTRODUCTION

"India lives in villages and its true spirit lives in rural areas". These words of the Father of the Nation, Mahatma Gandhi, are very much justified even in the New Millennium. He was not in favour of heavy and large industries. The reason is clear that large-scale industries can increase production but cannot provide employment to the millions of poor rural Indians. According to him, the crying need of India is production by masses through rural entrepreneurship and not mass production by heavy industries. The focus of rural entrepreneurship is, therefore, very clear. Firstly, it can produce self-employment opportunities, to the millions and thus, reduce unemployment. Secondly, it can augment employment avenues for others in backward areas and bring in balanced regional development to alleviate poverty.

Rural entrepreneurship can be defined as entrepreneurship emerging at village level which can take place in a variety of fields of endeavour such as business, industry, agriculture and acts as a potent factor for economic development. In short, rural entrepreneurship implies rural industrialization consisting mainly of agro-based industries, khadi and village industries and cottage Industries. Industries coming under the purview of Khadi and Village Industries Commission (KVIC), Government of India organization, are treated as rural industries.

9.2 RURAL INDUSTRIES UNDER KVIC PURVIEW

'***Khadi***' means any cloth woven on handloom in India from cotton, silk and woolen yarn handspun in India or from a mixture of any two or all of such yarn. ***Village industry*** or ***rural industry*** means any industry located in rural area, population of which does not exceed 10,000 or such other figure which produces any goods or renders any services with or without use of power and in which the fixed capital investment per head (in plant and machinery and land and building of an artisan or a worker) does not exceed Rs 15,000.

Recently, the KVIC has broadly regrouped the various village industries for the purpose of implementation of its programmes. The list of industries is given as under, both existing and new:

(i) Mineral-based industry—existing/new
(ii) Forest-based industry
(iii) Agro-based and food-based industries
(iv) Polymer and chemical-based industries
(v) Engineering and non-conventional energy-based industries
(vi) Textile industry
(vii) Service industry

According to a report of Development Commissioner, Small Scale Industries (DCSSI), the basic objectives of rural industries projects are expeditious growth of small scale industries and creation of opportunities for fuller and additional productive employment in rural areas so as to improve the earning of the artisans and entrepreneurs.

However, the definition of village industries has been recently modified by the government so as to enlarge its scope. According to the modified definition, any industry located in rural area, village or town with a population of 20,000 and below and which can have investment of Rs 3 crores in plant and machinery is classified as a village industry. As a result of this, the scope of village industries was enlarged.

9.3 ADVANTAGES OF RURAL INDUSTRIALIZATION

Modern small scale enterprises have been incorporated in rural industries. These enterprises benefit the rural industries. Modern small industry implies a small industry which caters to the needs of the emerging modern economy, is progressive in outlook and adaptable to changing conditions in its production process and applies reasonably up-to-date ideas of organization and management in its business operation.

W. Lockwod, in the *Economic Development of Japan*, writes: "To a far greater degree, the Japanese succeeded in modern techniques of small establishment. Most important, they strengthen it with external economics introducing large scale organization in supply of raw materials, working capital and market". The integration of industry into the rural way of life substantially lowered both the transport and social costs of industrialization. The advantages of rural industries can be summarized as under:

(a) Rural industries can produce the best type of products where skilled labour of specific nature is required. Products requiring special attention to the taste and the fashion of individual customers like ornamental goods, traditional crafts, can be best produced by rural units.
(b) Products like specialized components of large industries can be manufactured at a less cost in small units in rural areas by means of subcontract system. As per the need of the hour, small enterprises and cottage industries can very well shift their production to support large machinery firms and large scale sector to meet their order. Thus, they can become ancillary units.
(c) The rural industries can take advantage of local resources, locational advantage using local raw materials, local skills and local experience and catering to the local demand thereby avoiding transaction cost.
(d) Small and cottage industries can be started with low capital investment as they have got low overhead cost. This is not possible in case of large industries.
(e) Small and rural industries can sustain for a long period of time due to cordial personal relationship between employer and employees.
(f) Small scale enterprises in rural areas meet a substantial part of increased demand for consumer goods including mass consumption items.
(g) Small scale and rural enterprises assist in dispersal and avoid problems which unplanned urbanization tends to develop.
(h) Rural enterprises create jobs in the rural areas of the developing countries where unemployment is rampant. This will also help in reducing the migration of workers from rural to urban sector.
(i) Rural industries help in integrating rural economy on one hand and large scale industries on the other.
(j) The marketing of rural industries products can be easily done since the customers are mostly local.
(k) Rural industrial enterprises are training grounds for local entrepreneurs on decision making and excellence in production. They help the growth of economy by nurturing entrepreneurial and managerial talents.

The role of rural industries is of paramount importance in our country due to above-mentioned advantages. China represents a unique example of rural entrepreneurial development with prima facie importance to the use of local resources such as natural resources, human resources and material resources for local economic, social and cultural development and for reinvesting within the local area the surpluses so generated and at the same time effectively integrating rural development with modernization in the urban sector. China's successful rural development through less dogmatic and down-to-earth approach to rural industrialization is really worth emulating for our country.

The importance of cottage and village industries was acknowledged by Mahatma Gandhi by his policy priorities on village upliftment including khadi and other village industries since Independence.

Table 9.1 exhibits the financial provisions made in various five year plans for the development of rural industries. In all the plans emphasis, has been increasing in absolute numbers from Rs 97 crores in the First Plan to Rs 19,708 crores in the Seventh Plan.

Table 9.1 Plan Outlays on Rural Industrialization

Plan period	*Public sector outlay (Rs)*	*Plan Provision*		*Percentage of public sector outlays*	
		Industry as a whole (Rs)	*Rural industry (Rs)*	*Industry as a whole*	*Rural industry*
First Plan	1960	97	42	4.95	2.1
Second Plan	4672	1125	187	24.08	4.0
Third Plan	8577	1967	241	22.93	2.8
Annual Plan	6625	1636	126	24.69	1.9
Fourth Plan	15779	3107	293	19.69	1.9
Fifth Plan	39426	9581	592	24.30	1.5
1979–80	12601	2636	289	20.94	2.3
Sixth Plan	97500	15018	1780	15.40	1.8
Seventh Plan	180000	19708	2753	10.95	1.5
Eighth Plan	434100	45175	6334	10.4	1.6

Source: Government of India, *Economic Survey*, 1982–83 and Seventh Five Year Plan, Vol. 1, Planning Commission, 1985–90.

From Table 9.1, it is evident that the percentage of the total public sector outlays in the industry on the whole was declining after the Second Plan, from 24.08 per cent in Second Plan to 10.95 per cent in the Seventh Plan. The expenditure on rural industries was increasing from Rs 42 crores in the First Plan to Rs 6334 crores in the Eighth Plan. Thus, each successive plan gave more and more importance to the development of rural industries.

The Industrial Policy Resolution of 1948 and the Industrial Policy Resolution of 1956 declared by the Government of India emphasized on both small scale and cottage industries for the achievement of self-sufficiency, creation of employment opportunities, equitable distribution of income by the utilization of local resources.

The First Five Year Plan gave stress upon the development of agriculture, industry, infrastructure and social services whereas the Second Five Year Plan gave much thought to the revival of cottage and village industries. Rural Industries Projects (RIPs) were taken up during Third Five Year Plan in 49 selected areas. These programmes aimed at the following things:

(a) To develop SSI, cottage and village industries sector for employment generation
(b) To help these industries in increasing the production of consumer goods and producer goods
(c) To secure integration between small scale industries and large scale industries and to develop SSIs as ancillaries
(d) To promote the small scale industries in rural areas along with emphasis on training facilities in rural centres
(e) To set up more number of prototype development training centres (PDTCs)
(f) To establish quality-making centres

In the Fourth Five Year Plan, the above process of rural industrialization sustained. Agro-industries and dispersal of industries in rural pockets were accepted as crucial element for industrialization.

The Fifth Five Year Plan was conspicuous enough to ensure industrial development in backward areas. The District Industries Centres (DICs) were set up to provide all services to the entrepreneurs under one roof. Area development approach was accepted in which development of village industries constituted an integral part. Similarly, in the Sixth Five Year Plan, rural industrialization was the main focus of development strategies. During this plan, small scale industry status was given to the industries in which investment in plant and machinery was up to Rs 20 lakhs and in case of ancillary units, investment in plant and machinery was up to Rs 35 lakhs.

The Seventh and Eighth Five Year Plans gave emphasis upon the role of institution in marketing, credit and technology. In order to give a boost to rural entrepreneurship, a number of projects relating to rural sector were earmarked by KVIC, viz. pottery, leather goods, ready-made garments, food processing, etc.

The Ninth Five Year Plan was significant from the point of view of undertaking development strategies for the Village Small Scale Industries (VSSI) sector. The key features of Ninth Five Year Plan are:

(a) Incentives will be provided to the small and village industries.
(b) Credit facilities will be increased.
(c) The investment will be revised to Rs 3 crores.
(d) Technology development and upgradation will secure special attention.
(e) Special attention to sericulture introduction and better breeding practices.
(f) Special emphasis will also be given on wool industry.

The performance of rural industries is exhibited in Table 9.2. The table also reveals that production, sales, earnings and employment level were at the increasing trend from year to year.

Table 9.2 Performance of Village Industries

(Rs in crores)

Year	*Production*	*Sales*	*Earning*	*Employment*
1971–72	93.69	81.24	16.30	8.38
1972–73	109.13	97.04	17.80	8.40
1973–74	122.40	115.64	22.16	9.28
1974–75	136.31	133.17	28.05	9.82
1975–76	148.48	151.58	35.21	11.21
1976–77	171.73	174.71	40.19	11.72
1977–78	192.54	190.29	50.10	14.94
1978–79	242.97	242.01	59.79	14.96
1979–80	347.98	358.97	78.84	16.13
1980–81	451.24	476.47	101.34	18.10
1989–90	170.53	1895.47	546.85	27.89
1990–91	1994.07	2228.97	647.31	29.21
1992–93	2523.45	2801.13	845.58	36.20
1996–97	3760.21	3926.20	1126.25	46.25
1997–98	3895.21	4319.38	1275.57	42.49

Source: *Annual Report* of *KVIC*, 1971–72 to 1997–98.

9.4 MAJOR CHALLENGES IN THE WAY OF DEVELOPMENT OF RURAL INDUSTRIES

The major challenges in the way of development of rural industries are as follows:

(a) To evolve strategies for developing captive market for rural industrial products
(b) To safeguard the micro-enterprises and micro-rural industries from the onslaught of large scale and multinational industrial houses
(c) To ensure better allocation of resources and control for products of rural industries
(d) To make the regulatory policies better suited to the development of rural enterprises
(e) To promote more modern types of processing industries which have strong backward linkages with farm activity
(f) To find solution from the problem of sickness in the field of rural industries and micro-enterprise sector
(g) To ensure access to information, credits and technology to rural industrial units
(h) To cope with the rural infrastructure which is a major constraint to non-farm sector development
(i) To motivate professionals in the field of finance for timely help to the rural entrepreneurs
(j) To impart need-based entrepreneurship development programme for entrepreneurs of rural areas in the field of enterprise launching and management

9.5 RECOMMENDATIONS TO BOOST UP RURAL ENTREPRENEURSHIP

The following recommendations are important in order to boost up rural entrepreneurship:

(a) Modernization of rural industrial sector and upgradation of rural skills that the rural entrepreneurs need should be augmented.

(b) Continuous supply of raw materials at reasonable prices should be ensured. An urgent policy and programme action is required to strengthen raw materials base. To avoid delay in sanction and disbursement of loan to the rural entrepreneurs, effective credit planning through coordination of financial institutions should be done. The bank officials should be motivated to help and act as guide to the rural entrepreneurs.

(c) Rural enterprises are very much prone to sickness. Therefore, a specific action agenda to link the production centres to markets in the urban areas has to be worked out. Legislative measures should be taken to involve all the government departments to give preference to the products of rural enterprises while prescribing other required items.

(d) Training in government schemes like SGSY, PMRY, Women development, Entrepreneurship Development Programmes (EDPs) should be comprehensive to deal with various aspects including modernization and expansion of enterprises.

(e) Training institutions like Institutes of Entrepreneurship Development (IEDs) and Centres for Entrepreneurship Development (CEDs) should be strengthened to organize more number of training programmes in rural areas.

(f) Common production-cum-marketing centres should be set up with modern infrastructural facilities. This will help in promoting expert and bringing close interaction between buyers and sellers and thus, eliminate the middlemen in marketing business.

(g) The redefined village industries may be fully exempted from excise and sales tax so as to make their production cost-effective.

(h) Rural saving potential has to be harnessed by suitable strategies. Micro-finance organizations both at governmental and cooperative sectors should be set up for producing concessional finance to rural entrepreneurs.

(i) A common marketing complex in every block should be established by the District Industries Centres (DICs) for marketing the rural products.

(j) Growth of entrepreneurship, managerial skill and reduction in industrial sickness can be made possible by requisite training programmes that can be undertaken by the training organizations in an extensive scale.

It is heartening to note that manufacturing enterprises in rural areas generally suffer from disabilities of outdated technology due to lack of awareness among the rural people regarding marketing, finance, trading and above all various self-employment schemes implemented by the government from time to time. So initiatives by government as well as participation from the people at large are necessary factors for development of rural entrepreneurship in India.

9.6 ENTREPRENEURSHIP THROUGH POVERTY ALLEVIATION PROGRAMMES

The government of India and State Governments in India have sponsored several self-employment generation and poverty alleviation programme from time to time to create an atmosphere of entrepreneurship in both urban and rural areas, viz. Integrated Rural Development Programme (IRDP), Training of Rural Youth for Self-Employment (TRYSEM), Development of Women and Children in Rural Areas (DWCRA), Jawahar Gram Samrudhi Yojana (JGSY), Swarnajayanti Gram Swarojgar Yojana (SGSY), Prime Minister's Rojgar Yojana (PMRY), Rural Employment Generation Programme (REGP) by KVIC, etc.

The above programmes have been implemented by the government to alleviate poverty on one hand and increase the self-employment potentialities through development of entrepreneurial spirit among youths, including women in rural and other areas. The planned outlay for rural development in the Ninth Plan was Rs 74686 crore. The figure in the Tenth Plan's outlay on rural development was further rose to Rs 1,21,928 crores which is 63.25 per cent more than the Ninth Plan's outlay for the same ahead. Increased plan outlay, therefore, can expand the scope of rural entrepreneurship and rural development.

9.7 EXCERPTS FROM FORMER PRIME MINISTER'S ADDRESS ON YOUTH ENTREPRENEURSHIP AND EMPLOYMENT

Former Prime Minister, Sri Atal Bihari Vijpayee, addressed the Asian Summit on Youth Entrepreneurship and Employment on October 30, 2003 at New Delhi. The following are the excerpts from his address:

"Employment is not merely a means of livelihood for young people, it is also the enabler of discovery, self-discovery and self-development. Youth is the age when life is most creative and joyful. It is the age when idealism blooms and social consciousness is sharpened. It is when young people begin to dream, and learn to struggle to realize their dreams. But all this is possible only if the minds and hands of young people are employed in gainful work. Thus, a large part of human resources in the world is lying idle due to large-scale unemployment—unable to contribute to society and unable to achieve self-growth.

Both globally and locally, we have to reorient our economic thinking, planning and implementation to achieve the goal of full employment everywhere. We should be prepared to reform anything that needs to be reformed to achieve this central goal—be it the global financial architecture, the world trade regime or the growth-obstructing laws and institutions at national and local levels. Another thing is also obvious. In developing countries, including India, the mindset of young people wanting government jobs has to be changed. In the era of reforms, the role of the government has changed. Rather than being directly engaged in running enterprises, the Government has to facilitate the sprit of enterprise among the people to grow.

We need to create a proper awareness among the youths about the various employment and self-employment schemes of the government. And we have so many of them. If young entrepreneurs and self-employed persons face any problems, it is the duty of concerned government officers and bank managers to quickly attend to these problems. Often, start-up business of small entrepreneurs fails and folds up because of lack of support and guidance. It should be our endeavour to de-risk these initiatives as much as possible. There is also a big scope for private sector investment in mentoring and fostering small enterprise in informal sector through appropriate linkages. NGOs and producers cooperatives can provide these linkages.

Change in India is visible not only in a high-visibility sector like IT-enabled services. Entrepreneurship employment and self-employment, are also growing in India's rural and semi-urban economy. Here I would like to congratulate the Khadi and Village Industries Commission (KVIC) for its success in running Rural Employment Generation Programme. I am told that under this programme, over 1.5 lakh small-scale production units have been set up by rural entrepreneurs. They are partly financed by banks and partly through the Government's budgetary support."

"Our Government is working towards the goal of creating ten million employment and self-employment opportunities each year. The S.P. Gupta Committee, set up by the Planning Commission, has prepared a useful report on how to achieve this goal. I would like the concerned ministries and departments to implement this employment strategy with utmost seriousness. State Governments should also fully contribute to its successful implementation".

"However, this strategy cannot succeed through governmental action alone. ***Eradication of unemployment*** is a mission. In carrying out this mission, we have to learn from others around the world and also share our positive experience with them".

EXERCISES

A. Long answer type questions:

1. Define rural entrepreneurship. Explain the need for entrepreneurship.
2. What are the advantages of rural entrepreneurship?
3. Discuss in brief the importance of cottage and village industries in India.
4. What are the challenges in the way of development of rural industries?
5. What are the different poverty alleviation programmes adopted by Govt of India to boost up rural entrepreneurship?
6. What recommendations can your suggest for developing rural entrepreneurship?

B. Short answer type questions:

1. Write short notes on the following:
   (a) Rural entrepreneurship
   (b) Cottage industries
   (c) Khadi and village industries
   (d) Poverty alleviation programmes
   (e) Prime Minister's Rojgar Yojana (PMRY)
   (f) Swarnajayanti Swarojgar Yojana (SGSY)
   (g) Khadi and Village Industries Commission (KVIC)
2. Define rural industry.

CHAPTER 10

Role of Entrepreneur

CHAPTER CONTENTS

10.1 INTRODUCTION

Entrepreneur plays a significant role in economic development of a country. Economic development greatly depends upon entrepreneurial and industrial development. In western countries, entrepreneurs have contributed a great deal in making their country developed. According to **Harbison**, entrepreneurs are prime movers of innovation and **Sayigh** describes entrepreneurship as a dynamic force. Indeed, entrepreneur is the person who perceives business opportunity and converts it into a viable business plan culminating into a business venture ultimately. The entrepreneur, therefore, not only launches a venture but also contributes to the objectives of employment creation, output growth, technological upgradation, improvement in the quality of production, export promotion, import substitution and supply of goods at a reasonable price to the customers.

Therefore, growth of entrepreneurship and development of entrepreneurial culture in underdeveloped and developing countries are imperatively needed not only for employment generation but also for infusing entrepreneurial culture in the society which is not so far exposed to it. Entrepreneurship may also help in skill formation and technological upgradation in developing countries. Efforts made by a group of entrepreneurs in motivating the youths to change their attitude for self-employment, thus, may lead to further creation of wealth through enterprise creation. The important role that an entrepreneur plays are described in next sections.

10.2 ROLE OF ENTREPRENEUR AS AN INNOVATOR IN ECONOMIC GROWTH

Entrepreneurship development is getting a position of great importance for tackling evergrowing problem of unemployment due to rapid population growth. Though the last decade of 20th century experienced the growth of a large number of small entrepreneurs in our country, the number of innovating entrepreneurs is less than the imitating entrepreneurs; as a result of which, the country has been lagging behind in moving at a pace which the international communities demand. Therefore, to cope with the international order and the dynamism of the society, an entrepreneur's role as an innovator is of prime importance. According to **J.A. Schumpeter**, an entrepreneur is basically an innovator who introduces new combinations of means of production. Development consists of carrying out new combinations. A new combination may be carried out by utilization of both used and unused means of production. According to **Schumpeter**, as an innovator, entrepreneur forces the potentially profitable opportunities to exploit it. He is a risk bearer, problem shooter and gets satisfaction in confronting problems. As an innovator, entrepreneur performs the following activities.

1. ***Bringing about new combinations:*** As an innovator, entrepreneur brings about the new combinations in the following manner:
   (a) Introduction of new products
   (b) Introduction of new techniques of production
   (c) Opening up of a new market
   (d) Conquest of new source of supply of raw materials or semi-finished goods
   (e) The carrying out of new organizations of any industry like the creation of monopoly.

   Further, entrepreneur's motivation is directed by the desire to found private commercial kingdom, the will power to conquer and to prove superiority and the joy of creating and getting things done.
2. ***Making use of potential technical knowledge for continuous technological progress:*** According to **Schumpeter,** there always exists potential technical knowledge which entrepreneur can make use of. Continuous technological progress will spearhead towards innovation. Entrepreneur, in fact, depends upon the following two important things to achieve economic rewards:

(a) The existence of technical knowledge in order to produce new products
(b) The power of dispersal over the factors of production in the form of credit

However, innovation results in steady increase in total output and per capita output since historically diminishing return does not operate in case of technological progress. From the point of view of achieving economic development, it is necessary that underdeveloped countries should use ***innovation*** as an important tool of economic development.

3. ***Emphasizing on purposeful and systematic innovation:*** Like Schumpeter, Drucker also emphasized on the role of entrepreneur as an innovator. He pointed out that purposeful and systematic innovations begin with the analysis of opportunities and a successful innovation should aim at leadership. This quality is one of the most crucial attributes of the entrepreneur to bring about economic development. As entrepreneurship development and economic development are interlinked, changes in perception of the individuals are imperative. This will give rise to considerable innovative opportunities. Further, knowledge-based innovations are required for development of entrepreneurship.

   In fact, entrepreneurs with innovative traits are more common in developed countries than in underdeveloped countries. These entrepreneurs historically, have played key roles in the rise of modern capitalism, the factory system, enterprising spirit, hope of money-making, ability to perceive and explore opportunities thereby bringing about economic development.

4. ***Implementation of mechanical skills:*** According to Hoselitz, the founders of early industrial establishments in England, France and Germany were men with mechanical rather than commercial and financial skills. These men came from the ranks of artisans, labourers, yeomen and cottagers. A few of them were the sons of middle class parents. But the earliest entrepreneurs are men who worked with their hands, whose innovations were in the field of technology and who, in their majority, came from the lower, propertyless class. Thus, technology innovations and creativity played the crucial role in encouraging entrepreneurship and economic development.

   Innovations give rise to utilization of innovative talents which initiate and improve the economic growth in the following ways:

   (a) Improvement in per capita income
   (b) Increase in capital formation
   (c) Generation of employment opportunities
   (d) Balanced growth
   (e) Improvement in standard of living
   (f) Economic independence
   (g) Backwards and forward linkages
   (h) Technological advancement
   (i) Establishment of new form of organization
   (j) Entrepreneurial competency development

To conclude with B.V. Vaidya, a retired senior civil servant, the present age is an age of innovation. Doing a new thing or doing an old thing in a new way demands research and development section and this section is the most important from the point of view of unit's future progress. Hence, the role of entrepreneur as an innovator is considered the most crucial element for acceleration of economic growth.

10.3 ROLE OF ENTREPRENEUR IN GENERATION OF EMPLOYMENT OPPORTUNITIES

Entrepreneur plays a significant role in generation of employment opportunities. As we all know, entrepreneurship is a purposeful activity indulged in initiating, stimulating, promoting and maintaining economic activities for production and distribution of goods and commodities, the person behind these economic activities is, therefore, a critical factor as well as an integral component of socio-economic transformation. The development strategy of our country confronts two important problems—unemployment and poverty of the masses. These problems can be effectively minimized by activating the latent human potentials through entrepreneurship. This leads to the creation of self-employment and wage-employment avenues for large number of people.

For reduction of unemployment, entrepreneurship in small and tiny sector industries, both in manufacturing and service sectors, is imperatively needed. Thus, the role of entrepreneur and its significance in generation of employment opportunities can be depicted under the following heads.

1. ***Establishing tiny, micro and small scale enterprises:*** Role of entrepreneur in establishing the above types of enterprises is perceived as a powerful medium to address several socio-economic issues and the chief among them is generation of employment opportunities for millions. In a developing economy like India, where population pressure is quite high and the job employment is limited, the role of entrepreneur is very much significant. Entrepreneurial development gives rise to economic independence through self-employment. Creation of tiny, micro and small enterprises by the entrepreneurs can lead to creation of both self-employment and wage-employment opportunities, thereby solving the problem of unemployment in the economy.
2. ***Giving emphasis upon village and cottage industries:*** Upliftment of economically-backward sections of the society can be made possible if self-employment opportunities can be provided at the grass root level. To enable these people in backward regions of the state to set up village and cottage industries, government has implemented several antipoverty programmes like PMRY, TRYSEM, SGSY, REGP etc. and the importance of entrepreneurs in cottage and village industries sector has been clearly acknowledged by Mahatma Gandhi by his policy priorities in village upliftment including khadi and village industries in his famous ***constructive programme*** in 1922. Prior to Independence, cottage industries and handicraft production located in rural areas had occupied a distinct place in Indian economy because of their high potential in employment generation and income creation especially in rural and backward areas. As such, entrepreneur can play a significant role in setting up and

reviving the cottage and village industries, thereby creating employment opportunities to a large number of people living in rural and backward pockets of the country.

3. ***Utilising the surplus labour force in industrial activities:*** India is a primary producing country. This characteristic feature is further accentuated by the seasonality feature of the agriculture. Therefore, for a large part of the year, people remain unemployed. Disguised unemployment is a chronic phenomenon in agriculture wherein more people work in a field than actually required. So the surplus labour force is transferred and utilized by the entrepreneur in non-farm sector activities like small tiny, cottage and village industries which are labour intensive in nature.
4. ***Employment argument:*** It would be worthwhile to mention employment argument favouring the growth of small scale enterprise and the role of entrepreneur in accelerating this growth. In this regard, the report of Karve Committee can be quoted. According to the Committee: "The principle of self-employment is at least as important to a successful democracy as that of self-government. As the small scale enterprises are labour intensive, they create more employment per unit of capital employed. So entrepreneurs should be encouraged to put up small scale enterprises so as to create large number of employment avenues for others".

10.4 ROLE OF ENTREPRENEUR IN COMPLEMENTING AND SUPPLEMENTING ECONOMIC GROWTH

The classical economists like **Adam Smith** and **David Ricardo** did not recognize the role of entrepreneur at all. **Adam Smith** considered the rate of capital formation as the key component of economic growth. Ricardo suggested two policy variables namely socio-cultural environments and technological improvements which increase the marginal productivity of labour and capital. Thus, in both the analyses, the role of entrepreneur is totally ignored. But **Schumpeter** postulates that the rate of economic progress of a country depends largely upon its rate of innovation, which in turn, depends upon the entrepreneurial talents. According to **Schumpeter**, technological development cannot alone bring about economic growth unless they are put to practical use by the entrepreneurs. Similarly, **Peter Drucker** has also emphasized that this is the age of entrepreneurial society. Economic development and growth of a country depends to a great extent upon effective entrepreneurship. In his opinion, entrepreneur plays a crucial role for the creation of new small enterprises that energize the economic structure. Through constant creativity, new businessmen/entrepreneurs assure a strong economy and rising national income. Thus, the role of entrepreneur is important, as it not only complements but also supplements the economic growth of the country. To be more clear, entrepreneurs initiate, increase and sustain the economic growth in the following ways:

1. ***Generation of employment:*** Entrepreneurs generate employment opportunities, both direct and indirect, through establishment of small scale enterprises. These enterprises are conspicuous enough to create large volume of employment and as a result of which unemployment is reduced. As we all know, small scale enterprises create

immediate and permanent employment at a relatively small capital, and these industries are imperatively needed for our country which is rapidly heading towards economic growth.

2. ***Capital formation:*** Capital formation is the most crucial element for economic growth. It is always necessary to step up the rate of capital formation so that the economy accumulates a large stock of machines, tools, equipments which can be geared into production by the entrepreneur. Besides, capital formation in the economy can be brought about by the formation and upgradation of skills of human capital in terms of knowledge and skills which can be utilized to raise the level of productivity whereby economic growth can be accelerated
3. ***Increase in per capita income:*** We all are aware of the fact that economic growth is measured in terms of a sustained increase in real per capita income over a period of time. It is the entrepreneurial communities who complement and supplement the economic growth in increasing the per capita income and Net National Product of the country by identifying and establishing profitable business ventures.
4. ***Improvement in physical quality of life:*** Entrepreneurs supplement the economic growth in enhancing the physical quality of life. This implies that increase in life expectancy and increase in literacy. Establishment of enterprise leads to increase in employment avenues both directly and indirectly. Consequently, poverty is alleviated and per capita income grows. This results in improving the physical quality of life which is an indicator of economic growth.
5. ***Improvement in standard of living:*** Entrepreneurs establish different types of enterprises so as to improve the standard of living of the masses. They produce innovative products and help to improve the standard of living of the common man. Innovative and modern gadgets in a variety of designs and patterns manufactured by the entrepreneurs make the life of each individual easier. In this way, entrepreneurs complement the standard of living and economic well-being of the people.
6. ***Growth of infrastructural facilities:*** Entrepreneurs play a major role in the growth of infrastructural facilities such as roads, bridges, buildings, factories, etc. which are the cornerstones of economic growth. Establishment of factories and industries in a particular locality presupposes the growth of infrastructural facilities.
7. ***Economic independence:*** Entrepreneurship helps the country in achieving economic independence. In other words, national self-reliance can be ensured due to the growth of entrepreneurship. In augmenting the indigenous technologies and their uses in massive way in small scale enterprises, dependence on foreign technologies can be avoided. Entrepreneurs can also export their goods and commodities and thereby earn the scarce foreign exchange for the country. Hence, entrepreneurs act as the agents of economic growth.
8. ***Backward and forward linkages:*** Entrepreneurs initiate change in the economy by way of forward and backward linkages. Establishment of a giant unit generates several ancillary industries on one hand and several other industries which grow by utilizing the raw materials and bye products produced by the mother plant on the other. In this way, entrepreneurs supplement the economic growth.

As such, entrepreneurs play a significant role in supplementing and complementing economic growth. To conclude with the words of Meir and Baldwin: "Development in an economy does not occur spontaneously as a natural consequence when economic conditions in some sense are right. A catalyst or agent is needed. This agent is entrepreneur".

10.5 ROLE OF ENTREPRENEUR IN BRINGING ABOUT SOCIAL STABILITY AND BALANCED REGIONAL DEVELOPMENT OF INDUSTRIES

Entrepreneur plays a crucial role in bringing about social stability and balanced regional development. In each and every country, entrepreneur is considered as a valuable human resource. The responsibility of social stability lies on his shoulders. Entrepreneur, as a catalyst of change, tries to bring about social stability in the following ways:

1. ***Absorption of workforce in industries:*** Establishment of small scale units by the entrepreneurs leads to absorption of a large number of workforce at a relatively small capital cost and ensures social stability.
2. ***Alleviation of poverty:*** Entrepreneurs help in alleviating poverty by reducing unemployment through creation of large number of jobs by way of setting of small and tiny units. Thus, social stability is maintained.
3. ***Glorification of self-help:*** Enterprise creation glorifies the maxim of self-help. Self-help is the best help because it is a binding factor to unite family, clan, village communities, etc. and thus, ensures social stability.
4. ***Checking expansion of monopolies:*** Small scale enterprises help to bring about social stability by diffusing prosperity and by checking the expansion of monopolies.
5. ***Equitable distribution of income:*** Small scale entrepreneurs explore business opportunities in both rural and urban areas, thereby leading to equitable distribution of income and wealth in the society. This gives rise to reduction in social instability between rural and urban sectors.
6. ***Creation of social infrastructures:*** Entrepreneurs facilitate economic development and social stability through creation of social infrastructures like schools, colleges, health care centres, vocational institutes, banking and insurance facilities, roads and buildings etc. consequent upon establishment of industries.
7. ***Empowerment of women through enterprise:*** Women entrepreneurs are the prime movers of women empowerment. In this context, empowerment through enterprise involves access to resources and markets, actual ownership and active control. These things lead to equity and equality among men and women and act as a lever for social stability.
8. ***Supply of qualitative goods and services:*** Entrepreneurs can bring about supplying quality goods and services to the people. They manufacture both consumer's and producer's goods to meet the ever-growing demand which emerges due to population pressure.

The role of entrepreneur is also of paramount importance in bringing about balanced regional development. The following points justify this role of the entrepreneur.

(a) Setting up industries in rural and backward areas
(b) Establishing agro-based industries to coordinate the dispersal process and development of agriculture
(c) Utilizing indigenous technology for creation of enterprise in backward areas
(d) Developing handicraft and cottage industries sector for eliminating regional imbalance and to bring about balanced regional development
(e) Establishing industries in rural and backward regions and availing concessional finance, investment subsidy, transport subsidy, etc. provided by the government to reduce disparity

The strategy of balanced growth has been discussed by many economists like **R. Nurkse, H. Leibenstein, Rosenstein Rodan, W.A. Lewis,** etc. The whole idea revolves round the need for simultaneity of investment in many and varied industries. However, to bring about balanced regional development, the role of entrepreneur is very much important as far as the creation of industries in backward areas is concerned. As small scale industries bring about greater equality, it can stimulate the balanced regional development. Entrepreneurs can tap the local resources like raw materials, labour, idle savings, local talents, local experience and locally-available technology to create enterprises in the backward areas. Thus, it will improve standard of living of the people in rural areas by creation of employment and income.

In this context, the views given by the President of India Dr. A.P.J. Abdul Kalam, can be elaborated. Fearing instability in social structure in India, he suggested a multi-pronged strategy to make education more attractive and simultaneously create more employment potential. According to him: "Our employment generation system is not in a position to absorb graduates passing out from the universities leading to increase in educated unemployment year after year. This situation will lead to instability in the social structure. The educational system should highlight importance of entrepreneurship and prepare the students right from the college education to get oriented towards setting up of enterprises which will provide them creativity, freedom and ability to generate wealth".

President Kalam also strongly favours the banking system which can provide venture capital right from the village level to prospective entrepreneurs for undertaking new enterprises. According to him there is a need to identify marketable products and enhancement of purchasing power among the people. Thus, entrepreneurs can help economy not only by creating sufficient job opportunities but also by bringing about social stability and balanced regional development.

10.6 ROLE OF ENTREPRENEUR IN EXPORT PROMOTION AND IMPORT SUBSTITUTION

In recent years, liberalization, privatization and globalization have opened up a vista of export opportunities for entrepreneurs in India. They have evinced their interest in setting up industries which are export-oriented in nature. They also find it more lucrative to establish industrial units which produce import substitutes thereby making India self-reliant. As such, the role of entrepreneur is of fundamental importance as far as export promotion and import substitution are concerned. The role of entrepreneur in promotion of exports and substitution of imports for the development of the country is discussed further.

10.6.1 Export Promotion

1. ***Minimization of dependence on imports from abroad:*** Entrepreneurs are interested in manufacturing consumer goods as well as capital goods in the country in order to minimize dependence on foreign countries. Establishment of small industries for FMCG (Fast Moving Consumer Goods) as well as consumer durables makes the country self-sufficient and thus, they help in accelerating economic development.
2. ***Exploration of new markets:*** It is found out that market for certain goods within the country may not be sufficient to absorb the entire production and thus exploration of new markets is necessary. Entrepreneurs can explore the possibilities of new market abroad and can create conducive environment for sale of goods and services.
3. ***Foreign exchange earning:*** Growth of small scale industries gives rise to higher production of goods and commodities. In our country, industrialization particularly in small and tiny sectors resulted in higher level of production of qualitative products and as such our country is in a position to reap the advantage of getting large export earning consequent upon large volume of exports. Entrepreneurs, nowadays, come forward to establish 100 per cent EOUs (Export-Oriented Units) because of the availability of Export Processing Zones (EPZs) at several places in India. More of exports lead to more of export earnings and thus, increase of foreign exchange reserve.
4. ***Lessening the burden of debt servicing:*** The role of entrepreneur is important as far as the principle of debt servicing is concerned. Establishment of 100 per cent Export-Oriented Units (EOUs) for certain items by the entrepreneurs can bring about the benefit of earning foreign exchange on one hand and lessening the burden of debt servicing on the other. Moreover, expansion of the base of exports can reap the benefit of large-scale production.
5. ***Harnessing the available resources:*** India is rich with natural resources as well as manpower resources. In recent years, India has an increased supply of sophisticated manpower, especially in IT sector and highly-skilled human resources in streams like physical sciences, engineering and technology. They can be properly guided to set up their own industries. With this comparative advantage, entrepreneurs can establish industrial units in computer hardware and software, electronics, casting, machine buildings, metal products, transport equipments, consumer durables, animal husbandry and food-processing industries, etc.
6. ***Export of handicraft items:*** Entrepreneurs play a significant role in producing and exporting handicraft items. They generally use the local traditional skill, traditional technology, local knowledge and experience for producing traditional art and craft

and handicraft items which are having great demand, nowadays, in foreign markets, mainly jewelleries, carpets, stone carvings, appliqué works, etc.

7. ***Meeting balance of payments deficits:*** Expansion of exports increases the foreign exchange earnings and helps in meeting balance of payments deficits considerably.

However, to help entrepreneurs in exporting their items the following agencies have been set up by the government in the country:

(i) State Trading Corporation (STC)
(ii) Minerals and Metals Trading Corporation (MMTC)
(iii) Handicrafts and Handloom Export Corporation (HHEC)
(iv) Trade Development Authority of India (TDA)
(v) Trade Fair Authority of India (TFAI)
(vi) Department of Export Promotion and Marketing at the State level (DEPM)
(vii) Export Promotion Councils (EPCs).

In fact, establishment of these agencies has facilitated the scope and nature of exports in India and improved the trade relation between India and other countries.

10.6.2 Import Substitution

By import substitution we mean expansion of domestic production and replacement of the imports, mainly capital goods. This can be done by the entrepreneurs who can encourage the use of indigenous technology and reduction in dependence on technical know-how from abroad.

The role of entrepreneur in import substitution can be viewed mainly from the following angles:

(i) To achieve self-reliance in production of as many goods as possible
(ii) To save foreign exchange for import of goods

In a developing country, at initial stage, dependence on foreign technology is considerably high for the establishment of new industries; but in course of development, besides sophisticated technology, the emphasis is shifted to research and development of domestic technology to produce goods and commodities which are the import substitutes.

Again in our country, the policy of import substitution resulted in a great deal of change in import items. Many items which were imported earlier are not imported at all or imported in small quantities nowadays. Imports account for only less than 10 per cent of the total supply in many crucial sectors. The measures adopted by the government for import substitution in India are the policy of protection, heavy import duties, encouragement to use indigenously-manufactured technologies, use of local experience in innovative techniques of production etc.

Thus, the reason behind the policy of export promotion and import substitution is to prevent disequilibrium in the balance of payments and depletion of foreign exchange reserve which is vital for development and growth.

10.7 ROLE OF ENTREPRENEUR IN FOREIGN EXCHANGE EARNINGS AND AUGMENTING AND MEETING LOCAL DEMAND

The earnings of small scale sector have been increasing at a faster rate and so also the forex earnings. Increase in exports brings about increase in foreign exchange earnings and thereby helping to achieve a favourable balance of payments. We all know that expansion of exports is the kingpin of any policy of solving the problem of deficit and increase of foreign exchange earnings. The entrepreneurs of small scale units, therefore, play a great role in augmenting exports and thereby leading to earnings of foreign exchange reserve which is much needed for the development of a country like ours.

In order to earn more foreign exchange, entrepreneurs in India have come forward and motivated themselves to improve their exports and regulate their imports. The underlying aim of such export is to reduce the dependence on foreign assistance on any type and from any resource to the minimum. The balance of payments constraint is also eliminated.

Foreign trade acts as an engine of growth for the underdeveloped countries. Nowadays, entrepreneurs of developing countries are no longer exporters of primary products and importers of manufactured goods. According to GATT (General Agreement on Tariffs and Trade), they import only one-third of their total consumption of manufactured articles and even this proportion is on the decline. They produce the remaining two-third at their home. In fact, entrepreneurs in India today have given much emphasis on export promotion and import substitution. The exports mainly consists of textiles, light engineering goods, machine tools, steels, jute items, tea, gems and jewellery, machinery and engineering goods and leather products. Table 10.1 reveals the item-wise exports from small scale enterprises.

Table 10.1 Exports from Small Scale Entreprises.

Product group	*Total export*		*Share of SSI sector*		*Percentage share of SSI sector*	
	1992–93	1997–98	1992–93	1997–98	1992–93	1997–98
Non-traditional products:						
Engineering goods including electrical and electronics	6450	16376	1950	4400	30.23	26.86
Basic chemicals—pharma-ceutical and cosmetics	3623	10838	1992	6502	55.00	59.99
Chemicals and allied products	4299	8574	119	480	2.81	5.59
Plastic products	389	2339	175	985	45.02	42.11
Finished leather and leather products	3692	5875	2954	3263	80.00	55.52
Marine products	1767	4967	507	2692	28.67	57.31
Processed food	1293	7108	840	4620	65.00	64.99

(*Contd.*)

Table 10.1 Contd.

Product group	*Total export*		*Share of SSI sector*		*Percentage share of SSI sector*	
	1992–93	1997–98	1992–93	1997–98	1992–93	1997–98
Woolen garments and knitwear	595	1948	208	1353	35.00	69.45
Sports goods	94	241	94	241	100	100
Ready-made garments	8840	18389	7957	16551	90.00	90.00
Rayon and synthetic products	N.A.	3750	15	13.56	_	36.40
Processed tobacco stuff and bidi	382.06	508	1062	240	358	47.30
Traditional products:						
Cashew kernel and cashew nut shell liquid	749.23	1427	642.46	1427	85.75	100.00
Lac	53	65	51	64	97.85	99.00
Spices, oils, oleoresins	382	1408	10	14	261	10
Total	**32666**	**84097**	**17751**	**44442**	**54.44**	**52.84**

Source: Office of DCSSI.

According to the recently released data on foreign trade for 2003–2004 of the Ministry of Commerce, exports reached $161.8 billion and registered a growth rate 17.26 per cent which is far ahead of the official target of 12 per cent fixed at the beginning of the year. This has happened despite apprehensions by the exporting community that the recent appreciation of the rupee against the dollar had made Indian exports less competitive in world markets. Therefore, the exporting entrepreneurs needed to be complemented for their enterprise which, along with facilitating environment being created with the country, has helped India achieve this commendable performance in exports. During this period, India's imports stood at $ 75.2 billion. But considering the size of the country and the immense economic potential and skilled manpower, the achievement is dismal and therefore, entrepreneurs should take further initiative to produce import substitutions inside the country.

It is a good sign that India's foreign exchange reserve has been increased from $ 41 billion to over $ 116 billion and has been surging every week. This has been a major factor in appreciation of the rupee in recent months. Many South Asian countries had experienced this upward trend in their foreign exchange reserves. It is but natural that for India to assume a new global status in the changing scenario, the country should also have a more vibrant export sector entrepreneurs, rather than tinker with this vital economic activity.

In our country, opportunities exist for entrepreneurs to establish SSI units for production and exports of leather goods, plastic materials, processed food items and software. Simultaneously, a large number of constraints exist in the way of development of exports.

Major constraints are lack of infrastructure facilities, inadequate credit facilities and technological constraints. All the same, entrepreneurs are being encouraged to establish 100 per cent Export-Oriented Units (EOUs) by the Government and a package of incentives like tax holidays, land at cheaper rates, etc. are being given to the entrepreneurs. Through establishment of EOUs and production of quality items, entrepreneurs of small scale units play the most crucial role in augmenting exports for earning the much needed foreign exchange reserve not only for meeting fluctuations in the country's trade but also for generating employment opportunities mitigating fluctuations in balance of payments. Further, proper use of forex earnings is always expected so as to accelerate the tempo of economic development of the country.

Entrepreneurs also play a significant role in augmenting local demand. Focus of the entrepreneurs should spearhead towards production of such items which are demanded locally and can be manufactured through indigenous technology, locally-available skill, locally-available resources and local experiences. Government should encourage entrepreneurs to create demand for the goods which are locally manufactured as the prices of goods are normally low because of low cost of production due to proper guidance, provision of adequate incentives in the forms of capital investment subsidies price preferences, tax exemption, tax holidays, electricity duty exemption, etc. provided by the government from time to time. Specific industries are being promoted to augment local demand as well as to compete with the products of large scale enterprises.

While setting up enterprise, entrepreneurs should take into account the basic factors of the locality-like size of customers for the goods to be produced, frequency of demand for the goods, tastes and preferences of the customers, pattern of demand for the goods, availability of substitutes whether the items are traditional or non-traditional items, etc. In order to expand the local demand, small scale entrepreneurs in India are striving hard to expand at a faster rate than ever-increasing large scale sector. They can be capable of expanding it further if production of innovative goods with the help of locally-available resources, manpower, skill, technology, experiences can be made uninterruptedly by them so as to meet the increased demands of the local consumers. This will give rise to reduction of unemployment in the locality on one hand and generation of employment opportunities on the other; and consequent upon which the per capita income of the people will increase along with the increase in purchasing power leading to augmentation of effective demand of the people. Thus, the role of entrepreneur is of fundamental importance to a locality for augmenting local demand.

EXERCISES

A. Long answer type questions:

1. Discuss the role of entrepreneur in economic growth as an innovator.
2. Discuss the role of entrepreneur in generation of employment opportunities.
3. Explain the role of entrepreneur in complementing and supplementing economic growth.

4. Briefly discuss the role of entrepreneur in bringing about social stability and balanced regional development.
5. Discuss the role of entrepreneur in export promotion and import substitution.
6. Briefly discuss the role of entrepreneurs in forex earning and augmenting and meeting local demand.
7. Discuss the importance of the role of entrepreneur in augmenting and meeting local demand.

B. Short answer type question:

1. Write short notes on the following:
   (a) Regional balanced development
   (b) Export promotion
   (c) Import substitution
   (d) Foreign exchange earning
   (e) Export processing zones
   (f) 100 per cent Export-Oriented Units (EOUs)
   (g) Export promotion councils
   (h) Augmentation of local demand
2. Describe the following in five lines only:
   (a) Economic development through entrepreneurship
   (b) Economic growth through entrepreneurial initiatives
   (c) Balance of payment deficits and effective entrepreneurship
   (d) Export promotion organization
   (e) Indigeneous technology and import substitution.

Review Exercises

REVIEW EXERCISES 1

1. Define entrepreneurship. Explain the need for entrepreneurship development in India.
2. Discuss the characteristics of a successful entrepreneur.
3. Discuss the various steps in promotion of a venture.
4. Discuss various economic theories of entrepreneurship.
5. Distinguish between innovation and invention. State and explain the theory of innovation.
6. "Entrepreneurs are made, not born". Explain.
7. Elucidate briefly the scope and role of entrepreneurship in developing economies.
8. What are the objectives and functions of EDI?
9. Write short notes on:
   (a) Venture capital
   (b) Women entrepreneurship
   (c) Opportunity analysis
10. Distinguish between:
    (a) Entrepreneur and intrapreneur
    (b) Entrepreneur and professional manager
    (c) Entrepreneurship and enterprise

REVIEW EXERCISES 2

1. Define the term entrepreneur. What are the basic characteristics of an entrepreneur?
2. Explain the Theory of Achievement Motivation propounded by David McClelland.
3. Discuss the environmental factors affecting entrepreneur.
4. Discuss the need and relevance of EDP in India.
5. What is social responsibility? Discuss the social responsibility of the entrepreneur towards the various sections of the society.
6. Write short notes on the following:
   (a) Objectives of EDP
   (b) SIDBI
   (c) DIC
   (d) Venture capital
7. What are the national level promotional agencies working for the development of SSIs?
8. Define SSI. What are the national level financial institutions in India for providing financial assistance to SSI units?
9. Discuss the objectives and functions of NIESBUD.
10. Discuss the role of entrepreneur in promoting balanced regional development.

REVIEW EXERCISES 3

1. Distinguish between entrepreneurs and entrepreneurship. What are the functions of entrepreneur?
2. Briefly explain the emergence of entrepreneurial classes in India in pre-Independence era.
3. What are the social functions generating entrepreneurial growth?
4. Discuss the social responsibility of an entrepreneur.
5. Define women entrepreneurship. What are the problems faced by the women entrepreneurs in India?
6. Write short notes on the following:
   (a) IDBI
   (b) UTI
   (c) SIDBI
7. Distinguish between
   (a) Imitative entrepreneurs and innovative entrepreneurs
   (b) Drone entrepreneurs and Fabian entrepreneurs

(c) Export promotion and export financing
(d) Industrial entrepreneurs and agricultural entrepreneurs

8. Explain the objectives and various phases of EDPs.
9. Discuss, in a netshell, the entrepreneurial environment.
10. Explain the role of KVIC in promotion of rural entrepreneurship.

REVIEW EXERCISES 4

1. Discuss the characteristics of an entrepreneur.
2. Explain how opportunity analysis helps the entrepreneur in promotion of venture.
3. Explain briefly the need hierarchy theory propounded by Maslow.
4. What is EDP? State and explain the role, relevance and achievement of EDPs in India?
5. Explain briefly the social factors which influence the growth of entrepreneurship.
6. Discuss the role of entrepreneurs in economic growth.
7. Write short notes on the following:
   (a) IPRs
   (b) DICs
   (c) SFCs
   (d) EDPs
   (e) 100 per cent EOUs
8. Distinguish between:
   (a) Intrapreneur and ultrapreneur
   (b) Women entrepreneurship and rural entrepreneurship
   (c) Entrepreneur and enterprise
   (d) Small scale industries and tiny sector industries.
9. Explain the role played by an entrepreneur in import substitution and export promotion.
10. What are the objectives and functions of state level entrepreneurship institutes and centres?

Glossary

CB	:	Commercial Bank
CCEI	:	Chief Controller of Exports and Imports
CECD	:	Central Excise and Custom Department
CIF	:	Chief Inspector of Factories
CIPET	:	Central Institute of Plastic and Engineering Tools
CITD	:	Central Institute of Tool Design
CSIR	:	Council of Scientific and Industrial Research
DDCA	:	Director of Drugs Control Administration
DEP	:	Director of Export Promotion
DGSD	:	Director General of Supply and Disposal
DGTD	:	Director General of Technical Directorate
DIC	:	District Industries Centre
DWCRA	:	Development of Women and Children in Rural Areas
EB	:	Electricity Board
EDI	:	Entrepreneurship Development Institute, India
EDP	:	Entrepreneurship Development Programme
EPC	:	Export Promotion Council
FMCG	:	Fast Moving Consumer Goods

GMD	:	Geology and Mining Department
ICAR	:	Indian Council of Agricultural Research
ICICI	:	Industrial Credit and Investment Corporation of India
ICMR	:	Indian Council of Medical Research
IDBI	:	Industrial Development Bank of India
IDCS	:	Industrial Development Corporation (State level)
IEB	:	Industrial Extension Bureau (State level)
IFCI	:	Industrial Finance Corporation of India
IIC	:	Indian Investment Centre
IICS	:	Industrial Investment Corporation (State level)
IIFT	:	Indian Institute of Foreign Trade
IPB	:	Invention Promotion Board
IRL	:	Industrial Research Laboratory
ISI	:	Indian Standards Institute
LA	:	Local Authority—Municipal, Panchayat, etc.
LC	:	Leasing Companies
MDC	:	Mineral Development Corporation
MID	:	Ministry of Industrial Development
MMTC	:	Minerals and Metal Trading Corporation
NIDC	:	National Institute of Development Corporation
NIESBUD	:	National Institute of Entrepreneurship and Small Business Development
NIMSME	:	National Institute for Micro, Small and Medium Enterprises
NRDC	:	National Research and Development Corporation
NSIC	:	National Small Industry Corporation
PMEGP	:	Prime Minister's Employment Generation Programme
PTC	:	Polytechnology Transfer Centre
RD	:	Registrar of Companies
REGP	:	Rural Employment Generation Programme
RIMCO	:	Rural Industries and Marketing Corporation
RT	:	Registrar of Trademarks
SBI	:	State Bank of India
SC	:	Salt Commissioner
SCPO	:	State Chemical and Pharmaceutical Organization of India

SEC	:	State Export Corporation
SFC	:	State Finance Corporation
SGSY	:	Swarna Jayanti Swarojgar Yojana
SIDO	:	Small Industries Development Organization
SISI	:	Small Industries Service Institute
SSIC	:	State Small Industries Corporation
STC	:	State Trading Corporation
TC	:	Textile Commissioner
TCO	:	Technical Consultancy Organization of the State
TRYSEM	:	Training of Rural Youth for Self-employment
WPCB	:	Water Pollution Control Board

Bibliography

Books:

1. Agarwal, R.N., *Indian Economy*, Vikash Publishing House, New Delhi, 1980.
2. Arke Bauer B. James, *Ultrapreneurship*, McGraw-Hill.
3. Desai, A.N., *Environment and Entrepreneur*, Ashis Publishing House, New Delhi, 1989.
4. Desai, Vasant, *Dynamics of Entrepreneurial Development and Management,* Himalaya Publishing House, Mumbai, 1997.
5. Desai, Vasant, *Management of Small Scale Industry*, Himalaya Publishing House.
6. Dutta Ruddar and Sundharum, K.P.M., *Indian Economy*, S. Chand & Co, New Delhi, 1984.
7. Gupta C.B. and Srinivasan, N.P., *Entrepreneurial Development,* Sultanchand and Sons, New Delhi, 1992.
8. Jhingan M.L., *The Economics of Development and Planning*, Vikash Publishing House, New Delhi, 1989.
9. Kao, J.J., *Entrepreneurship, Creativity and Organization,* Prentice Hall, Englewood Cliffs, New Jersey, 1989.
10. Khanka, S.S., *Entrepreneurial Development,* S. Chand & Co., New Delhi, 1999.
11. Rao, Laxman, V., *Industrial Entrepreneurship,* Chugh Publications, Allahabad, 1986.
12. Ray, Rajat, *Entrepreneurship and Industry in India*, 1800–1947, OUP, New Delhi, 1993.

13. Rani C. and Raju, V.B., *A Trainer's Handbook for Developing Enterprise among Women,* Tata McGraw-Hill, New Delhi, 1999.

14. Sahoo, B., *Rural Industrialization*, Books and Books, Cuttack.

15. Schumpeter, J.A., *The Theory of Economic Development*, Harvard University Press, Massachusetts.

16. Cohen, William, A., *The Entrepreneur and Small Business Problem Solver* (An Encyclopedic Reference and Guide), Ronald Press, John Wiley & Sons, 1983.

17. Trivedi, M., *Entrepreneurship Among Tribals*, PWP, Printwell, Jaipur, 1991.

18. Zafar, Altaf, *Entrepreneurship in the Third world*, Groom Helms, 1988.

Research Papers

1. Akhouri, M.M.P. and Vinod Gupta, *Sustaining Entrepreneurship* (Seminar Proceedings), NIESBUD, New Delhi, 1990.

2. Patil, S.M., *Experience in Managing Technology in HMT*, Seminar at IIS, Bangalore, 21 Sept. 1999, organized by DSIR, GOI with ASCI.

3. Raju, U.B., *Sedme,* Journal, Special Issues on Entrepreneurship, Vol. 29, Number 4, December 2002, NIMSME, Hyderabad.

4. Rao, Jayasrinivasa, S., *Sedme,* Journal.

5. Sinha, S.K., *Experience in Managing Technology*, Balme Lawrie Seminar, ASCI, Hyderabad, 6 January, 1998, organized by DSIR and ASCI.

6. Patel V.G., *Entrepreneurship Development Programmes:* Problems and Prospects, Paper presented at national workshop on Entrepreneurship Education in Management Schools, 1991.

7. Devarajan K.M., *Export and Flourish*, The New Indian Express, BBSR, 26 April, 2004.

8. Soundara Pandian, M., *Rural Industries*, Kurukshetra, November, 1999.

9. Ramana, A.V., *Entrepreneurship and Economic Development*, Kurukshetra, November 1999.

10. Saif Siddiqui, *Rural Entrepreneurship and Poverty Alleviation Programmes,* Excerpts from PM's address at the Asian Summit on Youth Entrepreneurship, *Yojana*, Vol. 47, No. 12, 26–27 December 2003.

11. *Manu Smriti*, Chapter IX 328, 329, 330, 331–332.

Index